D0982987

Executive Integrity

Suresh Srivastva
and Associates

Executive Integrity

The Search for High Human Values in Organizational Life

Jossey-Bass Publishers

San Francisco • London • 1988

EXECUTIVE INTEGRITY
The Search for High Human Values in Organizational Life
by Suresh Srivastva and Associates

Copyright © 1988 by: Jossey-Bass Inc., Publishers
350 Sansome Street
San Francisco, California 94104
&
Jossey-Bass Limited
28 Banner Street
London EC1Y 8QE

Library of Congress Cataloging-in-Publication Data
Executive integrity : the search for high human values in
organizational life / Suresh Srivastva and associates. — 1st ed.
        p.   cm. — (The Jossey-Bass management series)
    Bibliography: p.
    Includes index.
    Contents: Integrity / Michael Maccoby— Quality of service /
Roger Harrison — Integrity, advanced professional development, and
learning / David A. Kolb — Paths to integrity — Marcia Mentkowski —
Integrity in effective leadership / Steven Kerr — Is there
integrity in the bottom line? / Donald M. Wolfe — Integrity
management /James A. Waters — Reciprocal integrity / Chris
Argyris, Donald A. Schön — Organizational alignments, schisms, and
high-integrity managerial behavior — Samuel A. Culbert, John J.
McDonough — International dimensions of executive integrity / Nancy
J. Adler, Frederick B. Bird — To thine own self be true / Harry
Levinson — Foundations for executive integrity / Suresh Srivastva,
Frank J. Barrett.
    ISBN 1-555-42085-0 (alk. paper)
    1. Business ethics.   2. Executives—Conduct of life.   3. Industry—
Social aspects.   I. Srivastva, Suresh, date.   II. Series.
HF5387.E94 1988
174'.4—dc19   87-46332
                                                                   CIP

Manufactured in the United States of America

The paper in this book meets the guidelines for permanence and durability of the Committee on Production Guidelines for Book Longevity of the Council on Library Resources.

JACKET DESIGN BY WILLI BAUM

FIRST EDITION

Code 8761

The Jossey-Bass Management Series

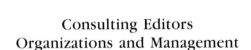

Contents

Part Two: Processes for Enacting Integrity

Part Three: Processes of Searching for Integrity

Preface

A recent issue of *Time* magazine (May 25, 1987) displays a cover that asks the pungent question "What Ever Happened to Ethics?" The subtitle offers the premise that informs the inquiry: "Assaulted by sleaze, scandals and hypocrisy, America searches for its moral bearings." We are reminded that more than 100 members of the current federal administration either have been indicted or face allegations of questionable activity. The insider trading scandal on Wall Street continues to expand as more executives and investment bankers become implicated. The secretary of education recently criticized U.S. schools as "languishing for lack of moral nutrition." These questions of ethical decay threaten to erode faith in our leaders and raise the disturbing awareness of something askew in the nation's soul. The appearance of this inquiry in *Time* is a historical coincidence for this preface; the questions posed in this book are perennial issues of inquiry.

It seems that we become aware of the urgency of ethical standards only after some code has been broken. As a result, discussions of morality tend to emerge in unpleasant contexts of censure after some instance of human behavior has been found wanting and disappointing. In such contexts we are likely to try to resolve dilemmas by proposing new codes and standards of behavior.

However, these themes of moral decay are expressions of a more fundamental, systemic issue. They point to the core issue of integrity that underlies every human endeavor. By paying attention to the symptoms only, we limit ourselves to the medical model of inquiry, in which doctors study disease in order to understand health. This volume provides an opportunity to study integrity in a more appreciative context. It calls attention to the conditions that enhance generativity and moral strength, not just to what we must do to prevent moral disease.

Executive integrity is more than a code of ethics or an articulation of standards. It involves the ongoing pursuit of value in the world. Integrity involves the search for standards of moral and intellectual cohesion and seeks to preserve the vital striving toward ultimate concerns that transcend expediency. Executive integrity as presented in this volume does not call for a codification of moral behavior but for an active, normative stance toward furthering processes of rejuvenation and fostering the life-giving properties of human relationships.

It was with an eye to these probing issues that some of the leading thinkers in the field of organizational behavior assembled at Case Western Reserve University in October 1986 for a symposium on executive integrity. The chapters in this volume are a culmination of the ideas developed and shaped at that conference.

This book should appeal to both academics and executives. For academics, it provides suitable material for advanced graduate courses; offers important concepts and highlights elusive processes that should help in formulating research and theory. For executives, it is a call to revisit some of the premises that inform managerial action and provides ideas for experimenting with new ways of organizing relationships toward the furtherance of organizational life. The book offers insights into the responsibility of proactively nurturing the conditions that further integrity in the workplace.

These chapters do not provide executives with prescriptive lists or action strategies, however. Rather, they encourage executives to be open to larger questions, to allow these ideas to percolate and to penetrate the assumptions that guide daily action. In this sense it is hoped that this book is a pleasantly disturbing interruption. It entices executives to slow down the culture of high velocity that often marks modern organizations. In this sense the authors seek not so much to provide information as to enhance awareness. Therefore, executives should read the volume introspectively, reflecting time and again on its lucid explications of processes and experiences that they may previously have guessed could never be shared, let alone discussed, with others.

This book is affirming in that it offers a fresh appreciation of the complex world of the modern executive and the dilemmas that resist unequivocal resolution. The book is also challenging. It is an opportunity for executives to reflect on their behavior and consider the multiple intended and unintended consequences of decisions that affect so many lives. Most important, this book is optimistic because fresh alternatives for organizing are envisioned. The assumption put forth throughout this book is that organizational members do not have to simply adjust their lives to existing social arrangements as if those arrangements were fixed structures with a force all their own. Rather, members are cocreators: They shape social arrangements and bestow meaning on activity and therefore are capable of choosing bolder forms of organizing and initiating actions that enhance integrity for many.

The book is also important, we believe, for the field of organizational behavior. Originally the choice of executive integrity as a theme for this work was guided by an effort to distinguish the field of organizational behavior from contributions to organizational theory by psychologists, sociologists, and others. The social sciences have traditionally advocated an objective, positivist strategy of research, modeled on the natural sciences, that calls for the researcher to assume a detached perspective toward the ''object'' of study and to beware of bias and contamination of data. Loyalty to these personal canons has demanded a price: We have too often avoided studying important topics that by their very nature demand personal involvement. As these chapters will make clear, organizational behavior is a field that strives to appreciate both ideas and the living processes of organizing, building theories that emerge from action and engaging in actions that feed into the formulation of new theories. We have not taken a hands-off attitude toward our subjects of inquiry but, rather, have taken advocacy positions for organizational change. In a sense we have assumed that research itself is an intervention for the better within an organization. These assumptions have informed our research action and our action research strategies. This book is true to the same tradition. It offers insightful theories that enlighten complex human behavior; at the same time, for the reader, this volume itself is an important intervention into the active processes of organizing.

Moreover, the nature of the topic of integrity requires an inward closeness to the "object" under study and an introspection of one's own life. For this reason, in order to enhance our awareness of a controversial and elusive topic, these authors have engaged in a high level of self-reflection and personal disclosure. We applaud their courage, and we hope that it will stand as an inspiration to others.

The spirit behind the preparation of this volume needs special notice. In addition to maintaining exacting standards of excellence in writing individual chapters, the participants exhibited many resourceful characteristics that made the book a gathering of ideas from colleagues who are inclined to celebrate knowledge and learning. The authors have used appreciative modes of inquiry and interaction; and their ability to learn from the ideas of others and their commitment to shared meanings are very noticeable in this volume.

The chapters in this book received special and thoughtful review by executive leaders in the community during face-to-face discussions with the authors. The book has been enriched by the searching contributions of Theodore M. Alfred, professor and former dean, Weatherhead School of Management, Case Western Reserve University; David E. Berlew, principal, Situation Management Systems, Inc.; Scott S. Cowen, professor and dean, Weatherhead School of Management; John J. Eversman, vice-chairman and chief operating officer, Cleveland Clinic Foundation; Roy Gentiles, former president and chief executive officer, Alcan Aluminum Corporation; William S. Kiser, chairman and chief executive officer, Cleveland Clinic Foundation; Peter B. Lewis, chairman and chief executive officer, Progressive Companies; Julien McCall, chairman and chief executive officer, National City Bank Corporation; Gerald McDonough, chairman and chief executive officer, Leaseway Transportation; Norton Rose, executive vice-president for human resources, Progressive Companies; and Ward Smith, president and chief executive officer, North American Coal Corporation. My colleagues and I are richer because of their generous contributions, and we owe them enormous gratitude.

A volume of this nature depends largely on the good will and unreserved support of friends and colleagues and on a creative learning environment. During the conception period I was supported most ably by my faculty colleagues, including Barbara Bird, Richard Boyatzis, David Cooperrider, Ronald Fry, Hank Jonas, David Kolb, Michael Manning, Eric Neilsen, William Pasmore, and Donald Wolfe. Splendid support was provided by a group of graduate students in my integrative seminar that included Gail Ambuske, Gaetana Friedman, Karen Locke, Joyce Osland, M. V. Hayagreeva Rao, George Robinson, and Michael Sokoloff. These students acted as shadow scholars to invited authors and created the community for exciting learning opportunities. My special gratitude goes to Karen Locke, as she carried the major task of organizing and managing the conference with thoughtful diligence and personal commitment.

Dean Scott Cowen of the Weatherhead School of Management provided personal encouragement and part of the financial support. I am grateful to all and to many others who remain unmentioned.

Warren Bennis, Richard Mason, and Ian Mitroff, as consulting editors to this volume, have been continuously supportive, thoughtful, and generous with their time and ideas. And, of course, my administrative aide, Retta Holdorf, has carried out the typing of this work, and I am most grateful to her.

Cleveland, Ohio   Suresh Srivastva
January 1988

The Authors

Nancy J. Adler is an associate professor of organizational behavior and cross-cultural management at McGill University in Montreal. Dr. Adler received her M.B.A. and Ph.D. from the University of California, Los Angeles. She has taught at the American Graduate School of International Management and at INSEAD, a European management school in Fontainebleu, France. She has published numerous articles, produced the film *A Portable Life,* and written a book entitled *International Dimensions of Organizational Behavior* (1986).

Chris Argyris is a professor of education and organizational behavior at Harvard University. He received his A.B. degree at Clark University, his M.A. degree at the University of Kansas, and his Ph.D. degree at Cornell University. Honorary doctorates include economics, Stockholm School of Economics (1979); psychology and pedagogy, University of Leuven, Belgium (1978); and law, McGill University (1977). Argyris is the author of 24 books and monographs and over 200 articles.

Frank J. Barrett is a Ph.D. candidate in organizational behavior at Case Western Reserve University. He received his B.A. (1975) in government and international relations and his M.A. (1977) in English from the University of Notre Dame. He is also an active jazz pianist. He has worked with the Cleveland Clinic, University Hospitals of Cleveland, General Electric, and municipal and county government agencies. His current research interests include the role of language, metaphor, and myth in group processes and the creative management of conflict.

Frederick B. Bird is associate professor of comparative ethics at Concordia University. He holds a B.A. degree in history from Harvard University, a B.D. degree from Harvard Divinity School, and a Ph.D. degree in religion and theology from the Graduate Theological Union in Berkeley, California. His current areas of research include business ethics, sociology of morality, and contemporary ritual practices.

David L. Cooperrider is assistant professor of organizational behavior at the Weatherhead School of Management, Case Western Reserve University. He received his B.A. degree (1976) from Augustana College in psychology; his M.S. degree (1982) from George Williams College in organizational behavior; and his Ph.D. degree (1985) from Case Western Reserve University in organizational behavior. Recently he has been engaged in research on the relationship among organizational ideology, executive power, and the management of change. Cooperrider's most recent studies have been "The Emergence of the Egalitarian Organization" (in *Human Relations,* 1986) and "Appreciative Inquiry into Organizational Life." He is also very active as a management educator and consultant.

Samuel A. Culbert is professor of behavioral and organization sciences at the Graduate School of Management, University of California, Los Angeles. He holds a B.S. degree in industrial engineering from Northwestern University and a Ph.D. degree in clinical psychology from UCLA. Culbert is widely recognized as an expert and theoretician in the management field, having authored several books and numerous professional articles and chapters. He holds the McKinsey award for an article published in the *Harvard Business Review,* and in 1980 his book *The Invisible War: Pursuing Self-Interests at Work* (written with John J.

McDonough) won an award as the best business and management book published that year. He and John J. McDonough are also the authors of a recent book, *Radical Management: Power Politics and the Pursuit of Trust.* Culbert has been a consultant to a diverse representation of the private and public sectors.

Roger Harrison is a management consultant and a principal of Harrison Associates, Inc., in Berkeley, California. He taught organizational behavior at Yale University and then spent eight years in Europe as an independent management educator and consultant. Harrison has contributed numerous articles to the management literature, including "Choosing the Depth of Organizational Intervention" (1970), "Role Negotiation" (1970), "Understanding Your Organization's Character" (1972), "Self-Directed Learning: A Radical Approach to Educational Design" (1977), "Startup: The Care and Feeding of Infant Systems" (1981), and "Strategies for a New Age" (1983).

Steven Kerr is dean of faculty and director of the Ph.D. program at the School of Business, University of Southern California. He received his Ph.D. degree from the City University of New York with major fields in management and organizational psychology. He is on three editorial review boards, has coauthored two books, and has published nearly fifty book chapters and journal articles. Kerr has been a consultant to many national firms and a regular participant in executive programs sponsored by Washington University, Oklahoma State University, and the University of Pittsburgh. His major research interests are in leadership and in evaluation and reward systems.

David A. Kolb is professor and chairman of the Department of Organizational Behavior at the Weatherhead School of Management, Case Western Reserve University. He received his Ph.D. degree in social psychology with concentration in personality research from Harvard University. He also received his M.A. degree from Harvard and his A.B. degree cum laude in psychology from Knox College. Kolb has authored numerous books, articles, and monographs in the field of organizational behavior.

His latest book, *Experiential Learning: Experience as the Source of Learning and Development,* is an integrative statement of fifteen years' research on learning styles and the learning process. Kolb has recently completed a major research project funded by the National Institute of Education and the Spencer Foundation concerning experiential learning and adult career development, focusing on midcareer changes in managers and on the role of professional education in preparation for a career of lifelong learning. In June 1984 he was awarded an honorary doctor of science degree from the University of New Hampshire School for Life-Long Learning for his contributions to adult higher education. Kolb has consulted for numerous public and private organizations.

Harry Levinson is president of the Levinson Institute; clinical professor of psychology in the Department of Psychiatry, Harvard Medical School; and head, section on organizational mental health, Massachusetts Mental Health Center. He received his B.S. and M.S. degrees from Emporia (Kansas) State University. In addition to numerous articles, Levinson is the senior author of *Men, Management, and Mental Health* and author of *Emotional Health in the World of Work: Executive Stress; Executive; Organizational Diagnosis; The Great Jackass Fallacy; Psychological Man;* and *CEO: Corporate Leadership in Action* (with Stuart Rosenthal).

Michael Maccoby is a social psychologist and psychoanalyst. He directs both the Project on Technology, Work and Character, a center for research and consulting in Washington, D.C., and the Program on Technology, Public Policy and Human Development at the John F. Kennedy School of Government, Harvard University. Maccoby received his B.A. degree in social psychology and his Ph.D. degree in social relations, both from Harvard. His major works include *Social Character in a Mexican Village* (1970, with Erich Fromm), *The Gamesman* (1977), *The Leader* (1981), and *Why Work: Motivating the New Generation* (forthcoming).

John J. McDonough is professor of management at UCLA's Graduate School of Management. He received his B.A. degree in economics from Dartmouth College and his M.A. and Ph.D. degrees from the Harvard University Graduate School of Business Administration. McDonough's research and teaching interests focus on issues of trust, power, and accountability at work. His most recent book (with Samuel Culbert) is *Radical Management: Power Politics and the Pursuit of Trust* (1985). An earlier book, *The Invisible War: Pursuing Self-Interests at Work* (1980), was voted the "outstanding" management book of 1980 by the Association of Publishers. McDonough is active in professional and community affairs, having served on the Los Angeles County Mental Health Commission for over a decade.

Marcia Mentkowski is director of research and evaluation and professor of psychology at Alverno College. She received her B.A. degree from Downer College, Milwaukee, and her Ph.D. degree in psychology from the University of Wisconsin–Madison. Mentkowski created the Office of Research and Evaluation at Alverno, where research findings have resulted in articles in the *New York Times* and *USA Today*. She is a prolific author, speaks at conferences across the country, and consults widely in colleges and professional schools.

Donald A. Schön is Ford Professor of urban studies and education at the Massachusetts Institute of Technology. He received his B.A. degree (1951) at Yale University and his M.A. (1952) and Ph.D. (1955) degrees from Harvard University in philosophy.

Suresh Srivastva is professor of organizational behavior in the Department of Organizational Behavior at the Weatherhead School of Management, Case Western Reserve University and served as chairman of the department from 1970 to 1984. He received his Ph.D. degree (1960) from the University of Michigan in social psychology. In addition to his work as a consultant for industrial enterprises and health care systems in the field of organizational development, he is the author of numerous articles in the area of psychology and management problems. His major books include *Behavioral Sciences in Management* (1967), *Human Factors in Industry* (1970), *Anatomy of a Strike* (1972, with

I. Dayal and T. Alfred), *Job Satisfaction and Productivity* (1975, with others), *Management of Work* (1981, with T. Cummings), *The Executive Mind* (1983, with others), and *Executive Power* (1986, with others).

James A. Waters is associate dean for academic affairs and associate professor of management policy at York University, Ontario. He received his B.A. and B.S. degrees in chemical engineering from the University of Notre Dame and his M.B.A. and Ph.D. degrees in organizational behavior (1976) from Case Western Reserve University. His work has been published in numerous journals of business and management.

Donald M. Wolfe is professor of organizational behavior at the Weatherhead School of Management, Case Western Reserve University. He received his Ph.D. degree in social psychology (1960) from the University of Michigan. He has maintained an active consulting practice in organizational development, conflict management, team building, professional development, and life/career planning for individuals and for industrial, governmental, educational, and health care organizations. His current research includes processes of learning and growth in adult development, the development and assessment of generic and professional competencies in the applied behavioral sciences and in management, and organization, group, and personal factors involved in relations among stress, health, and personal growth. He is the author of numerous articles and chapters and is coauthor of *Organizational Stress: Studies in Role Conflict and Ambiguity* (1964).

Executive Integrity

The Urgency for Executive Integrity

Suresh Srivastva
David L. Cooperrider

A human being is part of the whole, called by us the "universe," a part limited in time and space. He experiences himself, his thoughts and feelings, as something separated from the rest—a kind of optical delusion of his consciousness. This delusion is kind of a prison for us, restricting us to our personal desires and to affection for a few persons nearest us. Our task must be to free ourselves from this prison by widening our circle of compassion to embrace all living creatures and the whole of nature in its beauty [Albert Einstein].

We live in a time of decision. The awesome human option for living or destroying has led a number of historians to speak of our time as an Age of Terror. Whether or not one agrees with the force of such an assessment, few would deny the urgency of the challenges facing all of us in our national and international relations, in our communities and governments, in our schools and families, and in our public and private organizations of all kinds.

The need for leadership has never been so great. As evidence of this need, scores of volumes have been written in recent years exploring the dimensions of the executive task—especially as it relates to that overarching ideal which James McGregor Burns (1978) first called "transformative" leadership. Ever since his provocative formulation, we have been fascinated and drawn

1

by images of executives as "changemasters" and "pathfinders," as "gamesmen" and "entrepreneurs," and as "visionaries" and "social architects."

The modernist spirit, as embodied in each of these notions, has predominantly been one of novelty, of innovation, of transformation. Indeed, the idea of *change* wonderfully dominates the modern mind in all spheres of life, including life at the workplace. Executives everywhere continue to be called to envision alternatives that have never yet existed, to break the hammerlock of conventional notions of what is possible, to ignite the spirit of collective renewal, and to harness turbulent environmental forces to help transform their organizations in new and different ways. But in what ways? As Daniel Bell (1976) has cogently discussed, the thing that is so singularly apparent about this modernist emphasis on change, "the tradition of the new," is that novelty has seemingly taken on value in and of itself. The avant-garde has become the cherished and customary way of life.

This volume is offered in the belief that not only is effective change management an essential force in the leadership of vital organizational forms but there is another key aspect of the executive task that has largely been overlooked—namely, the management of social and organizational continuity. In our pluralistic rush to the future we have been intrigued by concepts of power and mind and executive vision. We want our leaders to make things happen. But power for what ends? Change in the service of whose values? Vision for the sake of what noble purpose? As people in all walks of life have been both dazzled and exhausted by novelty, they—we—are beginning to express a hidden hunger for continuity and community, for responsiveness and responsibility, and for the confidence that comes when everyday interactions are marked by simple trust and basic human care. This volume is based on a belief that integrity is *the* pivotal force behind organizational existence itself. Executive mind is impotent without power, power is dangerous without vision, and neither is lasting or significant in any broad human sense without the force of integrity.

The Contemporary Urgency

As we scan the scholarly reports on the ''global prob-
lematique'' or tune in the evening news, we are frequently
touched by feelings of disbelief and sadness, frustration and
helplessness. At other times, however, there is no feeling—only
a vague disquiet and a dispirited numbness. And why not?

How many times have we been warned of the consequences of a nuclear winter; mass starvation and poverty in the
midst of plenty; loss of faith in institutions; economic instability
throughout the globe; rejection of traditional values; and the
impending collapse of our ecosystem and species? The story is
so well known that it has become cliché to repeat it. But it is
our story.

Companies by the hundreds are cited annually for ethical
and illegal misconduct. In 1985 alone, for example, the *Wall
Street Journal* published over 400 articles reporting illegal or
unethical corporate behavior. The *Time* magazine feature that
we mentioned in our preface has observed that the *Wall Street
Journal* is starting to read more and more like the *Police Gazette:*
''Not since the reckless 1920s and degenerate 1930s have the
financial columns carried such unrelenting tales of vivid scandals, rascally characters, and creative new means for dirty-
dealing (insider trading, money laundering, greenmailing). . . .
What began as the decade of the entrepreneur is fast becoming
the age of the pinstriped outlaw, his prodigal twin'' (p. 22).

Well-known names such as General Dynamics, E. F. Hutton, Ford Motor Company, and Bank of Boston have been accused of criminal practices. Organizations devoted to ''high
risk'' technologies—nuclear energy, toxic waste, biochemical
engineering, genetic splicing—continue to be plagued by long
lists of technological failures, mismanagement, and subsequent
cover-ups. Many accidents have already occurred, pointing to
the fact that the potential for catastrophe on a large scale is very
real (Perrow, 1984). Add to this the facts that thousands of white-
collar crimes have been reported of seemingly respectable executives, professionals, and government officeholders and that con-

sumer fraud, including the illegal use of insider information, has turned into a $40 billion industry—one is left groping for words to describe the contemporary scene. For Jacques Maisonrouge, former CEO and chairman of IBM World Trade Corporation, we live at the watershed point of a new global era that will test the integrity of executives as never before. Drawing on the work of Edward Gibbon, he writes: "If history is little more than the register of crimes, follies, and misfortunes of mankind, ours is certainly an era future scholars will study with zeal. For the last few years we have witnessed the rise of a series of problems that for range, complexity, and seriousness have seldom been equaled" (1975, p. 11).

In our day, as never before, the human image embedded in our social and organizational forms has been injured to the point of near obliteration. As countless sociologists have shown, the staging of our organizational drama has lost its traditional script, leaving us with little direction, meaning, or central conviction of purpose. Even our moments of triumph are scarred by tragedy. The explosion of *Challenger,* the meltdown at Chernobyl, and the poison gas leak at Bhopal were not just technological failures—they were managerial ones. They loom as haunting symbols of our as yet childlike capacity to construct a global community congenial to the life of the planet and the preservation of the human spirit.

A question, then, that runs to the heart of our times might simply be this: How, in spite of what has happened, can human beings recultivate a modicum of trust in their organizational existence? How, in spite of Auschwitz and Hiroshima and countless other symbols of destruction throughout our century, are we to generate a solid and realistic faith in our capacity to cooperatively tend to one another and our civilization? The human option for living and dying, for connection or disconnection, is indeed our challenge. In the closing passage of his great *Civilization and Its Discontents,* Sigmund Freud (1931/1969, p. 92) put the question in a way that prophetically speaks to our times: "The fateful question for the human species seems to me to be whether and to what extent their cultural development will succeed in mastering the disturbance of their communal life. . . .

People have gained control over the forces of nature to such an extent that . . . they would have no difficulty exterminating one another to the last man. They know this, and hence comes a large part of their current unrest, their unhappiness and their mood of anxiety. And now it is to be expected that the other of the two 'Heavenly Powers,' eternal Eros, will make an effort to assert himself in his struggle with his equally immortal adversary. But who can foresee with what success and with what result?''

Defining Executive Integrity

Integrity, it is proposed throughout this volume, is one of the key *life-sustaining* properties involved in the *relational* nature of organizational existence. In its basic dictionary usage, the word *integrity* bespeaks a unifying process leading to a state of wholeness, completeness, or undividedness. The notion of integrity has historically been held in high esteem as a compelling ideal, as an aspirational image drawing opposing forces together into one integral whole. Whether one is referring to the integrity of a magnificent bridge, or of a beautiful symphonic performance, or of a loving and responsive relationship between a parent and a young child, the notion of integrity has always suggested a relational unity that makes a differentiated constellation of parts hold together as one. In a critical sense, then, *organization is impossible without integrity, for by definition organization is differentiation integrated.*

In the mood of caution and cynicism of our times, the public everywhere is critically examining its organizations. Stakeholders of all kinds—consumers, employees, stockholders, partners, regulators, communities—are crying out for integrity. They are searching for quality of service and product in every way imaginable and often in contradictory or conflicting ways. Consequently it can be said without exaggeration that today's executive task represents the world's most intensive course in integrity. At the same time, we understand so little about the nature of this phenomenon and have yet to spell out exactly what it means in managerial and organizational terms. What is *execu-*

tive integrity? And why is it so prized? Is it related to ethics or morality? To trust? To values? Is the quest for integrity a hard-nosed realistic aim, or is it merely a sentimental ideal, a romantic distraction? Is personal integrity the same as organizational integrity, and if not, how do they differ? Is integrity a way of seeing and thinking, or is it a way of acting? Is integrity an end in itself, or is it a means to profit or some other end? Why is it so difficult to talk openly and confidently about issues of integrity at the workplace? Is integrity viewed as a high standard of excellence or as a constraint on managerial action? Where does integrity in organizations come from? How is it enacted? Can it be developed?

These are but some of the questions raised by the authors of this book. One would think that the theme of integrity would pervade the literature on management. But it does not. Hence, the basic spirit of this work is exploratory and expansive. It is intended to open the avenues of discussion and inquiry and to outline the key features, boundaries, dimensions, and substance of the topic.

Somewhere between the common-sense and overly abstract definitions of a phenomena, there exists what Massarik (1985) has aptly termed a *working* conceptualization, a description that provides a beginning map, yet still requires rigorous inquiry. A working conceptualization of executive integrity that emerges from the common themes in this volume can be stated as follows:

Executive integrity is a process embedded in social *interaction* that involves the discovery and enactment of ever-new forms of organization that heighten responsiveness to the other. The development of integrity begins with a "dim awareness" of the fundamental wholeness or interrelatedness of an entire living system and is carried forward through the initiation of mutual *dialogue*. The movement of executive integrity is *directional* in nature, starting with one's immediate face-to-face relationships and then widening to include the organization as a whole, its relevant stakeholders, and the societal and natural environments in which it is embedded. And finally, the presence of integrity is *consequential:* In its discovery of new forms of responsiveness to the other, the enactment of executive integrity results in the construction of new meanings (values, culture) and forms (social arrangements) that reduce asymmetry (schisms) and enhance the relational life of the whole.

Four aspects of this definition deserve further note:

1. *Executive integrity is interactional.* By definition, executive work is fundamentally interactional, involving the management of relationships between one individual and the surrounding others; one group within the context of other groups; a department within a set of divisions; a subspecialty in relation to other subspecialties; a product or service in relation to the client or marketplace; and ultimately, perhaps, the organization within the ecology of the economic, political, and natural forces of the globe. In this sense, executive integrity is not simply an "ethic of honesty" or "living according to *one's* principles." Its axis or basic orientation is not the self at all but the *other.* It is continuously emerging within the context of a complex and ever-evolving set of relations.

2. *Executive integrity is dialogical.* Executive integrity is more than the presence of morality or the appropriation of values; integrity involves the process of seeking or creating values. Whereas ethical moralism is blindly obedient, integrity represents the "insightful assent" to the construction of human values. In this sense, organization is not viewed as a closed, determined structure but is seen as in a perpetual state of becoming. Through an "awakening" to the fundamental interdependencies of the workplace, executive integrity is carried forward through a quality of interaction called dialogue. Dialogue is the transformation of mere interaction into participation, communication, and mutual empathy. Executive integrity is, therefore, a breaking out of a narrow individualism and is based on a fearless trust in what true dialogue and understanding might bring, both new responsibilities and new forms of responsiveness to the other.

3. *Executive integrity is directional.* Through an awakening to interdependencies and through the choiceful establishment of dialogue, executive integrity evolves from the immediacy of the self to the other, from the local environment to the global environment. The development of executive integrity is the process through which the executive acquires a more extended (in both space and time), empathic, and valid conception of the broader and broader contexts in which the organization is embedded and in which it participates.

4. *Executive integrity is consequential.* The force of integrity is

evidenced each time a new form of organization emerges in which asymmetrical relations become more symmetrical, self-interest is replaced by an increased sense of solidarity with others, or complex differentiations are integrated into a coordinated unity. Whether one is talking about the birth of new values or social arrangements in revolutionary change (for example, the Gandhian movement in India) or evolutionary change (for example, establishment of new forms of responsiveness to the customer), the force of integrity is always followed by an increase in the relational health of the whole. The ultimate role of integrity is to promote unity and continuity in the organic development of social organizational existence.

What we have tried to show so far in this introduction is that the theme of integrity is both timely and important because there is a relational urgency to our times. During periods like this, there is, as Becker (1973) argued, "a great pressure to come up with concepts that help people understand their dilemma; there is an urge toward vital ideas, toward simplification of needless intellectual complexity" (p. 1). Becker also cautioned, however, that the urge for simplification often makes for big lies that may resolve tensions but in the process also distort reality. As our working conceptualization shows, the phenomenon of executive integrity is multidimensional and elusive and requires an interdisciplinary approach. In the rest of this chapter we will provide an overview of the diversity of views articulated in the various chapters and will elaborate further on the core common themes of executive integrity as interactional, dialogical, directional, and consequential.

Overview of the Content

The twelve chapters making up this book were written for this volume and are original pieces of work. Their character can only be described as thought-provoking—deeply sensitive, vibrant, expansive, and essayistic. The authors were chosen because of their leadership in the field and were asked, in the context of discovery: "to open new doors to understanding . . . to view this event as a forum for sharing new thoughts in collegial dialogue and for developing new hypotheses and directions toward the exploration of the functioning of executive integrity.''

The chapters divide themselves naturally into three parts: (1) "Processes for Developing Integrity," (2) "Processes for Enacting Integrity," and (3) "Processes of Searching for Integrity." As we now turn to a brief overview of each of the contributions, we hope to show that, taken together, this set of chapters has succeeded, at least in some small way, in opening the boundaries of our field to a humanly significant arena of inquiry.

Part One: Processes of Developing Integrity. The chapters by Michael Maccoby, Roger Harrison, David Kolb, and Marcia Mentkowski form a natural unity in their explicit concern for the processual and contextual factors associated with the *development* of personal and organizational integrity. Each author, in his or her own way, deals with at least three basic questions: (1) What is integrity? (2) Is it possible to consciously and actively develop, nurture, or educate for integrity? (3) If so, then how?

Michael Maccoby sets the stage, literally, with a fascinating "fictional dialogue" among a CEO and a diverse group of key organizational stakeholders. Besides the CEO, the cast includes a computer engineer, a union leader, a customer, a financial analyst, a personnel director, a political consumer activist, and an organizational consultant. As these participants sit around a circular boardroom table, the CEO begins the meeting by articulating one basic assumption: *that the way to develop a culture of organizational integrity is through open dialogue.* This principle, so deceptively simple in formulation, creates the stage for a candid and sometimes volatile meeting. The striking feature of the meeting, especially early on, is the sheer diversity in definitions of organizational integrity. The drama builds as parochial experiences and self-interested definitions are shared, debated, and compared. On its own merit each case is compelling and often contradicts or negates its predecessor. In the end, however, all participants have the shared experience of *giving voice to their values and being heard.* And each consensually agrees with the CEO's admonition that next on the agenda is to discover and nurture the organizational ground that transcends and encompasses them all. Indeed, one recognizes that this is *the* executive task.

Maccoby's medium is the message. One could simply take the title of his chapter and turn it into an entire course on the socially constructed nature of integrity. In its barest form, Maccoby is saying that integrity development *is* a fictional dialogue. The word *fictional* here is critical and should not be misunderstood in the literary sense of a piece of fiction. Maccoby's tacit message presents a theory of the human being as *Homo poeta:* Humankind is best understood as the creator and shaper of meaning. In short, what this metatheory signifies is that the integrative development of the self and the integrative development of culture both rely on one fundamental process—namely, that mind, self, and organization are developed as one in and through symbolic interaction. Taken a step further, Maccoby suggests that integrity for the individual as well as for the group develops not just through interaction generally but through a kind of interaction called dialogue. Although the author never defines what is meant by dialogical interaction, it is clear that it has something to do with an awakening to the fundamental interdependencies in the workplace and to the subsequent transformation of conventional monologic patterns of interaction into dialogical patterns where the basic assumption is no longer one of autonomy but one of connection. *Executive integrity, in this sense, is an interactional process that involves the discovery and enactment of ever-new forms of dialogic organization that heighten and sustain the relational life of the whole.*

In the next chapter, Roger Harrison treats the reader to one of those rare and penetrating essays that artfully blend sensitive disclosure with historical and conceptual analyses. Using himself and his past twenty years as a business consultant as an example, Harrison observes that because we have been living in such a competitive, abrasive, and insecure world, where relationships are often impersonalized and easily fractured, we are developing a "hidden hunger" to be loved a little bit. This is clearly evidenced, he notes, in the growing trend toward service to the other. Customer wants, for example, are changing: People are looking for transactions where they are treated as worthwhile human beings; where their opinions are genuinely desired, solicited, and heard; where they can relate in a mutual or participatory fashion; and where simple kindness and caring characterize the interaction. The pendulum, he argues, is swinging away from the rampant individualism and competitive aggressiveness that gave rise to the industrial revolution, toward the dialectically opposed pole of mutuality and compassion. The development of integrity, in this sense, is a process that synthesizes such opposing forces and requires an opening of our hearts in ways that seem foreign, especially in corporate cultures dominated by themes of power, impersonal roles, and achievement. Business organizations, Harrison recognizes, are tough places to nurture tender feelings. While privately many people do in fact harbor dreams of a more compassionate and responsive business world, most feel alone and unsupported—as if such thoughts were ridiculous or even subversive.

Drawing on the concepts of "alignment" and "attunement," Harrison fashions a theory of *executive integrity as the process that actively develops harmony between the twin forces of love and will.* Alignment refers to a state where there is intimate connection between members and mission, while attunement calls attention to the relational connections among members themselves. The executive task, Harrison infers, is to develop an organizational balance between high alignment (a collective will to achieve a shared purpose) and high attunement (a striving for caring and responsive connections). For Harrison, the ideal is a synthesis of what he calls the *achievement*-oriented organizational culture and the *support* culture. Developing such an integrated system is not an easy task, and few organizations have fully grappled with its implications. Like Maccoby, Roger Harrison urges more open dialogue on the subject but recognizes the sensitivity of the topic. Looking back over his own efforts, Harrison admits that it was one thing to peddle power and influence to his clients; it has been quite another "to prattle in public about love, compassion, and the Golden Rule in business."

In the third chapter, David Kolb takes a thrilling and scholarly look at *integrity as a concept describing the highest form of human intelligence.* Integrity, asserts Kolb, is not so much a character trait that one possesses more or less of but a sophisticated state of processing experience in the world in ways that encompass moral judgment, creativity, and intuitive and emotional capability, as well as rational-analytic powers. In this sense it is more accurate to speak not of integrity but of integration— the learning process by which intellectual, moral, and cultural standards are created and thereby used to strengthen and nourish the social bond.

Drawing on his research of the lives of executives and other "advanced professionals" (such as physicians, lawyers, and scientists), Kolb details the workings of the integrative knowing process and theorizes about the contextual factors that trigger its development. The lives of professionals and executives are marked by four major challenges: the challenges of wholeness, generativity, time, and complexity. Wholeness refers to the fact that the primary executive task is to take responsibility not for parts but for the development of an entire social system. The higher one develops in one's character, the greater the challenge of wholeness. Generativity refers to the challenge of taking responsibility not only for self but also for others and requires an executive to move beyond an egocentric state of self-preservation to an advanced sociocentric state of "species preservation." The challenge of time refers to the fact that executive work is carried out over long time spans of five to ten years or even more before results are evaluated. Finally, the challenge of change and complexity highlights the recognition that executives live and preside over a world where complexity is feeding on itself and growing exponentially. Each of these contextual challenges requires what Kolb calls an emerging *integrative consciousness.*

Obviously, not every advanced professional or executive responds successfully to the challenges of wholeness, generativity, time, and complexity. But those who do, Kolb observes, develop a higher form of human intelligence defined by the integrating responses of centering, caring, visioning, and proto- and retrolearning. Can these complex processes be developed? According to Kolb, the unequivocal answer is yes: If human beings somewhere and sometimes have developed those capabilities, even if by accident or without awareness, then surely integrity must be teachable. The implications of this kind of human potential research begin to stretch the imagination about the real needs of executives and the types of education required to respond to those needs. An executive college that fully addresses itself to processes such as centering, caring, visioning, and proto- and retrolearning has yet to be created. For Kolb this represents the next truly exciting and promising frontier in management education. The challenge, he argues, is to discover educational processes that creatively respond to the real lives and real dilemmas of executives and other advanced professionals.

In the last chapter in Part One, Marcia Mentkowski expands on Kolb's conviction that it *is* possible to educate for integrity and begins to synthesize eleven years of impressive research on the subject. Drawing on studies of close to 1,000 students at Alverno College, where integrity is taught and assessed in over 100 undergraduate courses across the curriculum, Mentkowski provides a comprehensive account of the promises, potentials, and difficulties of making integrity an educational aim.

For Mentkowski, integrity is a quality of human thought and action in its most idealistic form: *It represents the human pursuit of all that is worthwhile, the search for the transcendent in life.* Lying at the core of integrity is a process the author calls "valuing"—being able to make empathic, responsible, and morally sound decisions as well as to consistently act on those valuations in the service of one's vision of the true, the good, or the best in human conduct. The research has shown that through their education at Alverno, students will (1) become increasingly adept at discerning and articulating their own moral philosophy, including their vision of the good, (2) develop more and more sophisticated intellectual and moral reasoning, along with more imaginative and insightful perspective taking and empathy, (3) be able to take an increasingly self-directing role in initiating and analyzing moral action in increasingly complex environments of action, and (4) develop an increasing capacity to appreciate the ambiguities that arise when one compares their "ideal" moral philosophy and their actual moral "practice."

But how is integrity taught? What kinds of learning processes prepare future executives for integrity in the workplace? For one thing, Mentkowski argues that such an education must be based on an experiential learning process: It is not enough to give lectures on business codes of ethics or to issue a series of warnings about cases where executives ended up in jail. The human pursuit of all that is worthwhile requires engagement; it requires a "hands on" learning process that places the student in increasingly more complex decision situations requiring moral reasoning and responsible action. It also demands, the author argues, immersion in a social climate that fosters liberal arts learning values—values for dealing with multiple points of view and appreciation for the arts, philosophy, history, and humanistic traditions. Perhaps most important, Mentkowski concludes, the development of integrity requires a lifelong commitment to learning and needs to be pursued beyond the boundaries of the college and purposively taken into the everyday context of the workplace.

Part Two: Processes for Enacting Integrity. Many years ago the celebrated social philosopher John Dewey suggested that the primary outcome of organizational life is not so much the production of things but the production of people. In the last analysis, he argued, all organizations are morally educative in the sense of providing arenas of interaction and learning that shape and mold the character of every participant. In this sense, the enactment of executive integrity cannot be understood apart from the experiential context in which it operates and is shaped.

The chapters in Part Two converge around this notion of enactment with their emphasis on the everyday context of the workplace. They show how in pluralistic settings like ours, where relativity in viewpoints pervades, the actual enactment of integrity poses confounding questions. Confirming our basic proposition that executive integrity is among today's most urgent and challenging problems, this section covers, for example, the moral stress encountered by many managers because of the difficulties they experience in discussing issues of integrity in their organizations; it looks at the subtle but powerful factors promoting disintegrity; and it suggests that the realities of the current workplace require that we develop definitions of integrity that are simultaneously more pragmatic and more demanding.

The authors whose chapters are included in this section are Steven Kerr, Donald Wolfe, and James Waters. Each chapter adds uniquely to our understanding of the context in which executive integrity is molded, and each looks closely at the pragmatic considerations of integrity as it is actually lived on the firing line.

In Chapter Five, Steven Kerr begins with an unusually candid admission: that he, and almost everyone else he knows with his sort of executive responsibilities, can scarcely make it through a single workday without engaging in behavior that violates each of the prescriptions, canons, and guidelines said by the "experts" to constitute integrious behavior. Kerr boils down the conventional view of executive integrity (taken from the literature) into ten commandments: (1) tell the truth; (2) obey the law; (3) reduce ambiguity; (4) show concern for others; (5) develop and nurture subordinates; (6) practice participation, not paternalism; (7) provide freedom from corrupting influence; (8) always act; (9) provide consistency across cases; and (10) provide consistency between values and actions. The list looks great, he argues, until we apply it to ourselves and compare it with the way business is actually conducted. Using himself as the prime example, Kerr offers data that destroy the fantasy that executives have any integrity whatsoever—if one is using the conventional criteria as a standard. For example, in relation to the commandment "Tell the truth," the author points to the fact that virtually every administrator has at some time succumbed to the falsehood of intentionally assigning expenditures to the wrong category or has fudged on someone's performance appraisal so as to justify current salary action or lay the groundwork for future discipline. What, then, are the implications?

Kerr looks at three possible ways out of this apparent dilemma. First, perhaps the author himself is an unusually corrupt administrator who does not serve his position of leadership.

Second, one might contend that, yes, the author is corrupt, but
so is everyone else; organizations in general tend to have a corrupting influence on people, especially those in power. Third
(and the alternative Kerr clearly advocates), there may be a
critical weakness in the way integrity is conventionally defined.
Integrity cannot be boiled down to a simplistic list of ten commandments.
What is needed, argues Kerr, is a totally different kind of working definition of integrity that more fully reflects the dynamic
complexity, multidimensionality, and pluralistic nature of organizational life. Indeed, Kerr demonstrates that a clearer conceptual distinction must be made between the terms *business ethics*
and *executive integrity*.

The next chapter, by Donald Wolfe, is a careful and
penetrating analysis of the factors promoting *disintegrity* in organizations. In many ways it is a disturbing chapter because it speaks
so directly to the truth of the matter and does not whitewash
the issues by providing appealing but simplistic solutions. Its
purpose is not, however, to decry the moral lapses so clearly
evidenced in our organizational society. On the surface, the essay
is soundly critical—but at its core is a tremendous appreciation
of the context in which executives live and do their work. Virtually every decision that an executive faces, if it taxes integrity
at all, is incredibly complex, with implications for contradictory and competing values precariously hanging in the balance.
The enactment of integrity, writes Wolfe, poses a whole series of
confounding questions: Right for whom and wrong for whom—
and who's to say? And right in what time period? For the moment? For this quarterly report? For the next several generations? And right or wrong for what level of the system—the person, the family, the organization, the industry, the planet?

The central issue in the enactment of executive integrity
revolves around what Wolfe defines as *multivalence*. Whereas personal integrity may be an issue of being true to one's own values
and basic nature, executive integrity is a matter beyond the self.
*Executive integrity is an ecological and social matter operating in a dynamic
arena of multiple values, multiple realities, and multi-interactive consequences.* It is this multivalent nature of the executive context that
moves the author to assert that any conception of integrity that

makes it a private, personal matter sidesteps most of the issues that need to be discussed.

What needs to be better understood, Wolfe proposes, is the subtle and impersonal forces that prompt executives to oversimplify multivalent situations and enact integrity in disintegrious ways. Among the most powerful are the bottom-line mentality, one-dimensional thinking, the push for the quick fix, the misapplication of cost-benefit analysis to noneconomic values, and an overall marketplace ethos that fosters a sense that "it's all a game," removed from the real lives and existential consequences of real human beings. Most troublesome, however, is the possibility that the word *integrity* itself is becoming anachronistic—that increasingly public "image management," or public relations, is replacing genuine integrity. As Wolfe points out, a whole industry has grown up in recent decades whose sole purpose is to manage people's consciousness and beliefs. At its best, image management provides a useful communications and education function. But at its worst, the Madison Avenue mentality is premised on the notion "Let's change their minds, not our actions." When this happens, the enactment of integrity becomes a fraud and the organization's energies shift from integrious action to disintegrious talk—how to conceal flaws, how to put something across, and how to come out smelling clean. Eventually, however, this strategy is doomed to failure, Wolfe concludes, because ultimately organizations are relational entities whose foundation is not money, technology, or power but trust. And this begs the crucial question: At what price and with what consequences will any organization knowingly gamble with its public trust?

James Waters in Chapter Seven carries the theme of enactment an important step further. Pragmatically, he argues, organizations can no longer take the public's trust for granted. It has been shattered too many times in recent history. If management as a whole is to be worthy of society's continued investment, if it is to enhance us as individuals and as a planet, then the moral dimension of executive work must become prominent in the minds, hearts, and actions of senior managers in all our organizations. Somebody, Waters asserts, has to "bite the bullet" and say straightforwardly that the long-term vitality of the firm rests on *social* integrity. This involves not simply consistency between action and principle but *adherence to generally accepted principles of goodness and rightness in human conduct.* In this sense, Waters's concern is not with a definition of integrity as it relates to holy saints or even to the worst of sinners. His concern is with the basic social integrity of "us common folks."

Too often the failure of integrity in organizations is viewed as an individual's problem, a character flaw. This approach, the author contends, has serious limitations because it prompts an individualistic treatment plan (namely, let's remove the culprit from his or her position) and leaves the moral milieu of the organization untouched. The task of senior management, Waters contends, is to focus its efforts not so much on trying to change individuals' behavior as on creating a strong organizational culture that makes discussion of values permissible and encourages collective inquiry into the integrity dilemmas of the firm. The challenge is to move beyond the frame of management integrity (preoccupation with the individual level) and instead concern ourselves with *integrity management.*

Integrity management begins the day senior managers prepare an active and explicit position on the importance of the moral dimension in their organization. This is not, argues Waters, a specialized task to be departmentalized in some functional unit as an appendage "ethics division." Because the senior managers are the custodians of the organization's basic culture and are the symbolic interface with the larger society, it is their task to explain, model, and nourish the philosophy and values that are to guide the firm. Waters's earlier studies have shown that the issue of integrity is indeed a live topic for most managers, but its discussion is largely confined to the home; it is close to a nontopic among managers in the public arena of the workplace. The result, of course, is an increasingly alienated spirit about one's work which carries with it all kinds of dysfunctional consequences summed up by what the author calls "moral stress." The antidote to moral stress is good conversation: dialogue among two or more managers who are struggling to figure out how to do the best job possible in a situation while respecting and strengthening the value standards relevant to that situation. Armed more with questions than with unalterable positions, the participants in good conversation experience their interaction more as problem solving guided by values of inquiry and cooperation than as debate guided by values of strategy and competition. Waters concludes this section on a hopeful note with a series of ten specific actions that senior managers anywhere can use to help initiate and enact the philosophy of good conversation and integrity management.

Part Three: Processes of Searching for Integrity. In this section Chris Argyris and Donald Schön, Samuel Culbert and John McDonough, Nancy Adler and Frederick Bird, Harry Levinson, and Suresh Srivastva and Frank Barrett take a more theoretical look into processes of integrity search. The search for integrity is essentially a search for congruence, consistency, symmetry, and alignment. What unites these authors is their attempt to understand and explain one of the most pervasive and puzzling of all organizational phenomena—namely, that the organizational world is fraught with schisms where people think one thing and say another, where espoused beliefs are contradicted daily in practice, and where our own self-deceptive processes blind us to our consequences in the world but also serve as an essential defense to the ego and the maintenance of our self-esteem. The intriguing fact is that very few of us see ourselves as lacking in integrity, yet we can readily point to disintegrity in almost every institution in which we are involved. In this section, the authors thoughtfully explore the defensive routines, the evolution of alignments, the processes of multicultural distortion, and the workings of the ego ideal as they each, in their own way, attempt to understand the search for symmetry in a schism-riddled world.

Chris Argyris and Donald Schön challenge us immediately with the following paradox: Why is it that when individuals pursue a course of action they deem as having integrity, organizations tend to become less capable of effective moral action and then instill in those individuals a growing sense of distance, impotence, cynicism, and passivity? The question is intriguing because it hits so close to home. For example, who among us has not been witness to the situation where a superior and subordinate differ around some ambiguous value only to find that expression of their value-stances soon results in a widening series of polarizations, until each experiences a sense of futility about changing the other? Similarly, and directly building from this scenario, how many times have we observed the scene where the subordinate soon learns to avoid unmanageable polarizations (as well as surprises and informational threats) by restricting his most dangerous opinions to hallway conversation or by sending mixed messages?

According to the research of Argyris and Schön, when value differences are encountered, most organizations adhere to a set of norms or governing ideas (which the authors call "theories of action") that logically lead either to schismogenetic polarization or to the development of defensive routines. That is, either a vicious cycle of win/lose conflict is unleashed or else a set of defensive routines emerges that takes the conflict to a covert, hidden level. Defensive routines are most common and are insidious because they work in an automatic and camouflaged way. Their apparent purpose is to help people save face and to avoid conflict as well as to eliminate embarrassment, threat, or surprise. They serve a function in attempting to protect the eternally fragile social bond but usually only exacerbate the problems by triggering all kinds of unintended consequences: Unreliable information gets passed along, people say one thing in meetings and just the opposite in the halls, mistrust abounds, the rumor mill begins generating "noise," and more and more participants feel increasingly helpless and hence distance themselves from personal responsibility for dealing with the situation. Of course, such processes become self-sealing and over time lead to organizational deterioration, giving rise to the complaint "Somehow our communications have broken down."

The authors explain this complex process by describing the workings of espoused theories of action and actual theories-in-use. What they have discovered in their work over the years is that while most people espouse a "Model II" theory of interaction—norms of generating valid information, promoting free and informed choice, and encouraging personal responsibility for action—they usually work blindly in ways inimical to such values. The actual theory-in-use reinforced by most organizations, which Argyris and Schön call "Model I," is based on norms that state: (1) one should advocate positions in such a way as to win and not lose, (2) one should remain in unilateral control of the situation, and (3) at the same time, one should maintain the appearance of cool rationality by avoiding the expression of negative feelings. This is the theory most of our society adheres to in interpersonal relations, and it is so ingrained in our cognitive maps that we are virtually blind to its operations, the authors argue.

This analysis suggests that the greatest challenge in the management of integrity is the creation of a Model II organizational world. But as the authors point out, this requires competences few of us are able to display: *an ability to make our theories-in-use congruent with our espoused theories and an ability to create situations of inquiry into values whereby both parties advocate their beliefs and open them to confrontation in a setting of reciprocal dialogue.* Creating a behavioral world conducive to *reciprocal integrity,* Argyris and Schön insist, is the only lasting way to break the self-defeating cycle of deterioration built into Model I theories of action.

In Chapter Nine Samuel Culbert and John McDonough begin with the observation that executives want power and they want trust, but they rarely know how to get both. Without power they are unable to get the immediate job done. Without trust they are unable to sustain relationships into the future. And without both trust and power there can be no executive integrity, because there can be no long-term effectiveness for the organization. Forced to choose, Culbert and McDonough argue, most executives choose power, but this forces them to act schismatically: They publicly espouse trust but in reality practice power.

On the surface, this chapter presents the most controversial image of executive integrity. For Culbert and McDonough, integrity in organizations involves far more than mere congruence of thoughts and deeds or simple honesty in one's dealings with others. In fact, they argue, misrepresentations, convenient omissions, well-timed disclosures, and other acts of manipulation often constitute the actions required for an executive to maintain an empowered course in the service of the whole. Recognizing that truthtelling may not always equal integrity, they ask: What causes people to take liberties in their representations of the truth? Are there circumstances where deception is an organizationally constructive skill? If integrity is more than telling the truth, then what is it?

What exactly are Culbert and McDonough saying when they state that, in today's environment, honesty, truth seeking, and totally aboveboard performances are desirable but cannot be delivered irrespective of practical considerations? To understand this question is to go beneath the surface of the words and to grapple with their complex formulation of *alignments*. In its simplest meaning, the concept of alignment highlights three fundamental relationships that have to be taken into account simultaneously when considering any act of integrity: (1) self in relation to oneself, (2) self in relation to particular others, and (3) self in relation to the whole organization or system. An alignment is an orientation to this whole system of relations which allows a person to focus on a new situation and immediately act in ways that are simultaneously personally, interpersonally, and organizationally relevant; it is the arrangement in which doing for oneself, doing for the other, and doing for the organization are as interrelated as possible. It entails an active desire to produce win/win/win outcomes and often requires self-sacrifice where the needs of the organization and the needs of another are quite possibly pursued to the neglect of one's own self-interest. Of course, Culbert and McDonough note, this requires compromise, which is one of the realities of organizational life. Integrity in this sense is no simple matter. As they see it, the main obstacle blocking the search for integrity of the practicing executive or manager is the contemporary managerial environment itself. The problem is that today's managerial culture lacks a widespread commitment to even attempt to *link* self-interested behavior to every organizational act and pursuit. The concept of alignment represents an ideal as well as a practical challenge. It recognizes that as a collective phenomenon, integrity does indeed entail compromise but that compromise without an explicit desire to work toward alignment can never be said to be integrious.

Nancy Adler and Frederick Bird in Chapter Ten explore the theme of integrity search at a global level. As most of us know, since World War II there has been an extraordinary globalization of organizations throughout the world. And this, Adler and Bird suggest, raises all kinds of intriguing practical as well as conceptual challenges for the notion of integrity: As management has expanded from a domestic to an international base and is now of a transnational scope, our approaches to executive integrity must also expand. Not only does the globalization of the workplace imply geographical dispersion, but it brings with it exponential increases in heterogeneity and diversity, including all the attendant issues of parochialism, ethnocentrism, economic and cultural imperialism, cultural relativism, and cultural blindness.

Moving from a local- to a global-level conception of integrity, Adler and Bird raise their most important question: *Who is responsible for the world?* Do corporations have any global mandate or responsibility beyond that of making a profit? Traditionally the economic answer has been that organizations have responsibility to their shareholders, while the expanded answer is that they are responsible to each of their stakeholders or constituencies. The question, say the authors, is whether the time has come for organizations to acknowledge the state of the world as one of their "constituencies."

The issue is no ivory tower speculation, Adler and Bird suggest, because there are a myriad of global problems that transcend the boundaries of the traditional nation-state structure and therefore have no official organized body to preside over them. Issues of acid rain, ozone depletion, widening poverty lines, a fragile global banking system, millions living in states of degradation and human misery, as well as issues of radioactive waste accidents, atmospheric pollution, and depletion of precious natural resources—all these are examples of transnational, boundaryless problems that threaten the life and stability of the entire system. Clearly the license to freely exploit at will has run out. But can we expect executives to expand their concern beyond their own enterprise to the planet as an entire living system?

According to Adler and Bird, this is precisely what the

situation demands. The theme of *organizational* integrity demands a rejection of the theory of environmental determinism, that organizations are deterministically guided by their environments. We must now recognize, with more and more maturity and wisdom, that organizations create their external environments as much as they respond to them. By awakening to this unmistakable interdependence, the authors believe, we can construct a world where it is in the firm's best interest to actively and consciously create a positive external environment. For the transnational organization, this means creating a positive global environment and accepting a mandate of responsibility for the world. Unlike the nation-state, whose mandate is to take care of its own people within the national structure, the transnational corporation has a home and structure that span the entire earth. Acting with integrity at a global level is obviously heroic and overwhelming. But, the authors conclude, it is necessary if we are to have a healthy world.

In Chapter Eleven, Harry Levinson treats us to an empathic presentation of the dilemma-filled lives of the ordinary human beings we look to heroically as executives. Levinson's work is as special as it is sensitive because of his many years of consultation and research into the actual experiences of those he writes about. Using his clinical expertise, Levinson gives us a fresh look at the search for integrity from a psychoanalytic perspective by exploring the workings of the ego ideal.

The ego ideal, explains Levinson, is a picture of oneself at one's ideal best toward which the person is always striving. It is an image situated in the future and gives one a sense of promise and possibility. Though never quite attainable, it is an important conception of selfhood on which the ego seeks to pattern itself. Always in juxtaposition to the ego ideal is a person's current self-image, a picture of the self as one thinks one actually is at the present point in time. The degree of matching between one's ego ideal and one's self-image constitutes self-esteem. To understand this formulation, the author proposes, is to understand one of the truly powerful mainsprings of human activity—that people are continually engaged in advancing their self-image toward their ego ideal in the service of self-esteem.

Although the ego ideal is clearly unique to each individual, Levinson's research on CEOs has discovered a thematic unity shared by every participant interviewed. In a study of the previous chief executives of General Electric, IBM, the *New York Times,* Monsanto, Citicorp, and AMAX, Levinson found that they all defined themselves ideally as "stewards." Leadership for them was stewardship not only in the sense of perpetuating their organization's existence but also including a belief that their primary task was to turn over to their successors organizations that were stronger than they themselves had been given. Leadership as stewardship showed a heavy emphasis on the management of continuity and regeneration through the management of values, traditions, and all the elements of culture constituting the firm's identity. During their tenure, these leaders faced threatening problems. But in keeping with their firms' values, they led their organizations through a thicket of dilemmas and into an uncertain future. And they did so, writes Levinson, sometimes with horrendous failure and significant personal disappointment but never without hope and courage and ideals.

The message underlying Levinson's work is that, in the search for integrity, executives do not need to be preached at or given moralistic lectures on ethics. The problem, for most, is not their ideals or intent. What is needed, instead, is increased self-understanding and awareness of one's ego ideal as well as the threats to that ideal. To operate with integrity in an openly competitive society, one needs insight into the defensive processes of the ego and an understanding of the mechanisms of guilt, particularly unconscious guilt. Executives experience daily all kinds of pain and frustration and sadness in the decisions they are required to make. To be able to move freely from one experience to the next, executives need to be able to explore their feelings and gain insight into the joys and pains of their lives as they are experienced in continual progress. The essence of executive integrity, says Levinson, is to be found in the words of Shakespeare: "To thine own self be true . . . thou canst not then be false to any man."

In this final chapter Suresh Srivastva and Frank Barrett present a concluding essay on possibilities for enhancing the practice of executive integrity. Their work, marked by a spirit of faith in human potential, concludes that executive integrity is one of the highest values of human expression. It is important, they suggest, to isolate and study those rare "moments of integrity" because it is precisely in those moments that we begin to unlock the secret of the nature and mystery of the social bond.

According to Srivastva and Barrett, integrity can only be understood as an interactive event, a transformative process that becomes visible in those moments when an individual steps out of a self-oriented mode of existence and makes an effort to attend to the other's development. Executive integrity is based on a recognition of the relational nature of organizational existence and is embodied, therefore, in any deliberate attempt to nourish, strengthen, or enhance the delicate relational life of the whole system. But what exactly can an executive do to strengthen the relational life of his or her organization?

In answer to this question, the authors propose that executives must consciously and actively work to create norms that foster true *dialogue,* promote *diversity,* and support human *development.* They elaborate on each of these themes and propose a compelling framework for executive action that is designed specifically for anyone interested in fostering integrity in his or her own organization. In the end, Srivastva and Barrett argue that the choice of integrity requires both courage and commitment because, in its essence, integrity development means creating organizations that are in "full voice."

Conclusion

The chapters in this volume were written to open new doors for inquiry and understanding into the humanly significant topic of executive integrity. This book shows how integrity in organizational life is not a simple, unidimensional concept but is a multifaceted process that operates at many levels (intrapersonal, interpersonal, intergroup, organizational, societal) and can be viewed from many perspectives. As summed up below, the chapters present a provocative set of important understandings that expand the boundaries of the way we think and talk about integrity:

- Executive integrity is more than the presence of morality or the appropriation of values; integrity involves the process of seeking values in the world. Whereas moralism is blindly obedient, integrity represents an "insightful ascent" to the construction of human values.

- Integrity is more than the constitution of a system of beliefs. The presence of integrity involves a thread of consistency between vision and action, between espoused values and values in practice. Because executives with integrity are consistent in word and deed, they invite trust from others. Thus, a system marked by integrity will foster trust.

- Integrity represents the pinnacle of human development and is a concept describing the highest form of human intelligence. Integrity is not so much a character trait as a sophisticated state of processing experience in the world that encompasses moral judgment, creativity, and intuitive capability, as well as rational-analytic powers.

- Integrity relates to a way of knowing and thinking. As a synthesizing form of thought, executive integrity acts to preserve the whole by accepting polarities, appreciating differences, and finding connections that transcend and encompass all points of view.

- Executive integrity is not a personal matter at all but is entirely a system matter involving the organization's responsiveness and integration with its environment. It is a recognition of the social and ecological consequences of an organization's actions and an attempt to understand its vital role in the conditions of its community, its people, and its economy and ecosystem.

- Executive integrity is embodied in concern for the intergenerational continuity of organizational life. It involves a sense of stewardship that is generated by the consciousness "I am what survives me." It is concerned, fundamentally, with creating intellectual, moral, and ethical standards that will provide the cultural cohesion required for continued organizational life.

- Executive integrity defies simple categorization, and its meaning is highly context-specific. The importance of the word "integrity" may not even be its precise meaning; its importance lies in its apparent capacity to stimulate dialogue that leads to the *creation* of new meaning. Whenever it is raised to the level of group discussion, important issues begin to surface. Integrity, it seems, evokes "ultimate concerns."

Throughout this volume the authors are suggesting that executive integrity may be the pivotal life-sustaining property of organizational existence. It is pivotal because organizations are fundamentally relational entities and all relationships that are worthy of anyone's continued investment are based on integrity. As we have discussed, there is an urgency about our times that is real and palpable; it cannot be wished away. We do live, clearly, in a time of decision. And integrity is an active option. Times like ours require examination of those general, overall, suggestive conceptions that provide a positive pathway for dealing with our dilemmas and can move us to positive action; there *is* a need for "vital ideas." Integrity, we believe, is one of those ideas.

1

Integrity: A Fictional Dialogue

Michael Maccoby

Participants

Frank Fortune, the fifty-five-year-old chief executive of a successful computer company, Business Systems Incorporated (BSI), with 50,000 employees and sales of $15 billion a year. Fortune has an undergraduate degree in mathematics from the University of Washington and an M.B.A. from Stanford. He has worked all his career at BSI, starting in the marketing department. His company has been weathering tough times in the computer industry.

Mike Measure, a forty-year-old development engineer with BSI. Measure led the team that developed one of the company's most successful products, Network 4000. Measure has a degree in electrical engineering and a doctorate in applied mathematics from MIT. He started his business career at IBM but moved to BSI ten years ago because he felt he had a better chance to develop his ideas.

Dan Deal, age thirty-five, a customer of BSI, a vice-president of Financial Services Limited (FSL), an innovative, fast-growing company. Deal has an undergraduate degree in economics from a good small liberal arts college. Deal and two partners started FSL ten years ago and have built it into a company with revenues of $500 million a year.

Paul Price, a forty-two-year-old financial analyst with Wall Street and Company. He specializes in BSI stock. Price is a graduate of Princeton University and Harvard Business School.

Harriet Hire, a thirty-seven-year-old personnel manager at BSI. Hire is a graduate in English literature from a liberal arts college. She taught high school English for five years and became fed up with her low salary and joined BSI in the sales department. She did well and moved to personnel.

Carl Craft, a fifty-year-old union leader, vice-president of Information Workers International (IWI). Craft's union represents some 10,000 workers at BSI and is trying to organize more. Craft went from high school to work as an electrician and subsequently moved up the union hierarchy. He is active in Democratic party politics.

Vernon Vigilante, age twenty-eight, from the Council on Corporate Responsibility. Vigilante is a graduate in history from Notre Dame with a law degree from Columbia. He apprenticed with Ralph Nader and recently has been active in the campaign to force American companies to divest their holdings in South Africa. He is planning to enter the Democratic primary for Congress.

Sam Shrink, a fifty-five-year-old psychologist and consultant who works with both management and unions. Shrink has a B.A. from a liberal arts college in history and literature and a Ph.D. from the University of Chicago. He has written a bestseller about the culture of the information industry.

The participants are sitting around the circular boardroom table at BSI.

Fortune: I know this is a rather unusual meeting. I've invited you all here for a discussion about integrity. Let me tell you why. I believe integrity is an essential value for BSI. Our managers feel the same way. We have done some surveys in the company, and almost everyone believes that the key to our future success is integrity. We must be known as, and act like, a company that can be trusted. We must conduct ourselves with the highest ethical standards in our relationships with one another and with customers, suppliers, shareholders, and other stakeholders. I believe our good name is one of our most important assets.

Now, I realize I am taking a risk by inviting some of you here. You have been our critics as well as our associates, clients, and customers. Vernon, you have directly criticized our integrity. Dan, you are one of our largest and most valued customers; recently you have complained about us. Paul, you have had questions about the company's future. Carl and the union have had some harsh words to say about us.

I have not invited you to this meeting to make it easy for myself and BSI. I have even invited two of our own managers who have been critical of the company: Mike Measure of R&D and Harriet Hire of personnel.

The reason I have invited you is that I believe the way to develop a culture of integrity is through open dialogue. If we have made mistakes in the past, we are not going to hide them. Integrity to me means honesty and openness to continual learning.

I am not sure how to proceed, but I have asked Dr. Shrink to facilitate the discussion. Some of you know him. He has been consultant to both company and union in helping us to develop a more competitive culture. Sam?

Shrink: Thank you, Frank. I think it takes courage to have a meeting like this. If we can all be honest in expressing our views, we have a chance to improve our relationships by understanding one another better.

I would like to propose that we go around the table and each person give his or her view of what integrity should mean for BSI and where you see a problem. Once we have done that, each person will have a chance to respond. Is that agreeable?

(Everyone nods.)

Who will start?

(Deal raises his hand.)

Deal: Integrity for us, Frank, has to do with keeping your word. We have appreciated your technical integrity. When BSI makes claims about what its products can do, we rely on them. The quality is there. The problem is on-time delivery of meeting commitments. There were times last year when we kept getting different messages from different people in your organization. We were promised a new system and we counted on it. But BSI didn't have its act together. The person who made the promise could not deliver. He obviously did not consult the people who have to deliver the goods. Frank, for us your integrity depends on your organizational integration. We want to do business with you, but our lifeblood depends on data systems. If you can't deliver, there are a lot of vendors clamoring for our business.

Shrink: Let's just continue clockwise around the table. Paul Price?

Price: I feel I represent the shareholders, the owners of BSI. Integrity for us has to do with two things. The first is taking the hard decisions necessary for profitability. The second is honesty about the business and its prospects.

Take the first point. Frank, you are chosen by the owners as their representative to protect their investment. You have accepted that trust. It is a role that demands judgment and toughness. You may feel bad about letting people go who do not add value. You may feel bad about closing down a factory in the United States, but if you can produce the product at lower cost abroad, it is your obligation to do so. I might add that some CEOs who managed with their hearts rather than with their heads have been the victims of hostile takeovers. Frank, we must all recognize that we operate in a capitalistic system. That system has made us the richest society in history, and one that allows great freedom. To lead a great corporation requires talent, knowledge, and the kind of integrity I am talking about.

The second point has to do with the image you want to present of the company to investors. There is always the temptation to present a rosy picture, but if the facts don't back it up, the Street will start to question your integrity. Once they do, trust evaporates. A few years ago, when you were painting such a rosy picture of Network 4000, there were real questions about whether you could produce the big breakthrough you were promising. You can't make empty promises like that and maintain a reputation for integrity.

Craft: I may be out of turn, Dr. Shrink, but I can't listen to Mr. Price and just sit still. What he calls integrity, I call exploitation. How can anyone maintain his integrity and treat workers like disposable parts? Mr. Price, do you believe a company can succeed if workers don't trust management? You ask for commitment and motivation. How do you expect to get it with a pure market orientation? I often hear executives say: "Our employees are our most valuable resources."

Fortune: I say that and I believe it to be true.

Craft: Well, I cringe when you say it. Not because I don't believe you, but because I do believe you see people as resources, like raw materials. You don't give the workers credit for being partners with you in the company's success. It's like you are just using them.

Price: Mr. Craft, I don't think you understand that there will be no employment for your members unless BSI makes a profit. If it keeps people on the payroll out of loyalty, then it puts everyone's job in jeopardy. But I do recognize that you raise a real issue about motivation.

Shrink: Perhaps we can return to that issue. Let's first hear from everyone. Harriet Hire.

Hire: I have to admit that I've questioned my own integrity in coming to work at BSI. I probably would have continued to teach school if I had got the kind of rewards I've received here. As an English teacher, I never doubted that I was making a contribution to society. I believe BSI also makes a contribution, but I must admit that sometimes I question the integrity of top management. When I came to work here, I was told there was a commitment to affirmative action. This company is run by white men. There have been no women or minorities such as blacks or Hispanics at the top. I came into the sales department and did well. I was disappointed not to have been promoted into a significant line assignment. Personnel is a nice feminine-type assignment, but it doesn't lead to the top.

Fortune: Well, Harriet, I am sorry you take it that way. I believe if you do an outstanding job in personnel, you can move to another department. But I must remind you that you were offered a line job overseas and you turned it down.

Hire: I would have liked that job, but my husband was unable to move and it would have also been a hardship for my children. That was an issue of integrity for me.

Fortune: Many of us have had to make those moves. And it wasn't easy on our wives and children. But if you aspire to leadership, that's the price you have to pay. You can't ask others to make sacrifices unless you yourself are willing to make them. The corporation is not going to prosper unless its managers accept something like military discipline. We try to satisfy employees, but there are limits. As Paul Price points out, we have owners to satisfy.

Shrink: Mr. Vigilante?

Vigilante: I expected to arrive here in a fighting mood, but you surprised me, Mr. Fortune, by agreeing at your last board meeting to withdraw your business from South Africa. Compared with many companies, BSI has a good record in standing up for American values at home and abroad. You are fortunately in an industry that is not a major polluter. Overseas, you try hard to remain ethical in your dealings.

   I must, however, take issue with Mr. Price's view of your responsibilities. BSI makes use of resources created by this society. It hires some of the most gifted young people who are educated in public schools and universities, as you were, Mr. Fortune. It makes use of the infrastructure of publicly financed roads, bridges, and services. It asks society to defend its interests through foreign policy, trade agreements, and if necessary, military force. In turn, society demands that it contribute to social betterment.

Price: Companies pay taxes and obey the laws. It seems to me BSI contributes a great deal to society by providing employment.

Vigilante: I agree that it is an important contribution, and I also concede that, in the past, critics of business have given that too little weight. Of course, BSI must be competitive and profitable, but I do argue that the strength of the American capitalistic system depends on the continual development of the national culture. BSI needs highly educated people who understand the importance of integrity and feel protected when they tell the truth. In that regard, Mr. Craft's union contributes to America's industrial strength by guaranteeing rights in the workplace.

I also have some trouble with Mr. Price's concept of ownership. Many, if not most, of BSI's owners are not owners in the traditional sense of ownership tied to responsibility. They buy the stock and value it in terms of quarterly dividends, thus pressuring Mr. Fortune to keep profit high at the expense of investment and the long-term health of the company. We read that the successful Japanese companies pay very small dividends and put their money into R&D and gaining market share. These companies, Mr. Craft, do not treat workers as resources but as assets. If there is insufficient work, they cut the price of their products in order to sell more, and in the long run they gain market share, innovate, and prevail over companies that look at the people the way Mr. Price preaches. The companies that follow his prescription may boast a few fat quarters, but by the time they are foundering in the wake of the Japanese, you, Mr. Price, will have sold your shares and bought something more attractive, maybe real estate or gold.

Price: Hold on, Vigilante. These are complex questions. I don't disagree with everything you say, but the system works only if you play by the rules of the game. The Japanese tax dividends heavily, but they levy no tax on capital gains. The incentives are there for reinvestment. Now, if you think that is important, why don't you lobby for a change in the tax code? I hear you are planning to run for Congress, and if you will allow me to say so, I doubt that your liberal friends will be as excited about your helping to strengthen the corporation as they are about your speeches and sit-ins to force companies out of South Africa.

Fortune: In all honesty, Vernon, I feel guilty about accepting credit for moving our operations out of South Africa. We did it because you pressured us. We were uncomfortable. Some of the board members agreed with you that to stay in that country meant supporting a horrendous racist regime. Like you, they believed that American business could pressure the South African government to change its policies, eliminate apartheid, and give blacks the vote. But other board members disagreed. One who had visited South Africa believes that our presence there is an important civilizing factor. As you know, we have insisted on hiring people of all races. We are helping to educate new leaders. That director believes that there is no way the ruling South Africans will bow to pressure. He believes that as we move out, the Afrikaner right wing will take control. There may be a bloody civil war. It will not be just white against black. Many blacks will kill each other. They are already doing so. I voted with the majority to leave because of pressure and because, from a business point of view, the energy we put into South Africa did not pay off. But I don't feel good about it. I am not sure but that it would have been more courageous to stay there.

(There is a long silence.)

Shrink: Mike Measure, it's your turn to speak.

Measure: My concerns are in the technical area. For me, integrity means building the best computer systems that we can create. I am not naive about this. Some of my engineers want us to work to a level of technical excellence and reliability that would price our products right out of the market. I recognize that this makes no sense and that their concept of integrity is rather egocentric.

But I do worry about integrity. Mr. Deal, you complained about delivery of Network 4000. If I had had my way, we would have waited longer. The product was technically sound, but with more work, it could have been the big breakthrough. We can make a product that will really dazzle the customers.

Fortune: It was your enthusiasms that got us into trouble with Paul. We announced those wonderful innovations—

Measure: But you also promised a delivery date to Dan Deal. You couldn't have it both ways and maintain our integrity. Deal threatened that he would go to a competitor if we couldn't deliver by a certain date. We said we would not be ready by that date. When you insisted, we gave you what we could. But there was a loss of integrity.

Fortune: It was a compromise. Dan got what he wanted, but we did not give the market exactly what we had promised.

I am hearing a lot of different views about BSI integrity, as well as issues of personal integrity, and I don't mind saying that I'm more than a little confused. Dr. Shrink, can you help us out?

Shrink: It sounds as if we have different views about the meaning of integrity. Let me try to sort them out.

Some of you, like Dan Deal, define it as telling the truth. Is that right?

Price: That's basic.

Shrink: But if Frank is aware of problems with a BSI product, should he announce it immediately to the world?

Price: Well, the stock might plunge and the owners would lose a great deal. I'm not so sure that would be responsible.

Shrink: So integrity has to do with responsibility.

Deal: Don't leave truth out. Integrity means telling the truth about when I can expect delivery.

Shrink: Suppose Frank believes he is telling the truth when in fact the company can't deliver. Often people believe they tell the truth when they are mistaken. Sometimes they fool themselves.

Deal: Well, I don't care whether or not Frank believes it is true. That's his business. I care whether it *is* the truth. A company with integrity delivers. It meets its commitments.

Shrink: So integrity means telling the truth, meeting commitments, but doing it in a responsible way. Is this always possible?

Hire: That's a good definition as far as I'm concerned. The company made a commitment for affirmative action, and its integrity depends on meeting it. My integrity depends on meeting my commitments to my job *and* my family.

Shrink: So far, everyone's definition of integrity supports his or her self-interest. Harriet, you also mentioned a question of personal integrity leaving teaching. And Frank, you questioned your own integrity in bowing to pressure. Here integrity has to do with conflict between self-interest and an internal value judgment. It has to do with being true to yourself, to what you believe is right.

Measure: That's closer to what I mean by technical integrity. You can make a profit with an inferior product, but you feel you have betrayed yourself by going along with expediency.

Price: That's all very well. It's nice to have a clean conscience, and if you want one, you should go live in a monastery. In the business world, you make commitments, you cut deals, you accept responsibility. If on reflection, you don't like your commitments, you have the option of leaving the game. But integrity means being grown up, being the kind of person who can be trusted. If you don't keep your commitments, people will question your integrity and they won't want to play with you.

Shrink: So there may be a conflict between integrity as living up to commitments with others and integrity as being true to oneself. How should one resolve that?

Vigilante: I think people who make lousy commitments are sellouts. If you commit yourself to treating people as objects, there is no way you are going to feel good about yourself. I also have a question about your integrity, Dr. Shrink. How can you be a consultant to both management and the union? It sounds as if they have very different views of commitments and responsibilities.

Shrink: That's a legitimate question, Vernon. I was hired as a joint consultant to help create new ways of organizing work that are both more productive and more satisfying to workers. This is an area in which management and the union found they had a common interest. We have succeeded in creating new models where both managers and union leaders have been willing to be flexible and share power. As long as both sides agree on this goal, I can work with them both. But when they are in fundamental disagreement, I must withdraw.

I agree with you that integrity has to do not only with meeting commitments but with making the kind of commitments one feels good about meeting.

Craft: This conversation makes something clearer to me. Mr. Price and I have very different views of what Mr. Frank Fortune's commitments should be. My commitment is to the members of the union. They elected me to serve their interests. The union is a democracy, and we have open debate about what these interests are. Our goal is to establish the rights of workers. Unless we fight for those rights, they will not exist. Mr. Fortune's commitment to owners like the ones Price represents makes him treat workers like replaceable resources. It is our job to change that, to force the company to make commitments to the workers, to protect employment security, and to insist on training and education that enable workers to adapt to new technology. Of course, we recognize that BSI has to make a profit, but we don't accept the idea that the company should maximize its profits at the expense of employees.

I think if we push Frank to make this kind of commitment to his employees, he may actually be building a company he can point to with more pride.

Fortune: I can accept that. I don't like the idea of two cultures in this company, and I don't enjoy having to let go of committed employees. Competition demands that we work as a team. The difference between managers and workers is beginning to blur at the lower levels. Dr. Shrink has helped us to see that cooperation with the union can improve productivity and make BSI a better place to work.

Shrink: What I am hearing is that integrity depends on getting our commitments in line with our values. It means being true to ourselves and to others.

Measure: In this marketing society we live in, many people lose their integrity by trying to sell themselves. Their only values are making a sale. They don't seem aware that they tell people what they want to hear.

Hire: Yes, that's right. I have a question about that definition of integrity, Sam. What about a racist or sexist who says he is being true to himself? Some people have rather rigid values. Being true to themselves means forcing others to adhere to *their* views of truth. What if they are wrong? Vernon Vigilante believes integrity demands withdrawing from South Africa. Mr. Fortune suggests that form of integrity may hurt the South Africans.

Shrink: You make a good point. It's difficult to know the truth about what will happen in South Africa. In the name of integrity, an uninformed but self-righteous person can do all sorts of damage. Furthermore, a person may feel she is being true to herself, but unconsciously she is obeying parental dictates as the result of childhood brainwashing. One person believes integrity means being fully independent, neither lending nor borrowing. Another person believes integrity means helping others before anything else. Neither person has reflected on these values in terms of their consequences. For the first person, integrity can mean sacrificing the chance for meaningful relationships. For the other, it can mean letting oneself be used and feeling angry and resentful about it.

This conversation shows that there is no simple definition of integrity.

The issue of individual integrity is similar to that of an organization's integrity. If we doubt a person's integrity, we lose trust. It is a modern version of honor. In the past, a person lost his honor when he failed to live up to his commitments, to act courageously. As in the corporate case, personal integrity is not only a matter of honesty but of developing the capability to respond to commitments. Sometimes there is an internal dialogue among various internal voices that try to balance needs and wants with demands from others.

Hire: Perhaps this was easier when roles were simpler, when men were the providers and women the homemakers. When you have multiple commitments at home and work, it is not always clear where integrity lies. Suppose I am committed to go to a meeting, but my child is sick. There is no way I can maintain integrity by sticking to both my commitments. I have to prioritize and make a decision. I have to decide that some commitments are more important than others.

Shrink: That's true for all of us. To maintain a sense of integrity, we must be conscious of our values and recognize that we must make decisions. And sometimes we will make bad ones and feel we have betrayed ourselves.

Price: It may be easier to maintain a sense of integrity if you don't have much of an imagination. When you start to think of the effects of your decisions, you can paralyze yourself.

Hire: But if you do not, you sacrifice a degree of concern for people that makes them trust you.

Measure: Or you can lose your motivation to create. You can become mediocre.

Shrink: In any society, there are strong pressures to conform. People get along by repressing knowledge.

I suppose a slave can feel a sense of integrity as long as he recognizes that he is forced to submit to a master and does not fool himself into believing the master is wise and wonderful and *should* decide for him. If one is free, there is less excuse for not acting with integrity. But in a rich and complex society like ours, with so much freedom, there may be more temptations to lose integrity, to betray ourselves, not out of fear but because of ambition or greed.

Not only are we a culture that values integrity in commitments, but we also seek an inner integrity or wholeness. Our sense of dignity and meaning is based on this kind of integrity. We like ourselves when we feel we have resisted temptation to sacrifice integrity for advantage, and we admire others who do this. Our political tradition is built on the concept of liberty, freedom to make commitments, and rights that protect the sense of integrity. Our Judeo-Christian tradition deals with the internal freedom necessary to perceive the truth and act with integrity. It is built on the premise that God has given us free will and a knowledge of good and evil. We reject that knowledge and betray God when we worship idols, such as powerful leaders, and give up our personal responsibility to decide what is right and wrong.

We can even make idols of our *selves* by sacrificing our knowledge of what is right in order to sell ourselves. But in doing so, we lose our integrity.

But even if we avoid such secular idolatry, our knowledge is always limited, and so we can make bad decisions and the wrong commitments. Free people will not always make the right choices, but they can learn from mistakes and practice courage in making the right ones.

Measure: Do all cultures have the same concept of integrity? I've been to Japan and they tell me that, for them, integrity means accepting one's role gracefully. They don't see any need to feel a sense of integrity in acting according to conscience.

Shrink: Yes, for the Japanese, honor, or "face," has to do with how one is perceived rather than an internal sense of wholeness. But to maintain face, one must honor commitments. In that sense, there is a similarity to our concept of integrity. Japanese face is their way of expressing the universal human need for dignity.

Fortune: What is the relation of integrity to ethics?

Shrink: Ethics are commonly considered as rules that allow people to live with one another. But they can be judged in terms of values. The Old Testament ethic of desert justice—an eye for an eye, a tooth for a tooth—assumes different relationships than does the prophetic and Christian ethic of mercy and compassion for the sinner. Societies develop ethics, as do corporations. Craft and Vigilante believe they are fighting to improve corporate ethics. If Price and Fortune disagree with that, they can engage in a dialogue about ethics. Such a dialogue must clarify the values by which ethics will be measured.

Fortune: I believe BSI must have rules that allow people the freedom to argue different views. I believe the company needs people with integrity. But BSI cannot succeed unless everyone gets behind the decisions we make. This is not a democracy.

Shrink: Of course not. But in some companies, employees feel like slaves who must submit to keep their jobs; they protect their dignity and feel they maintain integrity by showing no enthusiasm and by playing power games that undermine corporate integrity. If you want more of a commitment from them, those people must have a real voice in developing corporate decisions.

People who cannot in good conscience accept your decisions should leave the company. Those who lack courage may stay and live with a guilty conscience, a symptom of a lack of integrity.

Many corporate managers I have interviewed feel they constantly betray themselves and accede to decisions they don't believe are right, not because to protest would cost them their job, but because it would dampen their chances for promotion.

You must decide, Frank, whether you want to create a culture that truly values integrity. If you do, you must be prepared to manage a process which will often be uncomfortable but which gives promise of gaining commitment and creativity. You can never fully succeed, but engaging in the process itself will strengthen your leadership and motivate the company.

Fortune: What, then, is our definition of integrity?

Shrink: For the company, as Frank pointed out at the start, integrity is defined as meeting commitments and acting according to ethical standards. Unless a company is seen as having integrity, neither customers nor investors will want to do business with it. But corporate integrity is not gained merely by honest executives. It requires building an organization that can meet commitments. It requires an open, honest, strategic dialogue among marketing, R&D, and production. It requires motivated people who are not afraid to tell the truth.

Let me stress the importance of the strategic dialogue. We see that the stakeholders of the company—managers, workers, customers, government—represent different interests and values. These may conflict. Simple dialogue only acquaints each person with the others' viewpoints and interests. Conflicting viewpoints get solved, if at all, either by negotiation or by appeal to higher authority. But it may also be possible to resolve differences through new approaches. Strategic dialogue goes beyond simple dialogue and negotiation. It involves everyone in a learning process, to answer a question through analysis, new ideas, and experimentation. Given the different stakeholders and the demands by the marketplace for innovation and profitability, organizational integrity requires many such strategic dialogues. Frank, it seems to me that your invitation to us today is an expression of exactly the kind of leadership needed by the corporation. But I don't think we have yet posed the right questions for this strategic dialogue.

Fortune: What are the right questions for a strategic dialogue?

Measure: If I understand Sam correctly, I'd say one question would be "How can we better meet our commitments to customers and at the same time satisfy our best technical standards?"

Hire: And how can we meet our commitments to affirmative action and also be efficient and competitive? We haven't begun to consider ideas to make it possible for women to contribute to the company and maintain integrity as mothers and wives. If we do ask this question, maybe we can also improve the quality of life for men.

Craft: What about the question of how to maximize employment security in an uncertain, globally competitive world?

Fortune: Thank you, Sam. And I thank all of you for speaking so openly. I see now that the larger question for our dialogue is not "what" is integrity for BSI, but "How can BSI be a company of integrity and produce real wealth?" That is a question which translates into many strategic dialogues and must lead us to new actions.

2

Quality of Service: A New Frontier for Integrity in Organizations

Roger Harrison

Someday, after mastering winds, tides, and gravity, we shall harness for God the energy of love, and then, for the second time in history, man will have discovered fire [Pierre Teilhard de Chardin].

At least a modicum of humility is called for in anyone presuming in this Age of Endarkenment to write or speak publicly on the subject of integrity or ethics. My obeisance in that direction will take the form of a personal confession. My own striving for integrity might be described by the oxymoron "rigid iconoclast." That is to say that I have passionately resisted the claims of rules, customs, and ethical conventions on my behavior while taking frequent stands on personal principle that have caused rifts and separations in my personal and business relationships. A somewhat more palatable way of putting it would be to describe me as a "principled contrarian." My behavior under this rubric convinced me, after I had bitten every hand that fed me during the first decade of my working life, that even the modest demands for conformity of the academic world were too constraining.

I have chosen to live by my wits during the twenty years since then. When I examine my ethical behavior as a management consultant, another oxymoron seems to describe the first

half of that twenty-year period: "compassionate buccaneer."
In my secret heart, I saw myself as a kind of latter-day Robin
Hood, driving the hardest possible bargains with the wealthy
organizations that were my clients while acting as a sort of guerrilla fighter for the liberation of the disempowered middle and
upper-middle managers with whom I spent most of my professional time. I took money from the rich and gave freedom to
the disenfranchised. It was a pretty good deal for me, since what
I took was tangible and scarce, and what I gave was intangible
and (theoretically) unlimited.

During the early seventies I began to experience burnout
and dispiritedness in my work, which I first associated with stress
and later came to see as a kind of spiritual emptiness. I felt that
I had painted myself into a corner by creating a reputation for
toughness, independence, and strength which left me without
much that was warm, nurturing, or healing in my work life.
Even when I asked for help and support, people tended not to
see me as needing it. I had certainly achieved the autonomy
I sought, but at the end of the day I found myself quite alone.
In due course I entered upon the search for wholeness and for
opening of the heart that currently engages me in both my personal and my professional life.

I have to admit that when invited to join this august company, I accepted more out of the hope of fellowship and con-
viviality than from an intrinsic interest in what I took to be the
subject. My old aversion to external control has given me a
distance for formal ethical standards and professional codes of
conduct, and I am not usually an enthusiastic participant in
discussions of moral issues. It wasn't at all immediately clear
to me how the topic of the conference connected to my primary
professional interest, the balancing of alignment (will) and attunement (love) in organizations.

Struggling with my ambivalence, I put off starting work
on the chapter as long as possible. However, when I finally
started the task with a look at the dictionary, my thinking was
greatly stimulated by the following definition:

Integrity. 1. The condition of having no part or element wanting; unbroken
state; material wholeness, completeness, entirety. 2. Unimpaired or un-

corrupted state; original perfect condition; soundness 1450. 3a. Innocence, sinlessness 1678. 3b. Soundness of moral principle; the character of uncorrupted virtue; uprightness, honesty, sincerity 1548 [*The Shorter Oxford English Dictionary*, 1968].

I have never thought of my personal or professional interests as having much to do with integrity in business, but the definition as wholeness and completeness sounded a lot like my own search and a lot like what I am working for in the organizations to which I consult. It also sounded like what my clients are reaching for when they ask in their middle years, "Is this all there is?" or "What's the deeper meaning of what we're doing?"

Intrigued, I looked up the definition of *ethics,* in the same source:

Ethics. . . . 3a. The moral system of a particular writer or school of thought 1651. b. The rules of conduct recognized in certain limited departments of human life 1789. 4. The science of human duty in its widest extent, including, besides ethics proper, the science of law whether civil, political, or international 1690.

That sounded more like what I first thought the conference was about. Ethics is the system of rules to which we are constrained to conform, or which we perhaps internalize and take for our own standard. It seems also to be what writers in the popular press mean when they decry the continuing decay in ethical standards in business and government, which leads to scandals on overpricing in the defense industry, wanton violations of pollution and safety standards in toxic waste disposal, cover-ups in the nuclear power industry, and the like.

I looked a bit more, and I found two statements that, looked at side by side, seemed to relate and contrast the two definitions:

The signs are clear. The intensity of the differences in our values is relentlessly escalating. It is evident that continuing the development of individualized ethics will *not* generate harmony and a cultural consensus or foster a concept of human dignity that can speak definitively to the issues of human meaning and purpose. . . . "Can the free enterprise system survive in a culture with metaphysical cancer that causes ethical schizophrenia?'' The answer is ''NO!'' The free enterprise system was nurtured in an environment with a strong ethical consensus—a necessity for its existence. That consensus has been shattered. The ability to appeal successfully to a moral standard for purposes of resolving value differences will diminish as long as the ethical schizophrenia remains. This being true, we will of necessity learn to rely more and more on a power structure for our solutions. Then, in time, the power structure will control the economic structure. When this is so, the cancer will have done its work [Chewning, 1984, p. 11].

We must make sure that our love, sense of truth, and intuition . . . are in good order. They are the tools we need to achieve our purpose . . . and our equipment must be up to the task. . . . Follow your heart when making decisions, and you will always be reacting constructively and living according to God's will. . . .

Lying deep within us is the knowledge of what is right for us and how to go about getting it. We must open up to ourselves by bringing our concentration down to the simplicity of true heart feelings. We must be willing to look inside to discover who we are and what to do with our lives [Bernard, 1985].

These two statements seemed to me to epitomize a dilemma in part modern and in part ageless. The modern dilemma is that our former consensus on business ethics and personal morality is not giving way to a competing unified standard but is being undermined by a kind of radical pluralism in which each considers himself or herself competent to choose, and in which the individual's choice of standards is perhaps as likely to be self-oriented as it is to be responsive to the needs of others. The ageless dilemma is, how do we know what is right? Do we seek and rely on direct knowledge from God or some inner voice, or do we get our guidance through the mediation of some human agency?

I can agree with both these statements. On the one hand, my personal journey has led me to rely increasingly on the kind of inner guidance suggested in the quotation from Bernard. For me, that is a path to *integrity*. It leads toward the kind of wholeness implied in the dictionary definition. The thrust of this chapter is toward the idea of wholeness as an ideal for executives and for their organizations. On the other hand, when I look at the world around me and the organizations to which I consult, I find the kind of disintegration of an *ethical* consensus that Chewning deplores.

When I think about the differences between integrity and ethics, I intuit that the major difference is that integrity is something that is characteristic of any living system, person, or organization: Integrity for that system is the state of being itself, of fully operating according to its highest purpose, of realizing its potential as a life form. The definition of integrity comes from within the individual or system. Ethics, in contrast, is a set of rules agreed upon or imposed from the outside. It cannot exist without a social system, for which ethics becomes the "rules of conduct recognized in certain limited departments of human life." It is clear that when people do not agree among themselves on those rules, the rules can be effective only if they are imposed by power. So Chewning is right in expecting that when the ethical consensus disintegrates, the application of power will be required in order to keep a code of ethics in place and observed.

During most of my professional life, those of us who serve organizations as behaviorally oriented advisers and consultants have been struggling with the basic issue that Chewning identifies, although I think many of us would be reluctant to draw his conclusions. We have taken our part in the dismantling of the ethical consensus. We have had high hopes for the flowering of human potential once people could be liberated from external constraints to their growth—and we have seen things turn out quite differently than we had hoped. I believe it is time for a reassessment of what is possible and desirable in developing human potential within organizations. A good way to start that reassessment is to review recent history, looking at the tension between ethics, defined as rules for personal conduct, and the search for personal integrity, defined as wholeness, within business organizations. Necessarily, my view of recent history is a personal one, but I make no apology for the limitations of my vantage point. We all have to look from somewhere, and I've at least moved around a lot!

During the sixties and early seventies, when the idea of "applied behavioral science" was acquiring meaning through the practice of sensitivity training and organization development, I think many of us believed implicitly in the replacement of ethics by integrity. We shared a vision of organizations that would operate on trust, instead of power and rules, and we exposed our clients to experiences such as T-groups and team development which we hoped would kindle that vision in them. We believed, more or less, that the liberated human spirit would turn toward openness, honesty, trust, and cooperation. Freed to cooperate, people would no longer need to be managed by power and by rules and regulations backed up by power. Perhaps in our hearts we hoped for the withering away of the organization, in the same way that Communists had earlier looked forward to the withering away of the state. The underlying assumption was the same: If you treat people right, they'll be good, and you won't have to motivate them through rewards and punishments. That theme has become a litany of liberal management thinking, expressed over and over in the writings of humanistic psychologists and management theorists over the last three decades.

The T-group and its successor, the encounter group, were, in fact, vehicles for the search for personal integrity. In managing the group as trainers, we began by dismantling the rules and norms (ethics) by which people usually live in social interaction, and we endeavored to build social supports for members to become whole persons and be accepted as such by the others. When it worked, it was beautifully liberating and fulfilling, and for a lot of people the experience became a powerful stimulant for their personal journey toward wholeness.

T-groups worked so well for groups composed of strangers that we were inspired to try to work with teams of managers in the same way. One way of looking at what happened is that we thought we could go beyond ethics (the normal organizational "rules of the game") and create structures and processes that would nurture the development of personal integrity (wholeness, being authentically oneself) within the organization.

It really didn't work out. In fact, these experiments probably put the kiss of death on the T-group as a force for social change, at the same time as their failure stimulated the develop-

ment of the body of techniques that came to be known as organization development. We did liberate people to a degree, but
they didn't always turn toward the light. Sometimes they turned
greedy or nasty. That's why *T-group* is often a dirty word among
managers old enough to know what it means. The T-group
didn't work out as an organizational intervention, because power
and politics didn't go away. We suspended the rules and customs
that normally hold people's competitiveness and power striving in check, but we didn't eliminate the impulses that the
"organizational ethics" is designed to control. Often power
issues and concerns blocked the trust-building and opening process, so that the group did not achieve its objectives. Sometimes
we seduced people into a degree of openness that was unwise
for them, and they were attacked and hurt by others whose
motives were far from pure. Sometimes their careers were dam-
aged as a result of exchanges in the group.

I think we were learning that most organizations are not
very good places to try to develop personal integrity. It took
me, like many others, quite a while to get the point. My first
interpretation of our failure was that we had used the wrong
methods. Like my colleagues, I spent most of the late sixties
and seventies in the search for better technology by which we
could free people in organizations to be "the best they could
be" (and of course at the same time to help the organization
to operate more effectively).

When we moved away from the T-group, we moved away
from the focus on trust and openness that had got us into so
much trouble. We developed names like "task-oriented team
development" and "role negotiation" (Harrison, 1972a) to
reflect the hardheaded attitudes that we believed more appropriate to working within organizations. I and many of my colleagues began to think of empowering the individual as the key
to the search for personal integrity within organizations. Ironically, I now think that the "ethical schizophrenia" to which
Chewning refers was fostered for many American managers by
the personal growth and empowerment for which I once considered myself to be a guerrilla fighter. The name of management training programs I used as tools give the flavor: "Labo-

ratory in Initiative, Risk Taking and Autonomy''; ''Positive Power and Influence''; ''Positive Negotiation''; ''Managing Your Boss.'' These programs were all to do with knowing what you want and getting it. They were long on skills and techniques, and they skirted ethical dilemmas whenever possible. Our avowed objective was to empower people to decide for themselves. Although we didn't come right out and say we thought the organization was the bad oppressor, and its members were the good people who could be trusted to make the right decisions, we certainly harbored that suspicion.

I spent most of that decade living and working in Europe. Europeans trust the innate goodness of the individual much less than we Americans do, and even when my work went well, I always considered it out of the mainstream. When I returned to the United States, I was surprised to see the extent to which a self-oriented transformation had occurred here. When I left in 1968, love and flower power seemed ascendant. In 1976, the first thing that struck me was the books in airport shops: *Looking Out for Number One; Winning Through Intimidation; The Gamesman*. Many of the young managers I met embodied the values implicit in these titles. They were self-confident and self-oriented, out for what they could get in work, in relationships, and in life. In their view, the organization was not so much an adversary as a source of satisfactions that could safely be exploited, an inexhaustible source of wealth and energy—somewhat the way we used to think about oil and gas!

The organizations were showing signs of the strain, as were our public institutions. People were taking out more resources and human energy from organizations than they were prepared to put back in, just when the environments in which the organizations operated were becoming more turbulent and uncertain, more demanding of the best that organization members could contribute. As a result the social fabric was coming unraveled.

There has long been a tendency in business to prefer machines to humans for any work where there is a choice, and that tendency seems to have been strengthened and accelerated by the individuality and feistiness of the ''Now Generation.''

A lot of people have lost their jobs, and a lot more are due to go. Many people are now afraid of the power of organizations that they briefly looked on as benign providers of the good life. Pension rights, seniority rights, rights to continued employment—all are weakening as economic conditions permit and perhaps require organizations to become "lean and mean." The replacement of consensus with power that Chewning refers to has become a reality for members of many organizations that were once seen as dull but safe and benign places in which to work: the telephone companies, the oil industry, the banks. The work may still be dull, but these organizations are neither benign nor safe any longer.

This change has been graphically illustrated to me by an event in one such organization, one of the world's largest and one known for its attention to the development and care of its managerial people. During one of the recent international terrorist scares, an internal consultant described to me the security measures that the top management group was taking on the "executive floor" of its world headquarters: special guards, bulletproof glass, the works. I remarked that they must be really concerned about Arab extremists, and he said, "No, we're in the process of shedding more than 20 percent of our managers, and what they're afraid of is that one of those managers will come gunning for them!"

If we look at developments in large organizations such as the one instanced above, we can interpret events of the last two decades as a struggle between the claims of an ethical consensus and the search for personal integrity, in which ethics lost and the search for integrity degenerated into hedonistic self-gratification. The outcome of the struggle is a victory for neither but, rather, a return to power as the means of social control.

We need not look far for evidence to support that conclusion. The media are full of our increasingly combative and amoral behavior in business relationships: public slander of one another's products by competing advertisers; unfriendly takeovers and mergers in which the winners get bigger jobs and the losers are out on the street; contract concessions forced on unions by the sincere threat to close plants or go into Chapter 11; endless proliferation of class action suits for everything under the sun; flagrant violation of air and water pollution standards by organizations large and small; prosecutions of high-level executives in some of our most prestigious financial institutions for insider trading and other illegal manipulations. Increasingly, it looks like a dog-eat-dog business world, in which the only ethics are those supported by power: the fear of the law and the fear of retaliation.

The evidence, however, is not all in one direction. We still live in a pluralistic society—indeed, a pluralistic planet—and for every current of change, we can identify several countercurrents. For example, the "search for excellence" and the emphasis on "high performance" and "high-performing organizations" seem to keep alive and vital our cherished notions of the perfectibility of the individual and of the institutions in which we work. Current interest in the quality of working life and in the improvement of service suggests that something other than naked power may be at work in the world.

Our time is reminiscent of the Renaissance, that period of ferment and change in the fifteenth and sixteenth centuries in which an earlier Chewning could also have said, "The intensity of the differences in our values is relentlessly escalating." It was a time that produced contrasts in values equal to those of our day. It pitted, for example, the integrity of "a man for all seasons," Sir Thomas Moore, against the opportunism of a Cardinal Wolsey and the self-indulgence of his master, Henry VIII. Nor does it overstretch the point to compare the great monastery land grab by Henry's opportunistic courtiers to the rapacious doings of modern-day corporate raiders. It was a time which produced a Machiavelli and a Michelangelo, which nurtured both the Borgias and Saint Theresa of Ávila, a time in which disintegration of the consensus on values allowed the basest and the most noble of human passions to overflow their banks and fertilize the ground for a new age.

I do not want to overemphasize the similarities between that time and ours, only to suggest that without destruction there can be no change and no creativity. I believe that ethical systems enforce a kind of moral mediocrity: Both sainthood and the diabolical fall outside their guidelines. Great good and great evil originate in choices made within the individual human heart, not in conformance to an external code. When a system of ethics breaks up, people gain freedom to make individual choices, both good and evil. The disintegration of the moral consensus releases altruism, love, and all that is finest in human endeavor, as well as selfishness, aggression, and all that is ugly.

I think that we who have spent most of our professional lives in what is roughly characterized as the "human potential movement" are just coming to appreciate the darker side of human potential and to acknowledge the possibility of evil in human behavior, beyond the behavior produced by social milieu, poverty, broken homes, and inadequate parenting. Perhaps we are the last to know. A quick look at the movie and television sections of any daily newspaper suggests that the popular mind is more fascinated by evil now than at any time in living memory. Here are the titles of six of the first ten films listed under "Alameda County Drive-In Movies" in the *San Francisco Chronicle* of August 31, 1986: *Lethal, Texas Chainsaw Massacre, The Fly, Psycho III, Aliens, Friday the 13th III.*

I would argue, then, that the disintegration of the consensus around ethics has the effect of giving each of us more freedom of choice and thus a more open road along which to seek personal integrity. By the same token, there are fewer barriers and sanctions to prevent our straying off the path. We should therefore expect what I actually find in my dealings with managers and leaders: that the range of ethical behavior is greater than three decades ago and that there is more preoccupation and concern over the moral choices that managers have to make.

Freedom of choice does not support us in making choices. I find little discussion of business ethics in the organizations I work with and even less discussion of personal integrity. One's search for integrity is considered a strictly private matter, for the most part, as though it were irrelevant to the conduct or success of the business. A curtain of silence exists that is a significant barrier to the development of personal integrity within business. It is a curtain that can be penetrated, but with difficulty, because it is located both within the individual and within the social system of the organization.

I have experienced this curtain myself in the process of changing the value base from which I work with clients. What follows is some more personal confession that I believe illustrates the dilemmas we all face when we work on our personal integrity in a business setting.

We all have different needs for developing wholeness and a sense of personal integrity. One of mine has been the lack of an open heart, but I had a long road to travel before I could do much work on it. As described above, for a number of years I was heavily involved in the development of interpersonal skills training that was devoted to the empowerment of individual managers. It fitted my personal development needs perfectly. I worked on becoming stronger, more assertive, and more autonomous, and I found little difficulty in translating my personal search into concepts and programs for my clients in business. Being strong and assertive is a value supported in many, if not most, businesses, and my colleagues and I found ready customers for the products of our own self-development. To me that was business integrity: acting out in my work the values I was trying to achieve in becoming most fully myself. When I was working on autonomy or empowerment both for myself and for others, I was energized by my work, and I was successful in business.

My rule of thumb for when I have finished working on something in myself is when I start to care more about the process than the outcome. I knew I was ready to move on from personal power when I could play with a negotiation or a confrontation and make a dance of it. It wasn't that I didn't care whether I won or lost, just that winning or losing was less important than the dance. And of course I wasn't always that detached. But when I started to play with power, it ceased to become an issue of personal integrity for me. At about that point, it began to lose energy and interest for me professionally. The programs weren't fun anymore, and I found it was no longer a matter of integrity to take up the challenge of each confrontation. Often I let a confrontation go and saved my energy for something else. I was ready to move on, but whither away?

I believe one can deal with ethical issues without having a clear sense of one's own personal identity or developmental path, because ethical codes come from outside the person. We can evaluate ethical behavior more or less objectively by comparing the standard with what the person actually does. For issues of personal integrity to arise requires a sense of who one is now and who one is becoming. The standard is known only subjectively, although it is no less real for that. For me, and perhaps for many people, it is more difficult to create the standard than it is to live up to it. Once I know what I need, that knowledge becomes a strong motivator for action, and the action is intrinsically fulfilling, even when painful. But the search for the standard itself begins in confusion, and the path to self-understanding is definitely a case of "management by wandering about."

Thirteen or fourteen years ago, I began to feel the lack of a spiritual connection in my life and work and began an eclectic process of experimentation that led me from Transcendental Meditation through the esoteric Arica programs of Oscar Ichazo and then, after my return from Europe, into a brief exploration of Tibetan Buddhism. Not all of it stuck, of course, but I came to feel that the meaning of my life was to be found in the spiritual journey. While working on the empowerment of the individual in organizations, I was also doing much hard but only modestly successful work on achieving higher states of consciousness. At about the time that the power game was beginning to pall, I realized that I had framed my quest as a kind of spiritual analogue to that game. I was looking for spiritual empowerment, for mastery of the higher states of consciousness. I began to understand that for me, at least, the attempt to achieve such states was like trying to build a skyscraper on filled land: without careful attention to the foundation, it would fall down in the first seismic disturbance.

I saw my spiritual search as trying to get high without first being good, and I realized that I had a lot of fundamental work to do in just cleaning up my act. I was trying to do graduate work without having passed Integrity 101, which I saw as about the Golden Rule: truly endeavoring to walk in the shoes of others; having understanding and compassion; giving without expectation of return; dealing with others as I would want to be dealt with—no mystical highs; just basic stuff. When I looked at the syllabus and considered the amount of time remaining in the term, I realized I might not have time for graduate work if I was to master the introductory materials.

What I was ready for was to move from a focus on the development of *willing* to a focus on the development of *loving*. That was when I began to experience, for the first time in my life, a serious crisis of integrity in my work.

Frankly, I was scared of bringing these insights into business, although I believed significant numbers of managers in midlife were stuck more or less where I was. It was one thing to peddle power and influence to my clients; it was quite another to prattle in public about love, compassion, and the Golden Rule in business. In the early seventies, when David Berlew and I developed something we called the ''Positive Power and Influence Program,'' we had a lot of prospective clients tell us that *power* was a dirty word in their organizations. Fortunately for our business, it was a dirty word in the same way that *sex* had once been: it attracted at the same time as it repelled. Once you got people into the back of the shop, they usually let themselves get into it, and they invited their friends. Our timing on bringing ''power'' out of the closet was just right. But ''love''— in business?

The world kept asking for power and influence, negotiation training, and the like. My inner voice kept saying that what I was offering to that world was as unbalanced as my own life had been. Not bad—just incomplete; not whole; therefore lacking in integrity.

I spent a lot of time between 1979 and 1981 at a place called the Institute for Conscious Evolution, meeting with other consultants in the San Francisco Bay area, talking about what we called ''organization alignment,'' and trying to work up the courage to put my energy where my heart was. Those conversations were frankly spiritual in tone, directed toward the question of how people could become more conscious of the relationships among themselves as individuals, their organizations as living systems, and the planet, considered as a larger living, evolving system of which all our other systems are parts. These conversations shaped my ideas of integrity as balance and wholeness, and I began talking and writing about the balance between "alignment" (the will to achieve a common purpose) and "attunement" (appreciation of connections, striving for love and harmony) in organizations (Harrison, 1983, 1984).

I have come to see the search for integrity as a kind of spiral alternation between opposites, developing first one pole and then the other, at greater and greater levels of differentiation and complexity. I see that alternation as a kind of swinging between "yin" and "yang," the two principles around which so much Chinese philosophy has developed. In business and in personal life, these principles can be understood from the following list of opposites:

Activity	*Receptivity*
(alignment)	(attunement)
Willing	loving
Resisting	yielding
Taking	giving
Differentiating	synthesizing
Controlling	nurturing
Competing	cooperating
Persuading	listening
Separating	joining
Changing	appreciating

As I came to see it, the search for integrity consists in exploring these two poles at ever higher levels of refinement (higher levels of spiritual development). At a lower level, the receptive pole might be "dependency" and the active pole "aggression." At a higher level, the receptive pole would be "mutuality" and the active pole "competition." At a still higher level, the poles would be expressed as "compassion" and "independence" (see Harrison, 1979). There are doubtless still higher levels, but a rule of thumb in spiritual development has it that one is unable to comprehend levels more than one above where one is oneself.

At any given time, then, the *expression* of one's integrity is in being fully who one is at that time. But the process, what I have called the *search for integrity,* consists in being willing and able to move on from where one is to the next phase of the process. Thus, one can have integrity and at the same time be completely stuck, unable to comprehend the possibility of a further development beyond the current state. When I stood at the pole of "competition," expressing my integrity meant playing power games, up to the time when that lost its edge, when it began to feel like "being stuck." Then, continuing to be involved in the search meant moving on toward "compassion," which I experienced as a need to open my heart, to be more generous and giving of myself.

After a lot of compulsive dithering about risks to my professional reputation and future income, I rather timidly did a paper on organization alignment and attunement (Harrison, 1983). My earliest effort received very limited circulation. I sent it to some friends and colleagues here and in Europe, and it was distributed to a small number of clients of SRI International. Then the feedback began to come in.

People who were "tuned in" to "New Age" ideas liked the paper all right and gave me some nice compliments. Outside of that inner circle, I got two kinds of strong feedback, both of which strengthened my belief that business organizations are not, by and large, good places in which to pursue the search for personal integrity as I was coming to conceive of it. One kind came from professional friends and colleagues, people who have liked and respected my work and who wish me well. The following is a good example:

You spoke of love at some length. After the initial shock of it my uneasiness did not go away. "You keep talkin' about love, boy, and you gonna get screwed royally" remained my basic sentiment. I mean, "love" in a high-performance organization? That's tossing a hot potato into a cold/cool medium. Even if you do warm things up with attunement, can you ever warm it up to "love" level and still keep an eye on business? . . . It seems to me, Roger, that using the term *love* for organization description stirs up people's deepest hurts and longings, and how you can meet their expectations and run a railroad at the same time is beyond me.

The second kind of feedback was from managers, people I didn't know who had received the paper through the workings of some mysterious network. The following quotation from a manager gives the flavor:

By the time I finished reading it, tears were streaming from my eyes. It is happening again, now as I write this note to you. For years, I have felt alone in thinking it was possible to work with people in such a caring atmosphere that the bottom line becomes a by-product of that atmosphere. Now, thanks to your report, there are many people around me who share that seemingly impossible dream.

Both men were focused on a basic truth: Business organizations are tough places to nurture tender feelings. People who do harbor dreams of a more compassionate and responsive business world feel alone and unsupported, except when something occurs that brings their feelings out into the open. Then they find that others have also harbored these same, seemingly subversive thoughts and feelings.

Seen through the lens of my current preoccupation with the development of an open heart, much of the business world is unbalanced and stuck, unable to support movement beyond the values of action, competition, and strength. The issue is not just one of personal growth. It is not just that organizations block development of caring and compassion on the part of organization members; the behavior of organizations in society is also frozen into a competitive/exploitative orientation. Viable alternatives to competitive behavior cannot even be perceived from that vantage point. We shall continue stripping the world of natural resources—polluting our air and water, replacing people who need work with machines that don't, manipulating one another into spending money we don't have for goods we don't need—so long as the development of the softer, responsive, compassionate side of people in business remains blocked. When we can't allow ourselves to take care of one another in business, we certainly won't allow ourselves to take care of the larger society, let alone the planet.

I do realize that elevating my personal search for integrity to the status of a vital mission for the welfare of our planet does make me the tiniest bit vulnerable to the charge that I am projecting my inner processes onto the world! It is that possibility which has always made relying on one's own intuition and heart feelings for guidance so suspect. Where, one asks, does intuition end and wishful thinking take over? I remember that during the sixties and seventies we did a lot of work with our clients around caring. Although it seemed for a time as though we were making progress, results seem to have been short-lived. What signs are there that in a business atmosphere that has become much tougher and more survival-oriented, the climate for attunement, for support, for love in organizations is any more promising than it was then?

I am not completely satisfied with any answers to these questions. Although I feel the time is right, I have seen a lot of wishes and fears put out to the world as intuitive truth, not least by members of my profession, and I do not completely trust my judgment in this. I do see some straws in the wind, however, which encourage me, and I have developed the beginnings of a strategy for helping organizations to open paths for their members to develop their compassionate, caring sides and to nurture the expression of that side in the conduct of business.

In looking for a promising strategy, I have identified *giving service* as an activity in which most organizations are involved and which is attracting increased management attention (see, for example, Albrecht and Zemke, 1985).

Service. iv. 1. The action of serving, helping or benefiting; conduct tending to the welfare or advantage of another [*The Shorter Oxford English Dictionary,* 1968].

What is responsive, customer-oriented service, if it is not love in action? What do we miss in our service relationships, if it is not caring? Of course, as we experience service between the parts of our organizations, and externally as customers, service is a lot of things that are not supportive or compassionate, or caring. It is in the giving of service that organizations and their customers most experience the lack of love, and it is in that area where improvement most depends on opening the heart of the organization and its members.

If we apply the "yin/yang" polarity, discussed above, to the giving of service, we get a diagram that looks like this:

Activity	*Receptivity*
(alignment)	(attunement)
Autonomous----------------------interdependent	
Rational------------------------------------- caring	
Systems focus------------------------person focus	
Initiating-------------------------------responsive	
Provider-controlled--------- customer-controlled	

There is a general understanding that in the United States today, service and quality are the next frontiers. We are making progress with quality, spurred by the Japanese. Really good service is still an unknown territory for many organizations, in the sense that they haven't yet developed coherent concepts or working theories of what constitutes service or how to achieve it.

Most organizations in the United States today are preoccupied with endeavors that fit the descriptive words on the left-hand side of the polarity described above, and their orientation to service is no exception. In the United States, our ideas of service are often synonymous with fast, efficient systems, designed to produce uniform and predictable outcomes. Such "excellent companies" as Federal Express and McDonald's have built reputations on the reliability of their systems in meeting customers' expectations. Their service is valued for cost/benefit and uniformity, rather than for making people feel warm and comfortable.

In public lectures on the relationship between organizational culture and service, I ask the audience to give examples of "service that makes you feel good." The examples almost always fit the right-hand side of the list above. People say things like:

"They really cared about me as a person."
"Somebody finally took the time to find out what my problem really was."

"They were willing to bend the system to fit my
  special case."
"They didn't mind admitting they were wrong."

It is clear that people want more than fast, efficient service. They
want to be treated as individuals, dealt with personally, cared
for, responded to. They see the public contact employees of large
bureaucracies as excessively rigid, uncaring, and unresponsive
to their needs. Customers are coming increasingly to place a
higher value on warmth, responsiveness, and support in their
search for service. They are looking for service transactions
where they are treated as worthwhile individuals; where their
opinions about what they want and need are respected; where
they are assisted by people to whom they can relate on a level
of equality; and where caring and kindness characterize the
human interactions.

    This is the trend I see over the recent past, and I am not
sure why. Perhaps the reason is the growing realization that we
are all going to have to do with the same or a lower standard
of material living as time goes on. If we don't look forward with
the same confidence to economic advancement, we may want
to enjoy the process a bit more. Perhaps it is the feeling that
too many of our transactions are with systems, too few with people, and we want those with people to be of a higher quality.
Perhaps it is the "high tech, high touch" trend John Naisbitt
talks about. Perhaps, living in a competitive, abrasive, and insecure world where relationships are often transitory and easily
fractured, we are developing a "hidden hunger" to be loved
a little bit in each human interaction.

    Whatever the reason, customers and the organizations that
serve them are growing more sensitive to service quality. It is,
I belive, the next frontier in American business, and it is a difficult frontier for most businesses to penetrate. When organizations become concerned about improving service, they tend to
see it through their own cultural biases. Customers talk about
wanting better service, and organizations think in terms of better systems. It isn't that customers don't want efficient systems
or excellent, innovative approaches to meeting their needs. They

want these, and more. Organizations that don't learn how to listen to customers from the perspective of the right-hand side of the "yin/yang" polarity don't understand what they are hearing, and they put effort into improving service in ways which customers are happy enough to have but which don't meet their deeper priorities.

Organizations should consult their employees if they want to understand what responsive, caring service is. The employees in many organizations feel themselves to be controlled and frustrated by the systems and structures under which they work. Most people, particularly those who choose work involving high contact with the public, enjoy being able to give service and satisfy people's needs. Often, their hands are tied.

Recently, the customer service people in an electric utility I work with got together the field supervisors in a series of meetings and asked, "What could we do in the short term to remove 'service inhibitors'?" Service inhibitors were defined as "anything which prevents our field crews and telephone contact people from giving customers the service they want, and which our people would like to give them." It had been expected that most of the ideas would involve additional personnel, money, equipment—commodities in short supply in any cost-sensitive operation. In fact, people enthusiastically contributed suggestions for short-term service improvements, only one of which required additional resources. The rest were matters of changing current practices and policies or giving field people additional discretion to decide which requests from customers were reasonable.

Tight, efficient systems do not permit people to respond from the heart. People who work in them become frustrated and irritated by their lack of freedom to respond, and they close down emotionally. They are not treated as individuals themselves; they do not feel cared for; and they pass on the treatment they receive to the customers. They check their compassion and their empathy at the door, because to experience those feelings would create too much internal conflict.

People who give service are more often frustrated by the circumstances, systems, and procedures under which they must operate than by the people they serve. And when I talk to leaders and managers about balancing the polarities in their organizations, there are far more wistful looks in the audience than antagonistic ones. Most people are urged by a sense of their own personal integrity to be kinder, more responsive, more supportive in their business interactions. Just beneath the surface is an unmet need to be more nurturing and responsive in their business lives.

Unfortunately, managers and employees alike are blocked by the driving, competitive climates of our organizations and by the rigidity of systems set up to ensure that customers have uniform service at a competitive price. Most organizations are too far out of balance to be able to integrate caring service with efficient systems and the drive for bottom-line results. They recognize the need for change, but they cling to what they know best, unable to let go of its security in order to reach for something that seems riskier at the same time as it offers improvement. For organizations, this is a crisis of integrity, similar to the personal crises that individuals face when they realize they have outgrown the values and assumptions of the current level of their personal evolution. They are ready for a ''jump shift'' to the next level, but they are afraid.

It is a genuine risk. In the same way that the disintegration of a consensus around ethics has opened the way for the development of both personal integrity and personal depravity, so the relaxation of controls can permit sloppy, uncaring performance, as well as service from the heart. Responsible managers will not let go of control unless they can have some trust and confidence in the improvements in service to be expected.

In this respect, service is like quality. So long as mistrust is behind the inspection of people's work, they will not assume personal responsibility for it, and quality is a persistent, nagging, unsolved problem, beset with adversarial relationships. When people are given and accept responsibility for their own quality, that situation improves, sometimes dramatically. I believe that service will prove amenable to the same approaches that have worked with quality: top management commitment, combined with systems designed to give the management of service over to the people who deliver it.

It will work only if the process is managed from the heart, not just because it is good business, but because it feels right. And it is not enough for business leaders to believe in caring service; they have to "walk the talk" as well, serving the services providers from their hearts, whether the latter are internal staff or work with customers.

That is very simple—and also very hard. It is hard because most organization cultures do not support development of the heart. It is simple because there are certain behaviors that, practiced faithfully, will open the heart of the practitioner and will warm the hearts of those affected. When the leaders I work with ask me what I mean by practicing love in business, here is how I suggest they treat other people and the organization:

- Give credit for their ideas and build on their contributions.
- Listen to their concerns, hopes, fears, pain: be there for them when they need an empathetic ear.
- Treat their feelings as important.
- Be generous with your trust. Give them the benefit of the doubt.
- See them as valuable and unique in themselves, not simply for their contribution to the task.
- Respond actively to others' needs and concerns; give help and assistance when it is not your job.
- Look for the good and the positive in others, and acknowledge it when you find it.
- Nurture their growth: teach, support, encourage, smooth the path.
- Take care of the organization. Be responsive to and responsible for its needs as a living system.

These are the signs and signals of love in business. I believe they are our next frontier in organizations that serve the public. For many of us, they also define a discipline that can lead us in the direction of greater personal integrity: across the frontier of our own hearts.

3

Integrity, Advanced Professional Development, and Learning

David A. Kolb

In the theory of experiential learning, integrity is an epistemic concept describing the highest form of human intelligence. The concept describes a way of knowing that is much more sophisticated than that measured by conventional intelligence tests, encompassing moral judgment, creativity, and intuitive and emotional skills as well as rational, analytic powers. Integrative knowing transcends the timidity of wisdom to encompass courageous action. It softens the dictates of justice with the mercy of love. Integrity is a normative ideal describing the kind of knowing process we humans value most highly, the process of human judgment that we choose to rely on for guidance in creating our collective future.

Integrity is not living by principle, but the process of choosing principles by which to live: "Honesty, consistency, and morality are usually, but not always, the result of integrated learning. One need only reflect on the 'immoral' behavior of men like Copernicus and Galileo to realize that integrity is the learning process by which intellectual, moral, and ethical standards are *created*, not some evaluation based on current moral standards and world views. It is misleading to confuse these products of integrity, absolute and reasonable as they appear, with the process that creates them, for creators precede their creations in time and must create with no fixed absolutes to guide them'' (Kolb, 1984, p. 225). I will, therefore, speak not of integrity but of integrating. As thus conceived, integrity is not a character *trait* that one possesses more or less of but a sophisticated *state* of processing experience in the world that one enters into in varying degrees, at different times, in different contexts. Mature adults have no monopoly on integrity. Integrating is a major developmental force at every stage of life. But in later adulthood, challenged by the integrative demands of adult life, integrity can reach its fullest flower.

Our Studies of Advanced Professional Development

This perspective on integrity was born out of an intense period of research. In 1979 Donald Wolfe and I wrote two research proposals in the hope that we might get one of them funded. The event we had not planned on materialized and both proposals were funded. The National Institute of Education funded our study of advanced professional learning and development, and the Spencer Foundation supported us in our investigation of the midlife transition in professional men and women. Over a four-year period these projects included some 20 researchers; 70 professional men and women in midlife transition who engaged with us as coinquirers in a continuing dialogue about their life situation and personal development; and questionnaire data, interviews, and psychological testing with a cross-sectional sample of 400 engineers and social workers, alumni of our university in the years 1955, 1960, 1965, 1970, and 1975 (Kolb and Wolfe, 1981).

The careful observations and theoretical formulations of Carl Jung provided conceptual guidance. In the perspective of history, Freud's work has had its greatest impact on understanding of child development, while Jung spoke most powerfully about the challenges and potential of adult development. What was impressive was how accurately Jung's theory described the dynamics of professional development as we observed them in our studies. Jung divided adult life into an early stage in which processes of specialization and individualistic orientation were dominant, a period of midlife transition, and a later life stage in which collective integrating processes dominated. This proved to be a powerful organizing framework for our data. The model fitted the retrospective life histories and future dreams of our midlife transition panel. It also fitted the professional development stages represented in the cross-sectional sample of engineering and social work alumni five, ten, fifteen, twenty, and twenty-five years beyond their formal professional education.

Our most significant finding was that advanced professional development presents integrative challenges to midlife professionals that are markedly different from the specialized demands of their early career. In addition, midlife professionals reach this transition point relatively unprepared for the integrative life challenges that lie ahead. Most professional education programs are vocationally oriented, focused on training for entry-level, specialized, professional roles. Problems of transition from specialization to integration were most evident in the science-based professions such as medicine and engineering, where intensely specialized professional education programs seem, in some cases, to produce a dysfunctional allegiance to a specialized professional mentality, even when that approach is no longer the best way to operate (Sims, 1983).

These studies offered a transprofessional perspective on adult learning and development. They helped to identify common life issues and work challenges across professional careers, for men and women, for younger and older persons. My current work is focused on the responses that advanced professionals make to the integrative developmental challenges they face. What is particularly interesting to me is the "expert" responses to these issues—the strategies for coping that promote further successful growth and development. It is in these mature responses of successful advanced professionals that one begins to see the detailed workings of the integrative judgment process.

The Challenge of Wholeness: The Response of Centering

> Our stability is but balance and wisdom lies
> in the masterful administration
> of the unforeseen [Robert Bridges].

The anguished cry of the midlife crisis is a cry for wholeness. Like a symptomatic fever, it is a painful but healthy cry, awakening one's self to the full appreciation of life. For most, however, the midlife transition is not a traumatic crisis but a series of adjustments to expectations, a time for reexamination of priorities, a growing awareness of one's specific mortality. How this passage is made is largely contingent on the person's life context—on the challenges for growth and the supports for self-insight, learning, and development that are present in work and in personal life.

It is in the life priorities of advanced professionals that growth toward wholeness can be seen most clearly. Figure 1 compares the life priorities of early-career, midlife, and advanced professionals in our alumni sample. For the young professionals (age twenty-four to forty), career is most important. They spend most of their time polishing their expert skills and establishing a professional identity, "making it" in their respective organizations. In midlife (forty-one to forty-five), family gains top

Figure 1. Importance of Major Developmental Tasks by Phases of Adulthood.

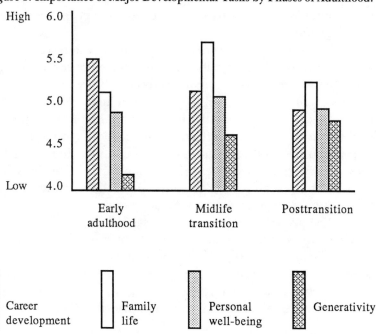

priority. Midlife is dominated by a host of personal life events—marriage, divorce, parents, children, education, finances. The advanced professional brings family and work into balance with a generative priority, a desire to make a contribution to society. He or she seeks a balance among career, family, personal well-being, and a desire to contribute to society.

Advanced professional work is filled with challenges for wholeness. Typically, successful young professionals rise to the peak of their professional specialty by perfecting their specialized professional skills in a work environment that is competitive and oriented toward rewarding the individual. At this peak, advanced professionals face a number of new tasks, requiring new skills—skills that in some cases are the opposite of the survival skills one has learned as a professional specialist. As Sir Noel Hall, the founder in postwar Britain of one of the first executive colleges, put it, ''Here we come to the central paradox. It is from individuals who necessarily have undergone this process of specialization, who have carried limited and restricted responsibilities that we have to draw for the higher posts those who are to be the synthesizers, the coordinators, those who have the quality of behavior which will draw other people to accept their guidance'' (1958, p. 9).

For professionals, these ''higher posts'' often come in the form of executive responsibility. The challenge for wholeness is seen most clearly as one assumes responsibility for an autonomous system—for example, as a general manager or CEO. The prime task here is to weld the functional parts of the organization into a coherent and effective whole, to give direction and purpose to the total enterprise. Advanced individual contributors, however, also experience a need to fit their specialty into the whole, to speak publicly for their profession, to mentor and lead younger professionals, and to serve society.

The process of advanced professional work is holistic, involving more synthesis than analysis. Problem solving is cooperative, typically involving integrated teamwork across different functions and professional specialties. Less time is spent solving problems, and more is spent selecting which problems should be solved, through agenda setting and priority setting. The environment outside the organization becomes more focal than the inside. The organization seen as a whole must find its place in the environmental whole. Generalized technical knowledge, the bread and butter of early professional life, must be coordinated with local knowledge—the unique situation-specific knowledge of opportunities, traps, resources, personalities, and techniques for getting things done in the organization's current environmental situation. Immense amounts of time in the executive role are spent networking, communicating, and representing in order to accumulate this local knowledge.

The developmental challenge to find wholeness has more personal dimensions. Finding a balance between "masculine" instrumentality/aggressiveness and "feminine" nurturance/expressiveness is often difficult in male-dominated organizations. The balance of body and mind becomes important, particularly when physical health becomes an issue or when work is heavily intellectual and abstract. Immersion in the straight lines and mechanical tools of the man-made world can cause one to lose connection with the curves and rhythms of the natural world where organic processes of growth and development thrive. Concern for self needs to be balanced with concern for and intimacy with others.

The growthful response to these challenges for wholeness is a process of centering. It begins with the emergence of a new attitude toward differences. Early adult development is fueled by the embrace of similarities, a process called "accentuation" because the effect of embracing similarity is to intensify and develop a particular skill or attitude—for example, by reading only opinions you agree with or specializing your performance in areas you are good at. This accentuation, unchecked by integration, inevitably leads to an imbalance, a one-sidedness, an overinvestment of the person's life energies in one area. This, in turn, creates an internal need, a counterforce, to balance oneself and regain one's center.

The path to the center lies in awareness and appreciation of differences. In the embracing of differences there is not only new stimulation and interest but also a renewal process that stimulates higher-order systems thinking. Jung called this

process *enantiodromia,* the Heraclitian philosophical term meaning that everything turns into its opposite: "I use the term *enantiodromia* for the emergence of the unconscious opposite in the
course of time. This characteristic phenomenon practically always occurs when an extreme one-sided tendency dominates
conscious life; in time an equally powerful counterposition is
built up which first inhibits the conscious performance and subsequently breaks through the conscious control" (Jung, 1923/1966,
p. 426). "The problem of opposites usually comes up in the
second half of life when all the illusions we projected upon the
world gradually come back to haunt us. The energy streaming
back from these manifold relationships falls into an unconscious
and activates all the things we had neglected to develop. . . . To
the man in the second half of life, the development of the function of the opposites lying dormant in the unconscious means
a renewal" (Jung, 1923/1966, pp. 59–61).

     In fully appreciating the different parts, one comes to
understand the whole. With holistic thinking comes the ability
to be choiceful in the way problems are selected and defined.
Instead of operating by implicit assumptions, choiceful problem
framing is possible. This process of choosing the perspective from
which to view problems, of issue formation, becomes more important in advanced professional work than specialized functional problem solving.

     Through all this, a strong, choiceful self and a deep sense
of personal authenticity emerge. Self-confidence, based not on
pride but on humble, accurate awareness of strengths and weaknesses, seems essential. It often comes with a sense of purpose,
a sense of calling, in which one's past, present, and future are
integrated into a meaningful life plan. Jensen (forthcoming),
for example, found such a concept of centering to be characteristic of the most effective managers in his sample of physician
administrators in a large clinic.

The Challenge of Generativity: The Response of Caring

An adult must be ready to become a numinous model in the next generation's eyes and to act as a judge of evil and a transmitter of ideal values
[Erik Erikson].

As a species, humans have two biological functional imperatives, two basic instincts—to preserve oneself as an individual and to preserve the species as a whole. The increasing concern for generativity in advanced professionals, as shown in Figure 1, suggests that the relative importance of these objectives changes from early to later adulthood. Childhood is for the definition of self and early adulthood for the development of self. But in later life it is the collective, species perspective that gains ascendance. This view is corroborated by a recent study of professional career development by Dalton and Thompson (1986), who found the early adult career to be divided into an apprenticeship stage and an independent contributor stage. In early adulthood the primary developmental task is moving from dependence to independence. Advanced professional development is divided into an initial mentoring stage and a more advanced director stage. The developmental tasks for the mentor and director are assuming responsibility for others and exercising power. These are the challenges of generativity. They are often first experienced in family life, where the natural response to care for the children is seldom experienced as self-sacrifice but more often as a fulfillment, a source of meaning and purpose.

What is less widely recognized is the pervasiveness of this need to serve others outside the family arena. Recent research on the key role that mentoring processes play in organizational life has shown that advanced professionals derive much personal satisfaction from quasi-parental relationships with younger co-workers. But focus on the mentor as a motherly or fatherly counselor has somewhat overshadowed how pervasively the generative instinct is woven into the fabric of organizational life. Work itself is often motivated by this need for meaning and for a sense of contribution. Organizational hierarchies, formal and informal, receive their fundamental legitimization from identification with the generative collective view "to promote the common good." The generative social contract is: Accept responsibility for the world and you are given the power to change it. As Chester Barnard said, "In a free society the reward for good service is a demand for more service." The generative challenge for each of us is: How much responsibility will I, can I, take?

For Erik Erikson, caring is the virtue that is born from the struggle to take responsibility: "Care is a widening commitment to *take care of* the persons, the products, and the ideas one has learned *to care for*. All the strengths arising from earlier development . . . hope and will, purpose and skill, fidelity and love now prove . . . to be essential for the generational task of cultivating strength in the next generation. For this is, indeed, the 'store' of human life'' (Erikson, 1982, p. 67).

Care is expressed in three ways in advanced professional work: through caring relationships, through careful work, and through moral leadership. Caring relationships are the most concrete and intimate forms of caring. The mentoring relationship, in which one shares knowledge and skills with younger colleagues, fulfilling a need to teach and be a role model for others, is one such relationship. All relationships, in fact, prosper in the appreciative attention of care. In careful work there is a desire to create something worthwhile, to make a contribution.

The third way care is expressed is more abstract and system-oriented, more related to the developmental task of Dalton and Thompson's director stage—the exercise of power. In this context, to care means that the power that is given for taking responsibility must be exercised for the collective good. How are the requisite judgments about good and evil, right and wrong to be made? As responsibility and power increase, decisions become more value-intensive, more moral than technical, more concerned with value priorities than with methods and tactics of goal achievement. Moral leadership, leadership in the valuing process, is the third arena for the expression of care in advanced professional life.

Values are the medium for the expression of care. In caring relationships one values and prizes the other, creating value in the relationship and feelings of self-worth in the other. The goal of careful work is to create value, to make a contribution. Moral leadership is leadership in creation, promotion, and preservation of values. For Jung, the achievement of integrity, a process of self-actualization that he called "individuation," was dependent on the creation of value: "Individuation cuts one off from personal conformity and hence from collectivity.

That is the guilt which the individual leaves behind him for the world, that is the guilt he must endeavor to redeem. He must offer a ransom in place of himself, that is, he must bring forth values which are an equivalent substitute for his absence in the collective personal sphere. Without this production of values, final individuation is immoral and—more than that—suicidal. The man who cannot create values should sacrifice himself consciously to the spirit of collective conformity'' (Jung, 1971, p. 450).

The challenges of moral leadership are the most difficult in advanced professional life. For many, caring relationships and careful work have been continuously growing since early career. The requirements of moral leadership are often sharply discontinuous, offering difficult new challenges—to be a public person, to represent others, to serve as a model for others, to be a leader and creator of culture, to choose right from wrong in the most complex of circumstances. All these activities require the management of values, while earlier career activities focused primarily on the management of factual knowledge. Professional education typically has offered little preparation for this focus on value-intensive decision making. In addition, the wider social context of Western society has seen deterioration of value-forming institutions such as religion and the family. The value neutrality of positivistic science encourages leaders to avoid dialogue about value issues, while at the same time fanatical single-value movements are on the rise. Morality and ethics, the ''sciences'' of value choice, are seldom discussed outside religious circles. The tasks of moral leadership are to make judgments about value priorities, to promote them in one's activities, and to preserve these values through the creation of a culture that sustains them.

From the point of view of advanced professionals themselves, value-intensive decision making is of primary importance. In Gallup's study of successful advanced professionals listed in *Who's Who* (Gallup and Gallup, 1986), ''a strong sense of right and wrong'' was the personal characteristic that 67 percent of the subjects said best described themselves. Furthermore, this was true for 78 percent of the most highly successful persons in the sample.

The Challenge of Time: The Response of Visioning

> If you plant for a season, plant budgets.
> If you plant for a decade, plant reorganizations.
> If you plant for a century, plant people [R. G. H. Siu].

Advanced professionals are preoccupied with time. The assumption of generative responsibilities brings a loss of control over one's personal time. To be responsible for people and projects requires responsiveness to their time demands and deadlines. Effective mentoring requires availability. The successful professional sees the financial value of his or her time increase as expertise increases. ''Free'' time correspondingly becomes very expensive. All this occurs at a time in life when one is more aware that one's own time is finite. Gallup's survey of successful professionals reports an average 63-hour work week, with a few top achievers working as many as 90 or 100 hours a week. It is little wonder that time management is one of the most frequently mentioned learning needs among advanced professionals.

More fundamentally, a change occurs in the advanced professional's conception and experience of time itself. It was Kurt Lewin who first observed that psychological development involves expansion of consciousness in the dimensions of time and space. The child's world is first the crib, then the room, the home, the neighborhood, and so on, in an expanding scope of awareness. Elliott Jacques (1979) maintains that a broad scope of time awareness, what he calls a long time span of intention, is the primary executive capability needed for advanced professional work. He argues that the hierarchical dimension of work, the ''size'' of a job, is best measured by its time span of discretion, the amount of time the person has to complete a task before his or her work is reviewed. Time span is measured by the time it takes to complete tasks in one's job role. A factory worker's output, for example, may be reviewed at the end of each eight-hour shift. An intermediate-level chief executive may take a year to introduce new machinery, or three years to open a new market, or five years to develop and market a new product. Higher-level CEOs will engage in formulation of strategic alliances and long-term projects with time spans of ten years or even more before results are evaluated.

To effectively meet the challenge of operating autonomously over long time spans requires the development of a correspondingly long time span of intentional action. With increased time discretion comes increased autonomy, and with that comes a need for intentional action skills—the capability of envisioning a project and carrying it out. Vision is the key to intentional action. It is at once the target, the plan, and the motive force for self-directed, purposeful action. To maintain intentional action over long time spans is an effort of will power that produces continuity and stability through focused commitment and persistence. The dynamics of will power have been no better understood than by William James. His ideomotor theory of action states that an idea held firmly in conscious focus issues forth automatically in behavior. The challenge of will power, therefore, is literally to keep the dream alive, to keep one's vision as the primary object of conscious attention.

The power of vision is limitless. Every man-made achievement was once only a subjective vision without any objective material existence whatever. Everything in human creation begins with the idea. But how are these visions created? Consider the nineteenth-century chemist Friedrich Kekulé, who, after struggling for years to find the formula for benzene, dozed before a fire one winter's evening. His dream: "The atoms danced before my eyes. . . . the small groups remained in the background. My inner eye . . . now distinguished bigger forms of manifold configurations . . . long rows more densely joined, everything in motion contorting and turning like snakes . . . One of the snakes took hold of its own tail and whirled derisively before my eyes. I woke up as though I had been struck by lightning . . . I spent the rest of the night working out the consequences" (LeBoeuf, 1980, p. 61).

Vision is not manufactured; it is born within us from our experience. It is more received than actively created. To receive vision requires an escape from the confines of objective, mechanical time. Vision is received in subjective, organic time, time felt rather than time conceptually understood. It is born in creative time—in a meeting of past struggle and future hope, in the most magical moment of all, the here and now, the only time in which one can actually do anything. It is communicated in the organic time of human relationships.

The Challenge of Managing Change
and Complexity: The Response of Learning

The human gap is the distance between growing complexity and our capacity to cope with it. . . .

We call it a human gap because it is a dichotomy between a growing complexity of our own making and a lagging development of our own capabilities. . . .

Learning can help to bridge the human gap. . . . Learning means an approach both to knowledge and life that emphasizes human initiative. It encompasses the acquisition and practice of new methodologies, new skills, new attitudes, and new values necessary to live in a world of change. . . . Probably none of us at present are learning at the levels, intensities, and speeds needed to cope with the complexities of modern life [The Club of Rome].

The challenge of managing change and complexity comes to advanced professionals from two directions—career advancement and a world that daily becomes more complex. In his study of a large manufacturing corporation, Lublin (1986) found that job complexity increased with organizational level on such dimensions as task variety, interdependence, personal responsibility, and required delegation. Similarly, Parcel and Mueller's (1983) study of jobs listed in the *Dictionary of Occupational Titles* showed complexity as the major vertical dimension of jobs in our society. In high-level jobs, long time spans of discretion require greater vision and intentional action skills. Holistic systems thinking requires simultaneous appreciation of specialized technical detail and understanding of the "big picture." Value-intensive decision making requires empathy, open-mindedness, and the capacity to constructively manage differences. At the same time, advanced professionals must use these skills to manage their responsibilities in a world where human-generated complexity is feeding on itself and growing exponentially (Botkin, Elmandjra, and Malitza, 1979). This final challenge to integrity is the most pragmatic: to master the bountiful products of differentiated, specialized knowledge and to unify them in the service of humanity.

To effectively manage change and complexity requires more than a status quo performance orientation: It requires an anticipatory learning orientation. Recent U.S. industrial history has dramatically shown that effective performance is no longer sufficient to guarantee survival. Failing to respond proactively to the changing world marketplace, one after another of our largest and most successful corporations has been decimated by international competition. During the same period, the U.S. economy has created jobs at an almost miraculous level. But these jobs did not come from large, established, effectively performing organizations. They came from creatively performing small businesses—entrepreneurs with an anticipatory vision of the future and a plan to make it happen.

The performance and learning orientations differ in four dimensions: time span, complexity, participation, and executive control. The time perspective of the performance orientation is short, mostly quarterly, perhaps yearly. The learning perspective enlarges the time frame through two processes. Protolearning, the formulation of scenarios, hypotheses, beliefs, and intentions, anticipates the future. The more articulated those expectations and models of the future are, the more quickly course deviations can be signaled. Retrolearning, the reexamination and debriefing of past experiences, establishes general operating principles, adding a cumulative quality to organizational efforts and a sense of historical continuity.

High performance is often achieved by simplicity and predictability, while learning requires a search for requisite complexity—matching the complexity of one's response to the complexity of the problem situation. For example, the choice of an appropriate time span in which to view an issue is perhaps the most important decision in defining a problem and finding a solution to it. To manage a complex situation in a simple framework is like trying to clear a fog with a hand grenade. Power is not the problem; the problem is the refinement of its application. With a simple framework, actions are too crude and the time span is too short.

Participation in the performance orientation is typically hierarchical and motivated by individual reward systems. It focuses mainly on specialized professional problem solving and implementation. Participation in the learning orientation focuses on issue formulation and problem definition as well as problem solving and implementation. It is a cooperative enterprise to share ideas and develop common vision labeled "egalitarian" by Srivastva and Cooperrider (1986).

The control process of the performance orientation is a goal-seeking first-order feedback loop typically called "management control," where deviations from given performance targets are the trigger for management attention and corrective action. The learning orientation adds a second-order feedback loop concerned with goal selection. This defines an executive action process involving strategic goal selection based on an overall system awareness. Both a performance and a learning orientation are essential for organizational effectiveness. Performance improves the efficiency of specialized organizational responses, and learning promotes integration and coordination at the strategic and developmental levels (see Table 1). Executives have to work in both these orientations, much as a sports team moves from game to practice to game in a continuing cycle of self-management.

Can Integrity Be Developed?

The worst of it all is that intelligent and cultivated people live their lives without even knowing of the possibility of such transformations. Wholly unprepared, they embark upon the second half of their life. Or are there perhaps colleges for forty-year-olds which prepare them for their coming life and its demands as the ordinary colleges introduce our young people to a knowledge of the world? [Carl Jung]

Can integrity be developed? The answer from our studies is, yes. By centering, caring, visioning, and learning, most men and women in our research were consciously responding to more

Table 1. Characteristics of the
Performance and Learning Orientations.

Characteristic	Performance Orientation	Learning Orientation
Time span	Immediate	Extended in future by protolearning; grounded in history by retrolearning
Tolerance for complexity and uncertainty	Predictability and simplicity maximized	Development of requisite complexity
Participation	• Focused on problem solving and implementation • Competitive/independent • Hierarchical	• Focused on issue formulation and problem definition • Cooperative/interdependent • Egalitarian
Control process	Management control • First-order feedback • Goal seeking	Executive control • Second-order feedback • Goal selecting

than one of the integrity challenges we have just described. The process of advanced professional development that we observed fits Nevitt Sanford's (1981) challenge/response theory of adult development. Integrity is developed primarily in response to the integrative challenges of advanced professional life. Those who, by choice or fate, do not face these challenges are less likely to develop the integrative responses of centering, caring, visioning, and learning. With regard to learning, for example, Gypen (1981) found that engineers in integrative management positions developed an integrated learning process, while those who remained engineering specialists maintained the specialized convergent learning style typical of the engineering profession. Sanford argues that self-insight is critical for the development of these responses. The absence of opportunity for self-examination and dialogue with others about integrative challenges and the appropriate responses is a significant barrier to integrity development.

A more difficult question is, can integrity be taught? The processes of integrative judgment—centering, caring, visioning, and learning—are highly complex, individualized, and largely subjective. Modern higher education, however, is primarily oriented to the production of specialized judgment, a vocational orientation to the entry-level demands of professional life. The traditional credit hours, mass production method of colleges and universities is perhaps consistent with this specialized orientation. To teach about integrity requires something more.

If integrity is learned, then surely it can be taught. But the educational program needs to follow an integrative method. It should, first of all, be integrated with the life purpose of advanced professionals. Any program of advanced professional studies should be based on careful study of how integrative judgment is learned from life experience and of how this learning is stimulated by the contextual challenges of adult life. As the nineteenth-century educator George Leonard said, "Education has only one basic requirement, a *sine qua non*—one must want it." For adults, especially, without purpose there is no learning.

A second requirement concerns the nature of the educative relationship. Authority-based knowledge conveyed through the teacher/student relationship is inappropriate for learning integrative judgment, which must often combine several coequal specialized authoritative views in order to deal with novel and uncertain situations. Integrative knowledge must be created, exchanged, and evaluated in a nondogmatic relationship of dialogue among equals. Integrative judgment is based on a relativistic epistemology. Somewhat paradoxically, relativity theory has not produced a more fragmented view of the universe, but a more unified, holistic one. Einstein's work showed that space, time, mass, and energy were not separate phenomena but parts of a unified whole. The most advanced work in physics today is synthetic, working toward a single unified law of physical phenomena. The lesson of relativity theory for the conduct of human affairs is most profound: Understanding comes only when the position of the observer is defined as clearly as the position of the observed.

Dialogue is a form of communication that acknowledges this relativism of all human views. In dialogue both abstract ideas and personal feelings about them are shared in a spirit of provisionalism, mutuality, and coinquiry. Adult learners learn best in situations where they are acknowledged as experts and equals. As adults, they have a need to teach as well as learn. Paulo Freire describes this learning relationship as follows: "Through dialogue, the teacher of the students and students of the teacher cease to exist and a new term emerges: teacher-student with students-teachers. The teacher is no longer merely the one who teaches, but one who is himself taught in dialogue with the students who in turn, while being taught, also teach. They become jointly responsible for a process in which all grow. In this process, agreements based on 'authority' are no longer valid . . . no one teaches another, nor is anyone self-taught" (1974, p. 67).

The paradigm of human potential development is a useful framework for thinking about these educational issues. This approach is the human resource development strategy followed by competency-based education and the development of expert systems in the field of artificial intelligence. It seeks to maximize human potential by studying the responses of human experts to particular complex tasks (for example, medical diagnosis) or wider role responsibilities, building heuristic behavioral models of expert performance. Human potential development is inspired by Maslow's self-actualization psychology. When first proposed in the 1950s, it challenged the deficit/normality model that today is the dominant rival paradigm in the human resource development field. In this quasi-medical model the focus for models of performance is the norm, and the focus of intervention is on returning to normal. Maslow's paradigm-breaking insight came in focusing on the creative, high-performance end of the human performance spectrum to build models of human potential. In so doing, he focused attention on the strengths of the human spirit—on the powerful human motivation to self-actualize, to realize one's full potential as a human being. The implications of this analysis of integrity for advanced professional studies programs can be summarized in the human potential development paradigm. Table 2 summarizes the integrative challenges of advanced professional careers and the "expert" self-actualizing responses we have observed. The third column sug-

Table 2. Integrity Development in the
Paradigm of Human Potential Development.

The Integrity Challenges	The Integrating Responses	Methods for Integrity Development
Wholeness	Centering	Individualized career planning
• Balancing work and personal life • System responsibility • Synthetic work process • Personal wholeness	• Embracing differences • Systems thinking • Choiceful framing • Authentic self • Purpose	
Generativity	Caring	Communication through networking and dialogue
• Taking responsibility for others • Exercise of power • The species perspective	• Caring relationships —mentoring • Careful work • Moral leadership • The valuing process	
Time	Visioning	Retreat and reflection
• Managing a scarce resource • Long time span of discretion • Living in subjective time and the here and now	• Intentional action • Will power • Creating vision	
Change and complexity	Learning	Experience-based learning
• Wide scope of responsibility • Long time frames • Value-intensive decisions • Growth of specialized knowledge • Rapid social change	• Proto- and retro-learning • Requisite complexity • Egalitarian participation • Executive control	

gests educational program components that are particularly suited to the development of centering, caring, visioning, and learning.

A career planning process that begins with a holistic assessment of one's current life situation, past experience and accomplishments, and future dreams and aspirations is a good starting place for a program of advanced professional studies. Advanced professionals are a diverse and unique lot. They all differ in the specifics of their life experiences and personal styles. If there is a common, successful response, it is the integration of one's strengths and weaknesses into a centered process of executive action. To develop this individualized, integrated executive action style would be the goal of a life/career planning process with three components: holistic self-assessment, setting personal learning goals, and personal development planning.

Skill in communication is essential for the expression of care. It has both a "macro" and a "micro" aspect for the advanced professional. The macro aspect is dialogue—the process of effectively creating and exchanging knowledge in work relationships. An advanced professional studies program should address itself to the need to develop relationships outside the organization and profession—to represent one's profession or organization to its diverse stakeholders. Integrative learning suggests an open-system, networking approach to the management of knowledge. A key function of education at the advanced professional level is to provide leaders with access to knowledge and relationship networks that can help them to learn about and manage the issues on their continually changing agendas.

Advanced professionals need time for retreat and reflection to broaden their scope of time/space awareness. The trap of expensive time is that it shortens time perspective, promoting symptom-oriented "fire fighting" rather than strategic problem solving. Advanced professional education should give the opportunity to reflect with peers, using the tools of protolearning and retrolearning to anticipate the critical issues of the future and learn from past experiences. In addition, global awareness should be stimulated by interorganizational and intercultural exchanges. Such reflection should stimulate new interests and perspectives. As Winston Churchill put it, "The tired parts of the mind can be rested and strengthened not merely by rest, but by use of the other parts. It is not enough merely to switch off the lights which play upon the main and ordinary field of interest; a new field of interest must be illuminated. . . . [It is only] when new stars become lords of the ascendant that relief, repose, refreshment, are afforded" (1932, p. 297).

Since integrative judgment is concerned with the management of complexity and change, it must operate at the front lines of knowledge. Integrative learning occurs best when the learning process is integrated with work in real time. Off-site sessions and training programs have some role to play in developing integrative judgment, but a greater payoff lies in the creation of organizational climates that allow learning from experience during work itself. Experiential learning approaches that emphasize these "real life," on-the-job learning experiences, such as Revans's action learning programs (1981), learning partnerships, and systematic career development processes that use careful assignment and rotation of job functions to develop the integrative general management perspective, are example programs to help manage change and complexity.

4

Paths to Integrity: Educating for Personal Growth and Professional Performance

Marcia Mentkowski

The very spring and root of honesty and virtue lie in good education [Plutarch].

Developing one's human potential for personal growth is a lifelong enterprise for each individual and a central value for our society. This book explores one aspect of personal growth, the functioning of executive integrity. Persons with integrity are trusted with leadership, executing our collective values and goals and making decisions that affect us all. They exemplify human values despite enormous pressures toward expediency and self-interest. Such individuals who have achieved respected leadership positions are held up as examples for us all to follow. Yet there are few guidelines for educators on what really distinguishes such an individual's path to integrity from that of another or how to educate for personal growth.

In this chapter, I argue that education for personal growth, integrated performance, and learning that lasts a lifetime is a major key to making the development of integrity happen. *Personal growth* refers broadly to the individual's search for maturity,

The author acknowledges direction and critique on earlier drafts of this chapter from Margaret Earley, Kathleen O'Brien, and Stephen Vogel, of the Alverno College faculty.

89

for realizing his or her human potential. Educating for personal growth is challenging for several reasons. First, the unexamined, conventional definitions implicit in our everyday discussions imply that an aspect of personal growth such as integrity is a personal characteristic, a stable personality trait. Second, maturity is too often viewed as an end point that particularly wise persons reach later in life through a sequential, but mysterious, process. For the casual reader, much of the psychological literature inadvertently reinforces a simplistic conception of development. Erikson's "generativity versus stagnation" and "integrity versus despair" are stages of development that humans reach later in life (Erikson, 1982); Kohlberg's "stage 6" and even "stage 7" are ultimates in the development of moral reasoning (Kohlberg, 1981a); the complex integration of personality as described by Jung (1950) is a consummative human goal; Maslow's (1970) self-actualization is the pinnacle of human fulfillment. Those who define integrity as a personality trait may compound the problem with a naive picture of the evolution of personal growth as a linear path; a pilgrim's progress toward maturity.

Third, although some centers are engaged in scholarship and research that identify complex moral and ethical development as an educational goal (for example, the Hastings Center, Institute of Society, Ethics and the Life Sciences; the Center for Business Ethics), there is little, if any, research that argues for the how and why of curriculum development (Kuhmerker, Mentkowski, and Erickson, 1980), and there are few examples of curricula in professional schools (this term is used here to include college majors and graduate programs) that deliberately intervene in personal growth outcomes. This chapter will provide research evidence that substantiates education as a major factor in personal growth, integrated performance, and learning that lasts.

The static, idealized quality of a term like *integrity*, together with a step-by-step notion of development, influences the way we think about educating for personal growth. One argument says personality traits like integrity are acquired too early for us to influence their development in professional school. Another claims that integrity is "too personal" or that professional school curricula cannot affect anyone's idiosyncratic odyssey toward wisdom; therefore, personal growth is not an educator's responsibility. A third view contends that professional integrity is learned through specialized knowledge. Finally, the paucity of research studies on professional school outcomes argues against developing a curriculum that intentionally educates for personal growth.

In capsule form, these arguments might sound something like this: "Personality traits like integrity are developed long before a student comes to professional school. We have to assume that students accepted into an undergraduate major or graduate program are personally mature, ethically responsible, and capable of integrated performance. We just have to measure maturity so we can select only those applicants who have it. Further, professional schools do not have a right to insist on personal growth as an outcome. Whether students become more mature is none of our business. Anyway, people develop at their own rates, and only tough, on-the-job crises can jolt them into new ways of seeing things. Besides, students are here to learn concepts, such as business and management. If you teach a manager or executive to be competent in the knowledge he or she needs on the job, you will guarantee integrity. Exercising integrity comes from being a competent professional. For a good executive, integrity comes naturally. Where is the research evidence that suggests otherwise?"

Some of these arguments break down if we consider that the integrity of an organization rests as much on the day-to-day decisions of entry-level managers as it does on the executive. Without the integrity of managers up and down the line, even the most outstanding executive cannot implement decisions that show integrity. Professional school educators, therefore, need to do more than point out stellar individuals who exemplify executive integrity as models for students. Educators need to develop curricula that recognize the complexities of personal growth. They need to shape professional competence by ensuring the integration of abilities, particularly interpersonal ones, that will continue to develop in a variety of organizational roles and settings through self-sustained learning.

The remaining arguments are addressed by my thesis that educators who create a learning environment and a curriculum that contribute to personal growth and integrated performance are making integrity possible and probable. If students leave school able to learn on their own, they will have lasting tools that can lead them to a life of integrated thought and action within a framework of values. In fact, the many forms of integration that are affected (for example, between intellectual and interpersonal abilities, between perceptions and performance, between knowing and doing) are essential to the development of integrity.

To support this thesis, I communicate four observations on the outcomes of educating for personal growth, integrated performance, and self-sustained learning that are emerging from the college outcomes research and studies of practicing professionals I have been directing since 1976 at Alverno College, as described in the next section. These observations are neither hypotheses nor conclusions. They represent what I believe now. Some of these observations are well grounded in several of the qualitative and quantitative data sets we have analyzed; others are intriguing possibilities given some of the results. The observations are broad generalizations usually supported by the findings, but at times the evidence is less supportive and raises other possibilities. I draw these four observations from the following research areas: (1) personal growth, defined as changes in intellectual, moral, and ego development, (2) whether curriculum affects development, (3) how development happens, (4) the integration of intellectual and interpersonal abilities on the job, and (5) elements of active, self-sustained learning that could account for continued development of these abilities across a lifetime.

It will help the reader to know that educators at Alverno College have implemented a learning process that educates for personal growth, integrated performance, and self-sustained learning. Faculty members focus their curricular intervention on those elements of personal growth that an education *can* affect and change (Earley, Mentkowski, and Schafer, 1980). While the curriculum has proved itself through teaching and assessment practice since 1973, Alverno has also been engaged in some broader research and evaluation efforts. In addition to analysis of classroom practice and assessment of individual student learning (Alverno College Faculty, 1985b; Loacker, Cromwell, and O'Brien, 1986), Alverno has invested in a research and evaluation program to validate the broad outcomes of college (Mentkowski and Loacker, 1985).

The observations I draw from the findings of this research program are as follows:

• Curriculum makes a difference in students' personal growth.
• Individuals recycle through earlier forms of thinking when they experience new situations: Development occurs in cyclical rather than in stepwise fashion.
• Students and professionals achieve integrated performance of intellectual and interpersonal abilities.
• Self-sustained learning that links knowing and doing is a causal element in integrated performance.

In sharing these observations with you, I provide arguments for educating for personal growth (defined in our studies as moral, intellectual, and ego development) and integrated performance of both intellectual and interpersonal abilities in the professional school and, by inference, in organizations. The "how to" is contextual for each institution. Alverno educators would not want others to imitate their curriculum. But the Alverno faculty shares an interest in the questions many professional schools are asking (Dentzer and Malone, 1986; "How Business Schools Deal with Moral Issues," 1986; Scott and Mitchell, 1985) about what personal growth outcomes can and should be taught. Alverno faculty members believe that research evidence on whether and how curricula can influence personal growth and integrated performance is essential both to starting up such an enterprise and to continuing to refine their vision of what is possible for the professional school student to achieve during college and at work.

Thus, Alverno educators want to know whether there are developmental patterns in individuals' intellectual, ego, and moral development that should influence how faculty teach for personal growth. They ask what accounts for integrated performance of intellectual and interpersonal abilities. They question whether their ability to educate for personal growth, integrated performance, and self-sustained learning is keeping pace with the demanding contexts and choices that graduates face in the world of work. And they continue to probe which curricular elements contribute to the development of personal growth, integrated performance, and learning that must last a lifetime.

Outcomes Research at Alverno College

Alverno College, a liberal arts college for women in Milwaukee, Wisconsin, has an enrollment of over 2,000 degree students in both weekday and weekend time frames. Generally, students are from southeastern Wisconsin, are first-generation college students, and work during and after college. Alverno, which has focused for a century on preparing women for professional careers, formally adopted an outcome-centered approach to its curriculum in 1973, accrediting students for progressive demonstration of certain broad abilities in all subject areas (Alverno College Faculty, 1985a): communication, analysis, problem solving, valuing, social interaction, taking responsibility for the global environment, effective citizenship, and aesthetic responsiveness. Valuing is explicitly defined through six progressively more complex levels that are taught and assessed in over 100 courses across the curriculum. Students identify and confront their own values; practice identifying value systems in humanistic works and historical and societal contexts; engage in self-assessment, peer assessment, and faculty assessment of valuing in decision making in a variety of professional contexts; and practice identifying the values inherent in a discipline or profession in both theory and practice. The faculty expects students to develop their valuing ability, to develop their own value frameworks and value systems, to be sensitive to moral issues, to make well-reasoned moral judgments, to create action plans to carry them out, and to reflect on their decision-making processes in ways that will lead them to more sophisticated and informed decision making in the future. Through the valuing ability, a student is expected to relate her value framework to those of others and to incorporate this framework into her decision making. This means thinking critically about frameworks in general and appreciating others' value frameworks. The college requires that students develop the valuing ability, learned in the context of the discipline, to graduate. The college does *not,* however, credential values.

The Alverno faculty believes that valuing is closely related to the ability to think analytically and critically, to interact with others in ways that respect their values and their basic human needs and rights, and to communicate one's ways of thinking and one's valuing clearly in words and actions. Thus, the faculty realizes that valuing must be integrated with the other abilities it has identified. Most important, if the valuing ability is to be an outcome of college, valuing must be integrated with work in the disciplines and professional areas.[1]

The four observations set forth in this chapter from the Alverno research (Mentkowski and Doherty, 1984a), now in its eleventh year, speak to issues related to educating for personal growth, integrated performance, and learning that lasts. Together with the Alverno faculty, the Office of Research and Evaluation has researched various questions concerning student change in college and the persistence of student outcomes beyond college. We have also studied the degree to which faculty-identified abilities match those of outstanding professional women who are not Alverno graduates but who are working in the professional areas our graduates generally choose, such as nursing (DeBack and Mentkowski, 1986) and management (Mentkowski, O'Brien, McEachern, and Fowler, 1982). The research results are based on 17,500 responses from 990 students, alumnae, and professionals who are not Alverno graduates, who were

---

[1]The Valuing Department has set forth how it educates for valuing (Earley, Mentkowski, and Schafer, 1980), has compiled its instructional materials (Alverno College Valuing Department, 1984), and conducts yearly workshops for college and graduate school educators (write Alverno Institute, Alverno College, 3401 South 39th Street, Milwaukee, Wis. 53215 for information). Perusal of these sources and others (Mentkowski, 1980, 1984; Read, 1980) will describe our educational program in detail.

compared cross-sectionally and longitudinally on twenty-six instruments drawn from five theoretical frameworks in a triangulated validation design (Mentkowski and Loacker, 1985). This extensive data base was gathered to enable large longitudinal sample sizes and to increase educators' confidence in the results. The design and findings are described in the overview and summary of the 2,000-page report submitted to the National Institute of Education, which partly funded the research effort (Mentkowski and Doherty, 1983, 1984b).

Observation One: Curriculum Makes a Difference in Students' Personal Growth

Most educators believe they devote a large share of their energies inside and outside the classroom to educating for personal growth. But there is little research evidence to show long-range effects of education as directly related to personal growth and little, if any, that points to the effectiveness of professional school curricula, although there are efforts in that direction (Bebeau, 1983). As educators, we believe that certain educational elements are essential, but we lack clarity about what works in what kinds of contexts. But first, can we make a case from the research evidence that *curriculum* does make a difference?

Changes Found in Personal Growth. Do students show growth and change in human potential as the result of the college's curriculum? Almost all colleges promise personal growth outcomes and expect that college will make a difference in broad abilities, lifelong learning, and life-span development. Studies of college outcomes have shown that college as a whole causes change (Astin, 1977; Feldman and Newcomb, 1969; Heath, 1977; Jacob, 1957; Pace, 1979). Few studies have demonstrated change linked to a particular curriculum.

Questions that guided the Alverno longitudinal research include: (1) Do students change on instruments drawn from outside the college that measure human potential for learning, abilities, and life-span development? (2) Can we attribute change on these measures to student performance in the curriculum?

In what ways is student development enhanced by the learning process? (3) Does the mature adult need education for personal growth, or is experience enough? What are the relative effects of age and performance in the curriculum on growth?

Consequently, alongside (1) student performance within the curriculum on five Alverno-designed ability measures and (2) the study of student perceptions researched through questionnaires and longitudinal interviews, we also researched (3) student potential through performance on twelve measures drawn from outside the college describing human growth patterns from three separate theoretical frameworks: cognitive-developmental theory (Kohlberg, 1981a; Loevinger, 1976; Perry, 1970, 1981; Piaget, 1972; Rest, 1979, 1986), experiential learning theory and learning styles (Kolb, 1983), and a recent thrust to identify and measure generic abilities that link education to performance after college (Watson and Glaser, 1964; Winter, McClelland, and Stewart, 1981). Because we can relate variation in performance on Alverno-designed measures to longitudinal change on these outside measures of human potential, we can examine whether performance in the curriculum contributes to changes in personal growth. Because the 750 women research participants ranged in age from seventeen to fifty-five, we can examine the relative effects of age and performance in the curriculum on growth as well.[2]

---

[2]More specifically, the twelve human potential measures were administered to two complete entering classes and one graduating class (altogether about 750 students). The entering classes completed the same battery two years after entrance and again two years later, near graduation. Thus, we have a set of longitudinal results that can be double-checked against results from a cross-sectional study of sixty graduating seniors compared with entering students who later graduated (controlling for retesting and attrition, with initial selection factors, such as disposition to change, probably uncontrolled). The data on 200 of the students who completed the twelve instruments on three occasions provide a parallel stream of longitudinal information alongside these same students' progressive performance on five college-designed measures. The design includes two age cohorts (age seventeen to nineteen and age twenty to fifty-five at entrance), to examine the effects of maturation, and two achievement cohorts (high and low, based on number of consecutive assessments completed in the learning process), to examine the effects of performance in the curriculum. Two class cohorts, with the second cohort analyzed for weekday versus weekend time frames, further

Students clearly show significant developmental changes across all three occasions when the battery of twelve measures has been administered (Mentkowski and Rogers, 1985; Mentkowski and Strait, 1983). Generally, the change that occurs can be related to student performance in the curriculum. This is the case even when we account for change due to the pretest scores, age, religion, parents' education and occupation, high school grade point average, prior college experience, marital status, year of entrance, residence at home or on campus, full- or part-time attendance, and type of major.

Looking at the results of all the external instruments together, we find that students appear to change more on these external measures during the first two years than during the second two years, but the changes in the second interval are more directly attributable to the student's successful participation in the college's curriculum. This finding suggests that there may indeed be a college atmosphere effect, as studies of college outcomes have shown, but the curriculum does have a decided, added value as well, particularly as students experience studies in their major or professional fields.

Moral, Intellectual, and Ego Development. Students became increasingly sophisticated in their use of principled reasoning in resolving moral dilemmas, as measured by Rest's Defining Issues Tests (1979). Older students showed generally higher scores than younger students at entrance to college, but both groups made gains during college. High achievers in the curriculum showed more change than low achievers. These curriculum effects were maintained when age and the other variables were controlled.

---

enhance representativeness, although only further longitudinal cohorts could truly control for societal change effects. The time series design holds time constant and allows performance in the curriculum to vary, so we can attribute change to performance in the curriculum in the absence of a control group of students who did not attend Alverno. We also control for several age, background, and program variables as well as pretest scores when we study the effects of performance in the learning process.

These results were less strongly realized on the production measure of moral judgment (where students had to generate their own reasons for moral judgments), Kohlberg's written Moral Judgment Interview (1981b). Graduating students showed gains over entering students in the cross-sectional study, but age was the statistically significant covariate. In the longitudinal study, change occurred during the second half of college. Results suggest that development shows first on a recognition measure like Rest's test, where students rank-order a list of reasons for a moral judgment, and later and less strongly on the production measure. This supports our general finding that change is gradual on production measures of life-span growth and suggests that systematic efforts, over time, are needed to affect cognitive development.

On Loevinger's levels of ego development, cross-sectional results showed that students entered college in transition between the Conformist and Conscientious levels, as measured by the Sentence Completion Test (Loevinger, Wessler and Redmore, 1970). At the Conformist stage, a person is characterized by preoccupation with social acceptability and conceptual simplicity. At the Conscientious stage, one's cognitive style shows complexity. One is concerned with self-respect and achievements and thinks in terms of self-evaluated standards and long-term goals and ideals. Students graduated at the Conscientious level or at the transition to the Autonomous level, where their cognitive style is increasingly complex. They can tolerate ambiguity and are preoccupied more with role performance in a variety of contexts; their interpersonal style shows respect for their own autonomy. Longitudinal results showed *no* change, however. This suggests that real change did not occur. However, since some studies of women college students show regression in ego development during college (Loevinger and others, 1985; Loxley and Whiteley, 1986), a finding of no change may represent personal growth. Any conclusions on change in ego development are premature until we sort out who changed, who did not, and why.

Students also made gains in the extent to which they demonstrated Piaget's conception of the logical reasoning and analytical thinking structures characteristic of adults (Test of

Cognitive Development, Renner and others, 1976). These changes appeared in the longitudinal study but not in the cross-sectional comparison.

Changes in Ways of Thinking. Perhaps the cognitive-developmental model most directly descriptive of college students (and of primary interest in describing the nonlinear change discussed in the next observation) is Perry's scheme of intellectual and ethical development, drawn from interview studies of Harvard undergraduates. This scheme describes phases through which students move as they respond to the diversity and ambiguity encountered in college learning.

According to the Perry scheme, students first approach learning with a dualistic focus, viewing learning as the teacher's responsibility to tell them *what to learn.* Later they are able to conceptualize learning as a process, and they center more on *how to learn,* with a concomitant appreciation of multiple perspectives. Then they move to emphasize *how to think,* ultimately understanding particular approaches to knowledge and evidence as contextually determined, as *relative.* Elaborated commitments to personal and professional choices and goals are reached even later. We studied three areas of development in relation to the Perry scheme: classroom learning, decision making, and career. Students wrote an essay in each of these areas, and it was rated for Perry's scheme using our tested method and criteria (Mentkowski, Moeser, and Strait, 1983).[3] We found that the measure showed definite student change in both cross-sectional and longitudinal studies.

Students show less change in understanding learning pro-

---

[3]The more complex model by Perry (1970, 1981) and the Alverno criteria explicating each position (Mentkowski, Moeser, and Strait, 1983) describe a much more elaborated picture of intellectual and ethical development. Our own intensive study of 3,000 essays from 750 students from the longitudinal and cross-sectional studies developed a valid method and sets of criteria for using expert judgment to code essays elicited by the three questions from Knefelkamp and Widick's Measure of Intellectual Development (Knefelkamp, 1974; Mines, 1982).

cesses and roles during the first two years of college and more during the last two. They use more sophisticated modes of decision making after the first two years of college, but after the second two years, they show a sharp decrease in level of sophistication in decision making. We hypothesize that when they are assessed near graduation, they are making decisions in areas related to future issues and begin by using less complex modes of thinking. Change on careering is upward and gradual, although this pattern is statistically significant only in the cross-sectional study.

Other patterns emerge when we compare older and younger students. Older (ages twenty to fifty-five) students have a consistent edge on younger (ages seventeen to nineteen) students in decision making and career understanding at entrance. And although both groups change, older students maintain their greater sophistication. Figure 1, a schematic presentation of these patterns across the three occasions of assessment, summarizes a combination of results from Mentkowski and Strait (1983).

But initial understanding of classroom learning processes and roles is *not* related to age at entrance to college. Older students are starting at the same place as younger students when

Figure 1. A Schematic Presentation of Patterns of Change Among Older and Younger Students over Three Assessments (at College Entrance, at Midcollege, and near Graduation) in Classroom Learning, Decision Making, and Career on Perry's Scheme of Intellectual and Ethical Development.

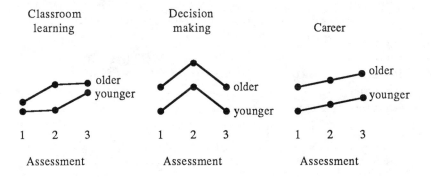

they enter. After two years, older students make more immediate progress in understanding such concepts as learning in multiple ways, learning from peers, and becoming independent in their own learning. But younger students do "catch up" during the last two years, when they make their leap in development. Formal learning experiences are necessary for this enhanced understanding of classroom learning processes and roles. Change for both older and younger students is due in part to performance in the curriculum.

Thus, our longitudinal studies indicate that older adults change just as younger students do. While age does indeed seem to confer some initial advantages as reflected in the intellectual and moral developmental levels of entering students, and educators can rely to a degree on age as an indicator of advanced ability with respect to broad cognitive patterns, older students do change. Their accomplishments reflect more than increased specialized knowledge; they show personal growth.

Clearly, personal growth continues throughout adulthood. This may seem an obvious assertion, especially after the publication of such books as *Seasons of a Man's Life* (Levinson, 1978) and *Adaptation to Life* (Vaillant, 1977) and in view of the current emphasis in developmental psychology on life-span development. However, many educational experiences, such as graduate courses, on-the-job training programs, and even intensive seminars, seem to rest on the assumption that in-depth learning stops after college. Further learning is often characterized by more "content" or "know-how" that serves as a stepping stone to some other course, task, or position. Few professional school curricula show commitment to teaching internalized lifelong learning patterns that lead to personal growth. We have not rid ourselves of the notion that our only responsibility is to select for personal maturity at admission, weed out the incompetent, or expel one or two "bad apples." Clearly, there are some qualities of character or elements of personal style that point to greater likelihood of developing one's human potential. (Such virtues as perseverance, promise keeping, and ability to make meaning out of one's life circumstances are examples.) But these results show that these characteristics do not tell the whole story of adult development.

What are some implications for professional school educators? Students cannot be expected to have developed all aspects of maturity as the result of college. The professional school needs to take the same responsibilities for educating for personal growth that traditionally were common to the mission statements of private liberal arts colleges. And indeed, if adults continue to develop, then I assume they will continue to develop as the result of interaction with the organizations in which they work. In sum, some of the changes in moral, intellectual, and ego development occurred as the result of the curriculum for younger and older adults. It is important to note, however, that changes were more likely to be gradual than dramatic. And these results leave unanswered several questions about change in personal growth. The next observation will address how development happens.

Observation Two: Individuals Recycle Through Earlier Forms of Thinking When They Experience New Situations: Development Occurs in Cyclical Rather than in Stepwise Fashion

A major goal in researching student outcomes, beyond pinpointing curriculum effectiveness, was to better understand the nature of personal growth and how it occurs. The study of student performance on outside measures of human potential helps us examine the nature of change itself—its themes and patterns.

What explains variations in personal growth? Patterns of change do not run neatly in parallel. We just noted increases at some intervals as well as some decreases on the Perry scheme. A measure of self-definition (Stewart and Winter, 1974) shows similar results. Self-definition encompasses the way one thinks about the world and oneself, the way one reacts to new information, and the way one behaves. People with high cognitive initiative are able not only to think clearly but also to reason from problem to solution and to propose to take effective action on their own. Self-definition increases during the first two years of college and decreases in the second two. My reading of the evidence on both these measures suggests that development is not linear and that both younger and older students show "recycling." That is, development proceeds in a gradual upward movement, but when individuals enter a new discipline, setting, or life phase, they cycle back to earlier, less sophisticated modes and strategies of thinking. This may explain why we see an increase in decision-making ability on the Perry scheme during the first two years and a decrease during the second two, when students are generally faced with the more unfamiliar decisions that leaving college brings. It may also explain why we see the same pattern on the self-definition measure. Figure 2 shows this gradual upward movement, with recycling. The three points of assessment show that we might see increases and decreases on measures, depending on when in the cycle we "catch" student thinking.

Figure 2. The Recycling Phenomenon in Individual Development.

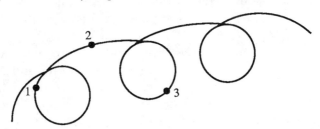

This pattern does seem to suggest the kind of complex developmental movement noticed by Piaget, in which a learner may revert to employing an earlier cognitive strategy when coping with new challenges, entering a new phase of growth, or focusing on a different ability. It will take considerable further study before we can say that these results document this phenomenon of *decalage*. But the possibility that we might validly record such developmental complexity is a promising one, particularly because our criteria and method enable us to measure the evolution of change as well as stability in cognitive level or position (Mentkowski, Moeser, and Strait, 1983).

Educators cannot assume that sophisticated levels of student thinking in one area are necessarily parallel in an unfamiliar area. Thus, even experienced adults can expect benefits from formal education. These findings argue for multiple, systematic assessment of abilities across disciplines to verify ability development and improve prospects for transfer to other settings. Indeed, during the second two years of college, high achievers in the curriculum decreased less on decision making as measured by the Perry scheme than low achievers.

What does this "recycling" phenomenon really mean for professional school education? It argues that professional schools cannot assume that if an individual has, as the result of earlier learning, shown a high level of intellectual or moral reasoning as an aspect of personal growth, this person will automatically show this level of reasoning in new situations like those he or she will experience as a professional. Let us take ethical and moral decision making as one example. Professional school educators will have to provide opportunities to do moral decision making and problem solving—and to behave in ethically responsible ways—*during* professional school. A course in ethics, an introduction to "codes of ethics," or a series of warnings emanating from cases in business where the executives ended up in jail will not suffice. Students will need concentrated experience in ethical sensitivity and moral reasoning. Opportunities are needed for students to engage faculty members about students' ethical dilemmas, especially interpersonal conflicts that students experience during field exercises, in order to provide practice and guidance in linking moral and interpersonal sensitivity, reasoning, and decisions to empathic, ethical action. And if this is true for professional education, is it not also true for the world of work?

Observation Three: Students and Professionals Achieve Integrated Performance of Intellectual and Interpersonal Abilities

Despite the need to recycle through earlier forms of thinking, one could argue that some stability and consistency do develop that can be counted on in new situations. Recycling through earlier ways of thinking in situations does not mean the person has nothing to rely on. If individuals are somewhat at sea in new settings, what do they use as a lifeline? The cognitive-developmental models of life-span growth describe ways of *thinking*. They do not describe what people *do* in situations, their ways of *performing*. To examine integrated performance that will enable on-the-job functioning, we need to move beyond intellectual, ego, and moral mind sets to actual behavior. To do that, we have researched broad, holistic *abilities* or *competences*, two terms we use interchangeably to describe learned dispositions to perform in ways that reflect specialized knowledge, attitudes, motivation, self-perceptions, and skills. What kinds of abilities are needed to carry the individual through a variety of new settings and situations? Do these abilities become integrated—that is, does an individual actively construct them into a complex whole and show coordinated use of multiple abilities in a situation, such that the performance of each ability is supported by the others?

      Our research suggests that the broad, faculty-defined abilities that students develop across the Alverno curriculum do become integrated and do allow for role performance. What is interesting for understanding the development of integrated performance is the combining of these abilities. While *intellectual* development and competence in intellectual abilities have long been the cornerstone of professional education, our research indicates that *interpersonal* abilities are just as important. Indeed, integrated performance on the job demands both sets of abilities. To examine the evidence, we now turn to three data sets from students, alumnae, and professionals who are not Alverno graduates.

      Students' Synthesized Intellectual and Interpersonal Abilities. In looking for interrelationships among the cognitive-developmental patterns, learning styles, and generic abilities we measured, we have found an unexpected but valuable result (Mentkowski and Strait, 1983). When students entered college, and again two years later, their performance on the battery of twelve measures tended to cluster statistically around two separate developmental factors—one we call logical or analytical thought and one we call socioemotional maturity or interpersonal ability. But after four years in college, the two clusters had merged. This may reflect one of the most desired outcomes of college—namely, that students are integrating their own understanding and use of these two kinds of abilities. If this is the case, personal integration may militate against the tendency to be intellectually and morally "undone" in unfamiliar territory.

Let's explore this integration theme further. Are intellectual and interpersonal abilities integrated once the individual faces the world of work? Because the Alverno faculty had identified intellectual abilities (analysis, problem solving) and interpersonal ones (valuing, social interaction, communicating) as curricular outcomes (Alverno College Faculty, 1985a), it wanted to know whether these abilities would lead to effective performance at work after college. Some interesting results emerge from studies of Alverno alumnae and from studies of practicing professionals who are not alumnae. Evidence from the two independent data sources shows that both intellectual and interpersonal abilities are critical for effective work performance.

Alumnae Stressed the Importance of Both Intellectual and Interpersonal Abilities. Of sixty Alverno seniors studied intensively near graduation, thirty-two participated two years later in three-hour semistructured, confidential interviews of their perceptions of their abilities, learning, and personal growth. In analyzing the interviews, we found two major categories of complex abilities that were equally important in managing their work roles and careers. Both younger and older women, across all professional groups, cited reasoning abilities—using such terms as *analysis, problem solving, decision making, planning,* and *organizational abilities*—as important to their career performance. But alumnae *also* consistently emphasized interpersonal abilities learned in college as critical to their effectiveness on the job (Giencke-Holl and others, 1985; Mentkowski, Much, and Giencke-Holl, 1983).

Some abilities identified as crucial to effective performance, such as reasoning abilities, on the face of it, are similar

to those identified by most college and professional school educators. In contrast, interpersonal abilities, long an expected result
from informal learning alone, are critical to effective performance
as evidenced in the observations of working alumnae. This vali-
dates the Alverno faculty's choice of abilities like valuing and
social interaction as similar in importance to intellectual abilities
(Earley, Mentkowski, and Schafer, 1980). The finding also suggests that *all* highly complex cognitive abilities should be integrated with high-level interactive ones. Clusters of abilities
carry forward from college to the world of work. When integrated
and adapted to the workplace, they contribute to effective performance.

*Practicing Professionals Also Used Both Intellectual and
Interpersonal Abilities.* The Alverno study of effective managerial
performance was designed to build a bridge to professionals who
were *not* Alverno alumnae in order to validate abilities the faculty
had identified (Mentkowski, O'Brien, McEachern, and Fowler,
1982). Local business leaders nominated 146 women managers
and executives as effective. Over 100 of these from fifty-three
private corporations met our criteria for "manager" and provided us with job performance interviews and careering histories;
perceptions were assessed through ratings of abilities critical to
education, selection, and performance (Klemp, 1978; McClelland, 1976). The job performance interviews were analyzed for
managerial competences (Boyatzis, 1982; Evarts, 1982) that
characterize effective on-the-job performance. The set of competences consists of four ability clusters: Socioemotional Maturity, Intellectual Abilities, Interpersonal Abilities, and Entrepreneurial Abilities. Each of these clusters is described by several
competences, and each competence is elaborated through a set
of behavioral descriptors. The four clusters, together with the
competences, are presented below.

Socioemotional Maturity   Interpersonal Abilities
   Self-control   Development of others
   Spontaneity   Expressed concern with
   Perceptual objectivity   impact

Accurate self-assessment
Stamina and adaptability
Intellectual Abilities
  Logical thought
  Conceptualization
  Diagnostic use of concepts
  Specialized knowledge

Use of unilateral power
Use of socialized power
Concern with affiliation
Positive regard
Management of groups
Self-presentation
Oral communication
Entrepreneurial Abilities
Efficiency orientation
Proactivity

Following is a list of these managerial competences in order of the frequency with which they were *actually performed* in our study, from most often to least often: proactivity, diagnostic use of concepts, development of others, accurate self-assessment, efficiency orientation, expressed concern with impact, conceptualization, self-presentation, perceptual objectivity, oral communication, use of unilateral power, self-control, management of groups, positive regard, use of socialized power, logical thought, stamina and adaptability, spontaneity, specialized knowledge, and concern with affiliation.

Intellectual and interpersonal abilities had equal importance for these professionals. Managers were equally likely to use intellectual abilities (thinking through problems, applying past experience to interpret events, using a framework to guide analysis and actions) as interpersonal abilities (using power, developing subordinates, managing groups). That these effective women managers and executives showed integrated performance of these abilities in situations is evident from the fact that, many times, several competences were performed in a single situation. To ensure effective career performance for their graduates, educators will have to focus not only on the development of cognitive skills but also on their integration with high-level interpersonal ones.

Given the pattern of competences performed, we created the developmental competence model in Figure 3 to examine relationships among the competences. The competence model suggests a sequence in the development of these competences.

Figure 3. Hypothetical Model of Competence in Women Managers and Executives.

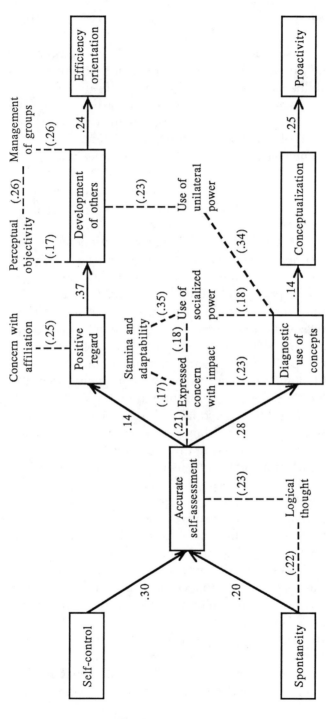

Note: Numbers not in parentheses are path coefficients indicating the strength of the relationship between competences (derived from a factor analysis showing independence) included in a final path analysis (solid lines). Other competences that show a significant positive relationship to competences included in the path analysis are linked to them by broken lines. The bivariate correlation coefficients are placed in parentheses. Three competences, "specialized knowledge," "self-presentation," and "oral communication," did not meet the criteria for inclusion.

Source: Mentkowski, O'Brien, McEachern, and Fowler, 1982, p. 114.

The findings underscore the importance of the competences in the Socioemotional Maturity cluster. Path analyses suggest that competences in this cluster that are (on the face of it) more related to personal growth do contribute equally to Intellectual, Interpersonal, and Entrepreneurial Abilities. Thus, abilities like "self-control," where managers hold back impulsive comments in tense situations or sacrifice personal needs for the good of the organization, as opposed to "spontaneity," where persons act out of immediate needs and feelings without regard for consequences, are important for effective performance. In particular, "accurate self-assessment," the ability to analyze one's own performance in situations and improve as a result, is essential for the further development of abilities.

For managers, some competences within Socioemotional Maturity and Intellectual Abilities preceded the development of Interpersonal and Entrepreneurial Abilities. This suggests that personal growth may be a key to development of the proactivity and efficiency orientation so essential to a manager or executive. In the sequential competence model in Figure 3, constructed from path and correlational analyses (see Mentkowski, O'Brien, McEachern, and Fowler, 1982, for technical details), "self-control" and "spontaneity" are prerequisite competences. "Accurate self-assessment" is third and is central in the sequence. This offers some support for self-assessment as a prerequisite for later competences, thus confirming that it should be developed in the undergraduate years for use early in a manager's career and reinforced systematically in graduate school. The ability to self-assess, to describe and evaluate one's own performance in a situation with recognition of personal strengths and weaknesses, expressing a desire to improve or taking action to improve, is important to developing more profession-specific competences related to interpersonal abilities like "development of others" or "using socialized power," as well as Intellectual and Entrepreneurial Abilities. What is of interest here is that two components of Socioemotional Maturity ("stamina and adaptability" and "perceptual objectivity") appear later in the sequence. This further supports the earlier finding that personal growth continues not only throughout adulthood but as the result of increasing job competence. It may also explain why these women managers, who were new to management and fairly young (67 percent were age forty or younger), showed less Socioemotional Maturity than they showed Intellectual, Interpersonal, and Entrepreneurial Abilities. In the 522 performance situations coded for competences, only 45 percent were coded for Socioemotional Maturity; in contrast, 80 percent, 83 percent, and 84 percent of situations were coded for Intellectual, Interpersonal, and Entrepreneurial Abilities, respectively. Even so, 80 percent of these effective women managers did perform some aspect of Socioemotional Maturity. However, 97 percent, 90 percent, and 95 percent of the managers demonstrated some aspect of Intellectual, Interpersonal, and Entrepreneurial Abilities, respectively. Personal growth is essential for effective performance, and it develops over time.

Education also seems to make a difference in at least some of the Socioemotional Maturity and Interpersonal Abilities that exemplify personal growth for the manager. Women managers who had completed a management training program showed more "stamina and adaptability" and more "use of socialized power" in dealing with subordinates. Those who showed more rapid advancement in their company, and most likely a broader range of experience, demonstrated more "accurate self-assessment" and better-developed "self-presentation" skills. Since "accurate self-assessment" seems, on the face of it, related to personal growth, we can take courage from these findings.

A more serendipitous finding also emerged. Most of the small group of women executives interviewed for this study of managerial competences communicate a holistic approach to life—as well as to management—that they want to teach and share. We did not set out to measure this, but it struck us that these executives were sure of their commitments and consistently acted out of them. These executives demonstrated integrated performance and involvement and tended to shape their own organizations.

But perhaps these few successful women executives are anomalies, honed by the experience of making it in management at a time when they weren't quite so welcome in the field.

Can management students today count on a well-defined and sustained education that contributes to integrated performance and to their personal growth? Will such an education really make a difference later, or will only a few develop their potential? The key to these questions lies in educators' ability to understand learning—the kind of learning that will last beyond formal education.

Observation Four: Self-Sustained Learning That Links Knowing and Doing Is a Causal Element in Integrated Performance

So far, I have examined some broad findings to develop the following argument: (1) personal growth (defined as intellectual, moral, and ego development) occurs during college as the result of a particular curriculum; and although (2) individuals may recycle through less sophisticated forms of thinking when confronted with new decisions and situations, (3) they can rely on increasingly sophisticated moral and intellectual mind sets as well as integrated performance of interpersonal and intellectual abilities in situations. Education seems to make a difference in development of personal growth and integrated performance for both Alverno students and alumnae, as well as practicing professionals in management.

But what learning processes account for these outcomes? Earlier, I cited recycling as one characteristic of life-span cognitive learning. But what kind of learning yields integrated performance of intellectual and interpersonal abilities, particularly at work?

To answer this question, we turn to longitudinal interviews of student perspectives. We gathered the student perception data through a confidential, open-ended interview ranging up to two hours in length, guided by a protocol of questions and probes (Much and Mentkowski, 1982, 1984). Because this measure is lengthy and complex, both to administer and to analyze, we selected samples for interviewing from both longitudinal and cross-sectional study populations. The results here reflect over 320 interviews from eighty-two students who provided interviews at one-year intervals at the end of each year in college. In all, almost 400 interviews were collected and transcribed. Interviews from traditional-age students and those from alumnae have been analyzed so far. The following description is adapted from Mentkowski and Doherty (1983, 1984b).

Self-Sustained Learning in Students. The interview analysis found that learning as described by students is a process of experiencing, reflecting, forming new concepts, and testing one's judgment and abilities in action. Two aspects of learning that students describe seem to be characteristic of a traditional liberal arts education: Students are taught to be objective, to stand back and reflect on their experience; and they are consistently exposed to opportunities to form new concepts, complete readings, and attend lectures on theory. But these students also came to realize that hands-on experience is critical for learning. They also avowed that using new knowledge is necessary to really learning it and that one must test new-found skills. From the students' perspective, these elements fit together as a process that describes how they learn.

One student, "Andrea," describes this process: "By learning something and going and applying it, you can find out what worked for you, what didn't, what you really don't understand, and then you can go back and question. Or in learning new theory, you can apply, you can think back to the clients you have had or the situations you were in and say, 'If I had known that then, it could have helped me a lot.' So I think the application and then going back to theory and questioning helps make it more solid in your mind—you can understand it better."

Changes in Student Learning Styles. Thus, our student interviews independently confirmed Kolb's (1984) recent description of the learning process as experiencing, reflecting, forming new concepts, and testing one's judgment and abilities in action. Kolb derived this experiential learning theory from theories by Lewin, Dewey, and Piaget and has researched it in part through measures of learning style.

Further evidence from the longitudinal studies of student changes in personal growth are the dramatic changes appearing in students' orientation to learning styles, using Kolb's Learning Style Inventory (1976). At entrance, both younger and older students showed marked preference for "concrete experiencing" over "abstract conceptualizing" and for "reflective observing" as against "active experimenting." In the first two years, they moved rapidly toward a more balanced pattern: By the second testing, they had come to rely equally on concrete and abstract modes and to show a similar flexibility in choosing either a reflective or an active approach. Additional analyses revealed that students who showed high achievement in the curriculum changed more and that when age, pretest scores, and other variables were controlled, the curriculum still accounted for change. Overall, achievement in the curriculum had a greater effect than age on changes in learning style preferences.

These results provide another clue that certain kinds of learning may be related to integrated performance. They also suggest that experiential learning is an important curricular element (Doherty, Mentkowski, and Conrad, 1978; Mentkowski, O'Brien, Cleve, and Wutzdorff, 1983). But which elements of the curriculum matter?

Curricular Elements Most Important to Self-Sustained Learning. To what curricular elements do students attribute "learning to learn"? The interview analysis identified three major components that describe the development of this process of learning to learn: *taking responsibility for learning, making relationships among abilities and their use,* and *using different ways of learning.* Figure 4 illustrates the learning outcomes and the curricular elements to which students attribute the development of their learning-to-learn skills.

Note that one of the more prominent causes gleaned from the interview examples is *experiential validation,* having to apply abilities within and across courses, demonstrating them on assessments and during internships, and using the abilities in multiple settings. This may be a curricular element essential for integrated performance.

Coming to Value Liberal Learning. While students are showing development of self-sustained learning, how do we know

Figure 4. Student Learning Outcomes
and Their Causes as Attributed by Students.

Student Attributed Cause   Student Outcome

Instructor attention and empathy   Taking responsibility
Feedback, Self-assessment   ──────────⟶   for learning

Experiential validation   Making relationships
Instructor coaching   ──────────⟶   among abilities and
Professional application   their use
Integration of abilities

Practice, Feedback   Using different ways
Modeling, Peer learning   ──────────⟶   of learning

that students *value* learning? Does learning become part of their value system? And do students' professional values include the kind of learning that would support integrated performance?

Student interview data confirm that students' commitment to personal, career, and professional values develops throughout college. There is also an important performance dimension to commitment; students consistently give examples of how they are acting out of their personal and professional value systems. Like their understanding of learning, their understanding of their own commitment develops throughout college, and they show more and more sophisticated behaviors that match their increasingly internalized goals and values.

Students also consistently broaden the settings in which they describe themselves using their abilities. As they progress, they cite instances from work, family, and other environments as often as their in-class assessments. This indicates that cognitively they have made the transfer that they claim to have made experientially. Through experiential validation of their abilities, students are able to construct a justification for liberal learning in which personal growth and effectiveness mediate between educational experience and concepts of professional role performance. Thus, there is reason to believe these students are capable of integrated performance. Our current, and fourth, interviews with these students, who are now five-year alumnae, suggest that we will be able to determine what value frameworks they use at work.

Self-Sustained Learning in Alumnae. But do two-year alumnae continue to show self-sustained learning after college at work? Do they value learning on the job? While Argyris and Schön (1974) have described the importance of a theory of action in effective performance and McClelland (1975) has shown that abilities are a basis for effective role performance, researchers and educators still must demonstrate how this happens. Educators want to know how and why abilities are developed so they can foster them in college. As we analyzed our thirty-two alumna interviews, a picture of active, self-sustained learning began to emerge as it was practiced at work. Several components of learning to learn characterized alumna behavior: (1) Learning is a continuous process; alumnae regard learning opportunities as motivating career development and job choice. (2) Learning to learn for alumnae means to tie knowledge, theory, and experience to productive action and to put these elements together in new situations. (3) Alumnae apply abilities in action, get a response, and adjust performance or ideas accordingly. (4) Alumnae show integration and adaptation of abilities based on the experience of "observing, thinking, retrenching." (5) Central to self-sustained learning is thinking and performing in particular settings and situations.

College learning and abilities form a foundation for role performance after college, but learning to learn is a prerequisite to adapting abilities in the role one has. Self-sustained learning is a process that enables adaptability to multiple settings; it enables students to perform abilities learned in college later, at work. Thus, this study of alumna and student interviews suggests another kind of integration, between knowledge and its use.

Linking Knowing and Doing for Integrated Performance. A central issue in whether integrated performance will accrue for the individual as the result of participation in an organizational climate other than professional school, and whether the individual will be in a position to contribute to an organization's integrity, has to do with the relationship between knowing and doing. From this initial study of student and alumna interviews, it seems that integration not only of intellectual and interpersonal abilities but also of thought and action in a particular context is key to a sustained pattern of growth and change. If we can center our educational experiences in consistently ensuring relationships between knowing and doing, as the students experienced in our interview studies, we are more likely to effect a general integration between thought and action that will generalize to a variety of situations, including those that call for integrated functioning within a framework of values.

It remains to be seen whether individuals taught in this way will continue to act responsibly in organizations, but there are enough examples in the interviews we are collecting in our current five-year follow-up study to indicate individual initiative in doing so. Clearly, the link between thought and action, between knowledge and behavior, seems developable during college and seems to develop further afterward. More important, it seems to be a central building block in the glimpses of integrated performance I have seen so far.

Our study of managers and executives also confirmed the importance of knowledge linked to action. Recall that we researched abilities through performance interviews and also asked participants for their perceptions of what outstanding professionals *should* do. Managers were invited to judge a range of performance characteristics. We found that these effective managers generally perform abilities they independently judge as characteristic of outstanding performers. The findings also allowed us to identify those abilities that professionals don't demonstrate but identify as important—such as negotiating and networking in management—thus signaling abilities that should be part of the manager's repertoire. Other abilities, such as demonstrating self-control and using socialized power, are more important for effective performance than the managers realize. However, the fact that we found this congruity between perceptions of managerial abilities and actual performance is evidence that the managers in this study have another element critical to the development of integrated performance—knowledge reflected in action.

Thus, application of abilities cannot be left to chance in professional school education. Traditional curricula have emphasized development of knowledge over action, just as they

have emphasized intellectual abilities and ignored interpersonal
ones. The Alverno curriculum demands *using* abilities across
multiple settings. Results from all three data sources—students,
alumnae, and professionals—confirm that the integrated performance of abilities is a developmental, learned process that
needs systematic teaching and opportunity for practice. Increasingly complex performance develops in concert with gradually
more sophisticated modes of thought.

Summary

Four observations from recent research on the personal
growth, integrated performance, and self-sustained learning of
students during and after college and professionals in management are used to draw implications for professional school educators who seek to contribute to the development of integrity. Personal growth, defined as intellectual, moral, and ego development, occurs during college as the result of a particular curriculum, although individuals may recycle through less sophisticated forms of thinking when confronted with new decisions and
settings. Yet people can rely on integrated performance of interpersonal and intellectual abilities in new situations that demand professional expertise, particularly because they use active, self-sustained learning strategies which help them improve
and which link what they know with what they can do.

One of the primary reasons that personal growth, integrated performance, and self-sustained learning cannot be left
to chance is that adults continue to develop throughout their
career. While this may not be startling news, what is intriguing is an emerging picture of how they do it. This profile argues
that development is not the step-by-step odyssey that the psychological literature and its popularized versions (for example,
Sheehy's *Passages,* 1974) imply. Consistency in thought and action and insightful decision making will not necessarily happen
when a person is faced with new and difficult challenges. Professional school admissions committees and personnel directors
in organizations cannot rely on selection of applicants "with
integrity," or other naively conceptualized personality traits,

and hope for the best. The most astute student and most experienced executive will find themselves recycling through less sophisticated ways of thinking and performing in the face of new situations, and unless they are well equipped with integrated interpersonal and intellectual abilities and a learning strategy that enables them to benefit from their mistakes and adapt to new contexts, even the most value-oriented individuals can persist in decisions and directions that do not reflect their potential for effective leadership.

The students and professionals we studied did show some of the forms of integration that might be essential to the development of integrity. Students' interpersonal abilities did become integrated with intellectual ones during college, and students used both sets of abilities at work after college. Effective managers showed socioemotional maturity and interpersonal abilities, as well as intellectual ones. In fact, these complex, personal maturity and interpersonal abilities, rather than specialized knowledge alone, are prerequisite to developing the more role-specific entrepreneurial abilities. Knowledge alone does not guarantee effective professional performance; some aspects of personal growth are a prerequisite. Therefore, educators cannot ignore their responsibility to educate for personal growth.

Interpersonal and intellectual abilities continue to develop and become integrated once students leave school because they use a learning process acquired in college that is active and self-sustained. The students we studied continued using these ways of learning on the job to improve their performance. Contextual thinking, decision making, and action resulted for many of the students we studied during college and afterward. For managers and executives, this kind of learning—that is, accurate self-assessment to direct and change behavior—is also a key ability that needs to be learned early in one's career. Individuals who value learning and who express that value in a lifetime commitment to learning continue their own personal and professional growth.

Observable linking between abilities and their use is another form of integration. Students make these links intellectually and validate them through experience inside and outside class. After college, they rely on such links to be effective at work. Effective managers' and executives' judgments of which abilities outstanding managers perform generally match the competences these professionals actually demonstrate in situations. The link between knowing and doing encourages consistency in judgment and action, which I believe is central to doing what one knows is right in the face of pressures to do otherwise.

Even so, we have found that it is the systematic application of certain educational principles across an institution that accounts for self-sustained learning, a causal element in integrated performance during college and at work. For example, instructor attention and empathy, expressed in part through detailed feedback on performance and opportunities to self-assess one's own work, are central to taking responsibility for learning. Opportunities to make relationships among abilities and their use, to integrate knowledge with performance, are key. Instructor coaching and opportunities for experiential validation of one's abilities in the classroom and through professional applications make integrated performance happen.

In sum, this chapter is meant to challenge commonly held assumptions about whether personal growth can be taught, how development happens, what abilities make up integrated performance, what some forms of integration are, how effective professionals use learning to continue to develop their abilities, and what needs to be included in professional school curricula. Evidence from a longitudinal study of students during and after college and a study of professional managers and executives helps educators describe more precisely the kinds of thinking, ways of performing, and self-sustained learning that characterize integration in students and professionals. Education for personal growth, integrated performance, and learning that lasts can and should happen, but it will not happen automatically. I believe that a curriculum with certain essential elements effects these three outcomes and thereby contributes to the development of a professional characterized by integrity.

5

Integrity in Effective Leadership

Steven Kerr

Columbus was not above using devious, even deceptive, techniques to keep his crew in good spirits and devoted to the common purpose. He did not forget his crew's concern for getting home, and in good time. To be sure that he would not discourage the men, he falsified his daily journal of the voyage. In noting down his estimates of distance traveled, "he decided to reckon less than he made, so that if the voyage were long the people would not be frightened and dismayed" [Daniel J. Boorstin, *The Discoverers*].

Upon being invited to a symposium on executive integrity and asked to speak on integrity in effective leadership, my initial thought was that the nomination made a good deal of sense. I do these days double as an executive, serving as inside dean or, if you prefer, "chief operating officer" for a large organization (nearly 300 full-time employees and a $37 million budget), and of course, who could ever question my personal or executive integrity?

Qualified as I obviously was, it occurred to me as I began to write this chapter that I would be even better qualified were I to learn something about the construct "integrity" and its close companions "ethics" and "morality." The briefest of excursions into the appropriate literature reaffirmed my belief in the wisdom of my selection—but for the opposite reason! Now I felt like the "before" side of a before/after marketing brochure for an ethics seminar, or like the poster boy standing sadly before a judge as the caption barks, "Don't let this happen to you!"

What I began to realize was that the organization for which I share responsibility, and all other organizations with which I have ever been associated, consistently and continually violate virtually all the prescriptions, canons, and guidelines said by the experts to constitute integrious behavior.

Let me underscore the seriousness of this last point. I am not engaging in a semantic exercise involving the word *integrity*, nor am I taking refuge in the occasional odd dilemma so popular in the textbooks (would you bribe the evil customs inspector in a country where it's expected?). The accusation being made is far more serious: that I, and almost everyone else with my sort of responsibilities, can scarcely make it through a single workday without engaging in behaviors that violate what are said to be the basic elements of ethics and integrity.

What are we to make of this assertion? It seems that there are three possibilities, and one of them must be true:

1. I am an unusually corrupt administrator and would-be leader, rationalizing my actions by alleging that "everybody does it." If this is the explanation, my participation in a seminar on integrity is probably a mistake—except, as mentioned, as a negative example—that provides no particular learning point or basis for further discussion.

2. Certainly I am corrupt, but everybody really does do it. This possibility is even more depressing than the first but at least provides a nice take-off point for discussion. Assuming it is not merely a case of societal bad genes, what is there in the character of organizational life that makes moral bankrupts of its leaders?

3. Suppose, for a moment, that I am not corrupt; even imagine that I, and people like me, really do possess leadership integrity when assessed intuitively rather than according to the textbook definitions. If this is true, what does it say about our working definitions of integrity? Are they still useful, or could they be made useful through revision? If they are to be rejected as not useful, what standards for ethics and integrity should be substituted for them? Such questions will occupy the remainder of this chapter.

Behavioral Components of
Integrity, Morality, and Ethics

With respect to identifying the set of behaviors that constitute integrity, a good place to start is with the remarks of
Suresh Srivastva, whose introductory letter (November 27, 1985)
served as an organizing device for the conference. According
to Srivastva:

> While the management literature has been relatively quiet in respect to
> the concept of integrity, it can be inferred that integrity is . . . a socially
> embedded phenomenon pointing to the unity and *connectedness* in all orga-
> nized relations. . . . Also, it is seen as a driving force in the movement
> toward *consistency* between values and action, or between espoused theory
> and theory-in-use. . . . Finally, integrity represents a generative concern—
> the concern for establishing and guiding the next generation of persons
> and institutions.

Another definition of integrity, consistent with Srivastva's,
is offered in Webster's *New World Dictionary:* "(1) the quality
or state of being complete, wholeness, entirety; (2) the quality
or state of being of sound moral principle, uprightness, honesty,
and sincerity."

Speaking about *morality* within the context of business
ethics, Solomon and Hanson (1983, p. 187) describe what they
say are the minimal conditions necessary for organizational
morality to exist. These include, among other things, *consistency*,
not in the sense defined by Srivastva, but in the sense that similar
cases are treated similarly. Solomon and Hanson argue that "if
two employees work equally hard for equally long, and the only
difference between them is that you enjoy a drink after work
with one, morality means that you should, in your position as
their superior, treat them the same, give them equal raises, and
give them equal consideration for promotion." A second condition that Solomon and Hanson name is *universality*, that is,
applying to ourselves the same considerations we apply to others.
A third condition is *giving reasons*, backing up our actions with
explanations and justifications. They say that the reasons "must

fit the first two conditions; that is, they must be consistent . . . and they must be universal, applying to *anyone* who might be or might have been involved in a similar position." A fourth condition of morality is *concern for others*.

To other writers and theorists, another important aspect of morality is clarity, or removing ambiguity. Wiener pointed out that, in law, "it is the first duty . . . to see that the obligations and rights given to an individual in a certain stated situation be unambiguous. Moreover, there should be a body of legal interpretation which is as far as possible independent of the will and the interpretation of the particular authorities consulted. Reproducibility is prior to equity, for without it there can be no equity" (1954, p. 107). Waters (1978) emphasized removing ambiguity not only with respect to rights and obligations but particularly concerning the relative importance attached to organizational priorities and to the general ethical standards of society. He argued that "if top management really wants to obey the law and operate according to the general ethical standards of society, it must say so unambiguously. It should state clearly that such constraints come *before,* and in that sense have a *higher priority than,* such traditional objectives as sales volume, market share, and profits" (p. 14).

A useful overview of *ethics* has been offered by Cavanagh, Moberg, and Velasquez (1981), who pointed out that ethical criteria have their roots in three basic kinds of moral theories: utilitarianism, theories of rights, and theories of justice.

Utilitarianism seeks the greatest good for the greatest number; therefore, organizational leaders "are required to estimate the effect of each alternative on all the parties concerned and to select the one that optimizes the satisfactions of the greatest number" (p. 365).

Theories of rights maintain that all people have fundamental rights that may not be denied even for the greatest good of the greatest number. According to Cavanagh, Moberg, and Velasquez, these include the right of free consent, such that "individuals within an organization have the right to be treated only as they knowingly and freely consent to be treated" (p. 366); the right to privacy; the right to freedom of conscience, whereby "individuals have the right to refrain from carrying out any order that violates moral or religious norms to which they adhere" (p. 366); the right of free speech; and the right to due process.

Theories of justice depend on various distributive rules and principles for administering these rules. The most important rule of distributive justice is that "differentiated treatment of individuals should not be based on arbitrary characteristics. Individuals who are similar in the relevant respects should be treated similarly, and individuals who differ in a relevant respect should be treated differently in proportion to the difference between them" (Cavanagh, Moberg, and Velasquez, 1981, p. 366). Principles of administration include that rules be clearly and expressly stated and consistently and impartially enforced.

To O'Toole (1985), ethics is a much less complicated matter: "Ethical behavior simply means adherence to a few common-sense principles, such as: Obey the law; Tell the truth; Stick to the Golden Rule; . . . Above all, do not harm . . . ; Practice participation, not paternalism; Always act when you have responsibility (that is, when you have the capacity or resources to act, or when those nearby are in need and you are the only one who can help)" (p. 349).

From all these sources, it is possible to derive a "Ten Commandments of Executive Integrity," which reads as follows:

1. *Tell the truth.* Communicate fully, honestly, and openly. Give reasons and justifications for decisions reached and actions taken. Absent full and honest communications, people cannot exercise their fundamental right of free consent.
2. *Obey the law.*
3. *Reduce ambiguity.* Clarify organizational values and priorities and individual rights and obligations.
4. *Show concern for others.* Obey the Golden Rule, which means treating people as you would have them treat you. Be faithful to the concept of universality, which suggests that artificial rank and status differentials should be minimized (as opposed to the doctrine RHIP: "Rank has its privileges"). Be faithful both to the principle of utilitarianism,

requiring those actions that bring the greatest good for the greatest number, and to the principle that all people have certain fundamental rights that cannot be denied.

5. *Accept responsibility for the growth and nurturing of subordinates.* Respect people's unique characteristics. Allow organization members to function as distinct, whole entities ("the human use of human beings"). Adhere to the most basic canon of medical ethics: *Primum non nocere* (above all, do not harm).

6. *Practice participation, not paternalism.* This suggests not only giving reasons and justifications for decisions but also communicating these decisions to subordinates before they become binding and irreversible.

7. *Provide freedom from corrupting influences.* It is necessary to protect organization members not only from overt demands that they act unethically but also from cultures and reward systems that subtly discourage integrity. Respect people's right to freedom of conscience.

8. *Always act.* When you have the resources to act integriously, or when someone requires your help, integrity requires that you take appropriate action.

9. *Provide consistency across cases.* If one person's problem is handled in a certain manner, all people with that problem should be treated in the same way.

10. *Provide consistency between values and actions,* between theories espoused and theories-in-use. To act otherwise is to be a hypocrite.

The Absence of Integrity in Everyday Organizational Life

Let me next present a number of examples of organizational behaviors that are in fundamental opposition to the components of integrity listed above. Some of these examples violate only one of our ten commandments. Other examples violate several commandments at the same time. Please note that these examples do not pertain merely to the odd, unusual event, nor do they reference decisions by impotent leaders who are powerless to act otherwise, nor do they describe decisions that must be made under great stress or time pressure, nor are they limited to organizations with shrinking markets or in collapsing industries. Rather, the examples describe immoral, unethical, unintegrious actions (according to our consensual definition) taken in the course of everyday organizational life by those at or near the top of nearly all private- and public-sector organizations. Several are actions I myself have taken and expect to continue to take in the future. Those that do not reference me personally are nevertheless extremely common, and I have witnessed them many times as an employee in my current or in previous organizations or in those I served as a consultant or researcher.

As you scan these examples, keep in mind the alternative possibilities offered at the start of this chapter. Do the examples reflect (1) unusually corrupt behavior by the chapter's author and his colleagues, with no implication beyond the obvious unsuitability of the author to hold a position of leadership, (2) generically immoral behavior by those who head our organizations, which speaks in some sense to the corrupting nature of leadership or of organizations in general, or (3) some weakness in our consensual definition such that the behaviors described might, through a different lens, be viewed as not necessarily inconsistent with integrious behavior?

Tell the Truth

Examples 1–4: Misassignment of Expenditures. Among the most frequent administrative falsehoods is the intentional assignment of expenditures to the wrong categories. Often a budget or a grant or an authorization permits money to be spent on one thing but not on another. Thus, students who are funded as teaching assistants (TAs) and who are supposed to have teaching responsibilities may be carried on the books as TAs but in fact are assigned to faculty members as research assistants. (Other TAs do work as TAs; this practice violates not only the principle of honesty but also the commandment of consistency across cases and, when funds come from government sources, the canon "Obey the law" as well.)

Another example of a deliberately dishonest assignment of funds that may violate several of our commandments is the subterfuge practiced by numerous organizations with respect to moving allowances. In some cases such allowances are forbidden altogether, while in others the maximum permitted is woefully inadequate to cover costs. In such cases it is often routine practice to advise incoming employees to forward a phony billing for an imaginary colloquium or nonexistent consulting, which is then paid by the organization and used by the employee to cover the costs of moving.

Another illustration of this type concerns the common practice of burying salary increases or performance bonuses in the budget by disguising them as different kinds of payment. This may be done to circumvent organizational regulations concerning maximum salary increases or to keep other employees from learning how much has been paid to particular individuals. (The leader can then lie to subordinates that each of them received "the top of the pool," whereas in fact some got more than the stated maximum.)

Sometimes the false category into which expenses are assigned is not a type of expense but a calendar or fiscal year. For example, in organizations mandated to operate under a balanced budget it is often common practice to spend beyond budget, then literally throw unpaid bills into a drawer where they remain until the new year begins—while lying to creditors that "the check is in the mail."

Examples 5–6: Creating Turnover. A highly orchestrated web of deceit often accompanies the involuntary termination of an employee. First, the organization communicates to other employees that the individual has resigned, implying if not stating that the resignation was voluntary. The terminated employee may then be invited to write not only his letter of resignation but a letter *to* him, allegedly from the president or department head, thanking him for his years of highly productive service. In keeping with the theme—blatant dishonesty and hypocrisy—a going-away party may then be arranged for the soon-to-be-departed, at which the same officers who fired him will extol his virtues and mourn his passing. The charade usually ends with a flourish, in the form of absurdly favorable references for the individual to carry with him to his next employer.

A variant on this method, often used in settings where termination is impossible, is to offer outrageously favorable references about a poor performer in hopes that they will fool some gullible outsider—or, in case of transfer, insider—into making a job offer, whereon the employee leaves voluntarily. (In such cases the going-away party is optional.)

Example 7: Being a Fire Hydrant. [1] Among the more entertaining of charades, this one usually begins with a clandestine visit by a department head to a dean or corporate officer. The dean is warned that an unreasonable request is about to be made of him by someone in the department. The department head is unalterably opposed to this unreasonable request but, of course, must appear to be supportive because of the need to maintain intragroup harmony. The charade is then played out in predictable fashion—everyone saying his or her assigned lines—and ends with the department head walking from the meeting room with his arm around the aggrieved petitioner, assuring her that everything that could have been done was done, but unfortunately the dean is anti-research, anti-female, or whatever.

Examples 8–9: Remaining Mute. In stark contrast to the precept that communications should be honest and complete, and truthful reasons and justifications for action should always be given, many administrators soon come to believe that it is often better *not* to give reasons, that, as Calvin Coolidge once argued, "you never have to explain something you didn't say." Consider, for example, the following reasons for nominating a particular person to a particular committee: (1) the university requires that such-and-such committee include someone from your school; (2) such-and-such committee has performed no

[1]Lyman Porter once observed that "a dean is to his faculty as a hydrant is to its dogs."

useful work during its twenty-six years of existence, and you feel confident that its best years are behind it; (3) fortunately, a perfect fit suggests itself inasmuch as you have on your staff a faculty member who has performed no useful work over *his* lifetime. What most executives learn to say to the appointee in such a circumstance is either (a) such-and-such committee is poised on the edge of greatness and only your participation can bring this potential to fruition or (b) nothing. Telling the truth in such a case would confuse the appointee and seem odd to everyone else.

A more compelling reason to refuse to explain appears in the case of an employee whose contract is not to be renewed, because he is a horse's ass and no one can stand to be around him. You are uncertain, and your legal counsel is uncertain, whether being a horse's ass is job-related (in academe). You are certain that half your staff will quit if the individual's contract is renewed. In this circumstance, many executives will decide not to renew his contract and will use as an explanation something more elegant—and more legally defensible—than the truth.

Obey the Law

Example 10: Hiring One's Cronies. Lawmakers expend considerable time and energy creating legislation to protect the right of prospective employees, particularly women, minorities, and the elderly, to be considered fairly for position openings. Organization leaders expend at least as much time and energy circumventing this legislation. As one example, imagine that someone well known to an organization as a high performer becomes available to be hired. The organization wishes to move quickly to permit this to happen. However, the law requires that the position must be publicly advertised and posted for a certain period of time. Numerous well-intentioned job seekers then appear, who are put through bogus selection and interview procedures that raise their hopes and waste their time. The law may require that this go on for quite a while. At the end of the specified period, the employee known to the organization is hired. Whose rights have been protected? Whose justice has been served? A goodly number of our ten commandments are violated by such procedures, but few executives are easily persuaded to employ a stranger in lieu of someone whose skills and work habits are known and valued.

Example 11: Rigging the Files. Another common, illegal practice is the intentional distortion of performance appraisals and the rigging of personnel files for the purpose of justifying current salary action or laying the groundwork for future disciplinary action. Perhaps most common is the practice of completing performance appraisal forms from the bottom up, that is, first making a subjective determination about what summary rating or salary increase a leader wants a subordinate to receive, then working backward through the forms so that the subdimensions or components "add up" to the desired total.

An important paradox in today's litigious environment is that, to many managers, the commandments "Obey the law" and "Nurture subordinates" seem increasingly contradictory. This is because the law is much less insistent on remedying employee deficiencies than on documenting and even perpetuating them, at least until the employee's track record has become sufficiently long and dreary that legally defensible disciplinary action may be taken. Many a would-be mentor has been advised by legal counsel to refrain from making shifts in responsibilities or workloads aimed at improving an employee's low performance, lest the record of unacceptable behavior be interrupted and the legal basis for discipline removed.

Provide Consistency Across Cases

Although they are in clear violation of the prescription that there should be consistency across cases, the following examples are extremely typical in both industry and academe.

Example 12: The Order Effect. Unfortunately, the order effect is a major determinant of which cases will be approved and which disapproved. Often something is approved on an ad hoc basis the first few times it is requested. Human nature is such that once a few persons have been granted a personal computer, grader, extra file cabinet, or whatever, numerous requests for the same item soon follow, even from those who have no need for the item. Management's response is inevitably to institute some allocation policies whose net effect is to create distribution criteria that are far more restrictive than those governing the earlier cases, resulting in inconsistency across cases and within the same cases over time.

Example 13: Gossip and Rumors. Although everyone agrees that it shouldn't happen, invariably gossip, rumors, and stray bits of unconfirmed data become bases for decision making. This violates the consistency doctrine in that some individuals are allocated resources and are found wanting as a result of a kind of "test" that others did not undergo.

Example 14: Nepotism. Even in the best-run organizations, it often happens that nepotism and cronyism become bases for promotion or appointment to an attractive position. This is held to be among the least integrious of all organizational behaviors (in our society; in many cultures it is considered an honorable, superior basis for selection). Yet it is a simple truth that most executives feel more comfortable working with people they know and like. Nepotism is generally seen as a violation of the consistency principle, since employees with similar performance records are not treated similarly. It could, of course, be argued that the records are *not* similar in the important respect that one candidate enjoys the confidence of higher management while the other does not.

Example 15: Undue Influence. A final example of this type is that, in academe, children of influential alumni and family members of wealthy donors are likely to be admitted even though other students with identical records would not be. (Note that in the so-called good schools this is true only at the margin; that is, prospective students with terrible records will be denied admission regardless of lineage. Moreover, good schools may let people in because of who they are or whom they know but will not let them out—that is, graduate them—unless they perform at acceptable levels.)

Accept Responsibility for the Growth and Nurturing of Subordinates

Examples 16–17: Creating False Career Hopes and Career Paths. It is common practice in many organizations for top management to permit employees to believe, and go on believing, that they are likely candidates for some higher-level job while secretly interviewing other candidates for that position. Often the person being passed over is not really unqualified for the job but is considered unqualified because of unfair stereotyping or pigeonholing. For example, once someone is known to be good with computers, the only positions mentioned in connection with her are computer-related.

It is also common practice for organizations to assign employees to tasks that are in no way compatible with their skills, interests, or future growth potential but, rather, because the organization presumes it will benefit from having the person in that position. In extreme cases, placements are made that thwart personal and professional growth, induce high physiological and psychological stress, and endanger the employee's marriage and family situation. It is also becoming increasingly common for organizations to pressure people into taking early retirement, whether or not it is in the employee's best interest and irrespective of what the law says on the subject.

Show Concern for Others

Violation of the prescription to show concern for others permeates many of the previous examples. I would add to those the following:

Example 18: RHIP. In opposition to the concept of universality, rank has its privileges in most American organizations. Deans, for example, often enjoy special parking, have access to the best secretarial and office help, can obtain computers, electronic typewriters, and other equipment without the hurdles and delays experienced by others, and may even enjoy the benefit of spending the organization's money as though it were their own.

Example 19: Denying People's Individuality. It is very common for organizations to violate the principle that people should be treated as individuals. What seems to an individual employee to be a unique problem is often viewed by higher management as "situation 104," calling into motion a generalized response that leaves the individual feeling ignored and unappreciated. Individuality is, after all, contradictory to uniformity and standardization, and it also threatens organizational requirements for predictability. For that matter, individuality may also be largely incompatible with consistency across cases.

Let me illustrate this point with a case that, as I write, has occupied my attention within the last twenty-four hours. The holder of a D.B.A. from the University of Southern California petitioned the School of Business to have his degree converted to a Ph.D. My first thought was to conduct a review of his thesis and other evidences of scholarship to see whether such conversion was warranted—in short, to treat the case as a single event and consider it on its individual merits. My superiors at the university level soon put an end to such foolish notions, however. Here is the actual language of their response to me:

. . . We cannot legally and ethically make a change like this for one person; we would have to review all D.B.A. degree recipients during the same time period (early 1970s) to see if their degrees should also be changed and make the same offer to them. Even if we tried to do this for just _____, I can assure you . . . that many others would demand the same treatment. And where would we draw the line? 1975 D.B.A.'s? 1960 D.B.A.'s?

The remainder of the letter dealt with the steps necessary to determine whether these students' training while at USC justified conversion of their degrees. These stated requirements were so onerous that it would be irrational for me to pursue this matter further. Thus "showing concern for others" is once again to be sacrificed to some (undefined) greater good. Even though this is the *only* petitioner who has ever come to me seeking a degree conversion during the nearly five years I have been a dean, the organization has decided that it cannot "legally and ethically" treat the case on an individual basis.

Example 20: Disempowerment. Let me close with a particularly interesting example: the intentional, premeditated effort by an organization leader to *lower* the self-esteem of a subordinate. The situation involved an employee who continually complained about being underpaid. The comparison group consisted of other full professors at the nation's best universities. The manager had tried to solve the problem by negotiating future performance targets whose attainment would trigger a merit adjustment. The subordinate was unreceptive to this approach, claiming that the only relevant data were the average salary figures of his peers at Harvard, Chicago, and so on. The approach the manager finally took was to accumulate a number of vitae of full professors at the schools referred to and, in a memorable session with the subordinate, to demonstrate in a most explicit fashion that the subordinate was nowhere near as productive as his colleagues at Harvard and Chicago—indeed, that he would never have been promoted or tenured had he been at Harvard or Chicago. The subordinate left the session much better informed but with his ego in considerable disarray. How can such an approach be reconciled with such principles as showing concern for others, nurturing subordinates, or "doing no harm"?

Conclusion

Among the three earlier-mentioned possible ways to make sense of the preceding examples, I would, however tentatively, like to rule out the first. Doing so suggests to me that organizations, and particularly those who lead them, tend to operate against the consensual definition of integrity in both subtle and unsubtle ways. The idea that organizations can corrupt the powerful and alienate the rest is, of course, not new. For example, in his review of the Marxian perspective on the sources of alienation, Nord (1974, pp. 570–571) has pointed out that, to Marx, "the division of labor under capitalism is a source of social tensions. . . . It produces people who are alienated from one another. . . . Since men's activities are not voluntary, the power generated by the cooperation of individuals becomes an 'alien' force which they do not control . . . . In short, the capitalistic social-economic system embodies a vicious circle. The division of labor and private property generates alienation which, in turn, increases the emphasis on material products, which further accelerates the division of labor and the stress on accumulation, which results in further alienation." (For more detailed treatments of this topic see Morgan, 1980, and Burrell and Morgan, 1979.)

A number of authors have made good suggestions about how we might modify our organizational practices so that they operate more in accordance with our definition of integrity. For example, Maier (1970) has discussed ways of reducing status differentials, and he and others (see Vroom and Yetton, 1973) have helped us to understand how participative management can be used to better advantage. Numerous authors have discussed ways to nurture organization members. With respect to honesty, Bennis (1984) suggested that "to build openness and integrity from the ground up, the organization can provide direction by making a conscious effort to reward truthtelling." Waters (1978) elaborated on this point by suggesting some concrete things organizations can do to foment a climate in which internal whistle blowers would feel free to operate. Work by Jansen and Von Glinow (1985) and my own work (see Kerr, 1987) have described some ways that reward systems might be altered to serve such ends.

Alternatively, there may be something to the third possibility I identified earlier—namely, that there is something wrong with, or at least seriously incomplete about, our working definitions of integrity. Such statements as O'Toole's (1985) that "ethical behavior simply means adherence to a few common-sense principles, such as: Obey the law; Tell the truth; . . . "may strike you as they strike me, in the wake of my examples, as perhaps a bit ingenuous. For one thing, as I hope has been illustrated to some small extent, these "common-sense principles" do not appear to be particularly compatible with one another. In particular, those principles pertaining to the more cognitive elements of ethics and integrity often seem attainable only at the cost of jeopardizing the more affective elements. For example, consider once more our ten commandments, arrayed in the following manner:

Obey the law	Match values to actions
Tell the truth	Nurture subordinates, do no harm
Provide consistency across cases	Show concern for people
Reduce ambiguity	Respect people's freedom of conscience
Act when you have authority	Practice participation

It can be argued that each principle on the left is often incompatible with most principles on the right, and vice versa. Thus, "Obey the law," "Tell the truth," and "Provide consistency across cases" may be incompatible with "Practice participation," "Nurture subordinates," "Show concern for people," and so on.

It seemed to me as I reviewed the literature that, with a few exceptions, the more confident were the prescriptions about how to behave with ethics and integrity, the further removed was the author from the life of the everyday manager. A good deal of this literature derives from the work of ethicists, philosophers, and social scientists. As noted by Fritzche and Becker (1984, p. 166), "Little effort has been made to try to link ethical theory to management behavior."

Though woefully incomplete, this chapter has attempted to widen the lens so as to consider both ethical theory and management behavior. Certainly management behavior—at least my own and that of most other managers I have known—has been found wanting in important respects. I have also tried to suggest that our definitions of ethics and integrity may be unsatisfactory. I think the literature would greatly benefit from a different kind of working definition of executive integrity, one that provides a greater measure of internal consistency and more fully reflects the complexity and multidimensionality of organizational life.

6

Is There Integrity in the Bottom Line: Managing Obstacles to Executive Integrity

Donald M. Wolfe

Undershaft: (to his nonworking son, Stephen) Well, come! Is there anything you know or care for?

Stephen: I know the difference between right and wrong.

Undershaft: You don't say so! What! No capacity for business, no knowledge of law, no sympathy with art, no pretension to philosophy; only a simple knowledge of the secret that has puzzled all the philosophers, baffled all the lawyers, muddled all the men of business, and ruined most of the artists: the secret of right and wrong. Why, man, you're a genius, a master of masters, a god! at twenty-four, too! [G. B. Shaw, *Major Barbara,* Act III]

Right and wrong. That must have something to do with integrity. But even in moderately pluralistic societies it poses confounding questions. Right for whom and wrong for whom— and who's to say? Right or wrong in what time perspective— for the moment? for this quarterly report? for the sequence of generations? And right or wrong for what level of system—the person, the family, the organization, the planet?

The secret of right and wrong is never simple and never linear or unidimensional. There is no master value for which all others must take second place. We have no algorithm to sort out multiple stakes in a given situation or even to compute "the greatest good for the greatest number." We cannot do without a concept of commonweal—a public good, a common welfare— but it is never easy to discern.

Nor can we avoid living in a normative society. However local and culture-bound are our beliefs, customs, and laws, one will always be faced with value systems and value conflicts. Even the most alienated, indifferent, apathetic, cynical, or misanthropic among us must reckon with others' and with societies' values and preferences. A value-free profession (like a value-free science) is not only nonsense but a most dangerous kind of nonsense.

Executive integrity is among today's most urgent and most perplexing problems. It is urgent because of the distressing increase in shady and unethical actions by corporations large and small, by executives in many fields, by money managers on Wall Street, and by fast operators everywhere looking for a way to beat the system. It is urgent also because we are reaching the limits of resources to be exploited wastefully and of the earth's capacity to receive pollutants dumped on it without serious consequences.

The problem is perplexing because the underlying issues are complex and because the guiding spirit of the past no longer seems to work. We have learned more and more about the vast interdependence of organizational life, of national and international economies—indeed, of the world as a living system. But with that we also have become more aware of just how relative and incomplete are the moral standards and beliefs that used to provide guidance and stability (or at least rationales) for appropriate social and institutional conduct.

We have been disabused of most of our absolutes and too often have concluded, therefore, that "anything goes." Opportunity and advantage—the competitive edge—too easily displace integrity when we are not up to addressing the complexity that real integrity involves. Equally vicious is the temptation to deny the complexity—to latch onto simplistic catch phrases or to buy into closed-minded, fundamentalist moralities that only cloud the difficult choices to be made and that brook no honest differences or contrary evidence. No! Integrity *is* complex, and trite efforts to come up with simple solutions will not do.

The central issue in executive integrity is *multivalence.* Every human system, from individual to society, is guided by multiple needs and values and thus has a stake in a multitude of conditions and possibilities. Moreover, every living system contains the potential to develop in various directions, and this expands the range of factors of importance to the system. The measure of integrity, therefore, is not just how well one succeeds in pursuit of a single value but also how well one manages the complex of values that are inevitably interdependent in action, if not in conception. To the extent that integrity is a matter of being true to one's values and one's basic nature, questions of integrity are deeply bound up with the integration of dynamics within the self. The same can be said of the integrity of organizational systems.

Interdependence is the fundamental character of human life, regardless of all our strivings toward autonomy and dominion over the conditions of our lives. The outcomes of one person's pursuits, particularly in organizational settings, are influenced by the actions of others, just as one's own actions influence the well-being of others. Moreover, to live in more than fantasy, one's endeavors require the cooperation of nature; the successful pursuit of one's values implies a consequential change in conditions outside one's self. Thus, integrity involves the integration of self and environment. It is an ecological, not just a personal, matter. A confounding problem is that you cannot do just one thing. Each act by a person or organization has multiple consequences, intended or not. While pursuing A, one gets B, C, and D as well. Whether for good or for ill, one must live with all the consequences of one's acts. Integrity involves an integration of purpose, action, and outcome.

Integrity is also a social issue. We are social animals. Our values are socially derived—consensually validated and reinforced. I have a stake in your values, not only in my own, and you have a stake in mine. When my conduct in pursuit of my values disadvantages you in the pursuit of your values, then you will *care* about whether I value the *right* things or not. Integrity becomes a social matter in that you will gauge my integrity not by how satisfactorily I meet my ends but, rather, by how my conduct influences outcomes you value. Thus I have a private integrity, to be assessed within my own frame of reference, and a public integrity (still mine), judged by others with whom I am interdependent. As children, we know little of the former but much of the latter through the praise or castigations of parents, teachers, peers, and the like. In fact, we come to value (and thus incorporate into our private integrity) many things because they have produced praise and reward or headed us off from punishment.

The point here is that any conception of integrity that makes it only a private, personal matter sidesteps most of the issues that need to be discussed. One cannot be a person of integrity in the absence of significant resonance with others who share the same social system.

Integration of self and environment implies coming to grips not only with one's own multiple values but with the multiple values of others as well. And in this public, this social, sense, problems of integrity almost always become matters of *trust*. Can we trust one another to avoid doing us harm, if not to promote our well-being? This is a tall order even among people who care deeply about one another. It is even more difficult to establish with regard to the complexity of organizational life. Anything we do that undermines trust casts integrity into doubt, at least in its public meaning.

This reciprocity of values in social settings has led to several rules of conduct (for example, majority rule), not to mention vast codes of law that work more or less well in many situations. Games of fair division like "I'll cut and you choose" serve somewhat the same purpose. The best-known maxim is the Golden Rule: "Do unto others as you would have others do unto you." Less well known is the Silver Rule, which fits better when the two parties' values are at greater variance: "Do unto others as they would be done unto." (Then, of course, there is the more modern but less civilized Brass Rule: "Do unto others and cut out.")

I have mostly been addressing integrity at the personal and interpersonal levels. But many of the same dynamics operate at the organizational level as well. Every organization has its multiple needs and values, its stake in various conditions and outcomes, its environmental interdependencies. Here, too, one can question the extent to which it forms a unified whole, in which the parts fit together in harmony and its efforts produce valued outcomes.

In analogy to the distinction between private and public integrity discussed above for an individual, one can address how well the organization meets its own multiple objectives and manages its own multiple values—its *multivalence*—and how well it meets the questions of public integrity that organizations must face. The latter questions concern the organization's impacts on other systems and other stakeholders. Those impacts, as in the individual case, will be judged within the value frameworks of those other systems and groups. And here again, trust is the central dynamic. Will the organization conduct itself in ways that at least do not harm others around it?

Modes of Managerial Thought That Undermine Integrity

There has been a disturbing rise in the number of white-collar crimes—fraud, embezzlement, illegal uses of inside information, tampering with public records, and misuses of public trust for personal gain. These are all matters of central concern in any discourse on integrity. To cast them aside as the dirty work of a few rotten apples in an otherwise good barrel would be contributing to the same mentality that gives rise to these problems in the first place. Moreover, these kinds of acts represent only a small portion of the disintegrities found in organizations today.

What is at issue here is more subtle, more pervasive, more insidious ways of thinking that have gained wide currency in professional and managerial circles and tend to undermine integrity, directly and indirectly. They are apt to be implicit assumptions—unarticulated rules of thumb or habits of thought—rather than espoused beliefs. I do not expect any manager or executive to raise his hand and say, "Yes, this is the way I operate."

The Bottom-Line Mentality. Beyond its meaning as a technical term in bookkeeping, *the bottom line,* in its popular use today, means either the financial consequences of whatever activity is being discussed or (even more generically) "a final summing up," "the result that counts," "what is worth paying attention to while everything else is disregarded."

Five fallacies in the bottom-line mentality often contribute to a loss of integrity:

1. *One-dimensional thinking in multivalent situations.* Virtually every situation or decision that a manager faces, if it taxes integrity at all, is complex, with implications for various values hanging in the balance. The temptation, of course, is to oversimplify, to treat the situation as if there were only one value at stake, one objective to strive for. Generally the various values that enter into a given situation do not line up uniformly. There are trade-offs to be made—and such trade-offs are indeed made, whether one thinks them through or not. Being blind to some possible outcomes of a course of action does not prevent those outcomes. It only means that one is more apt to be taken by surprise if the action leads to disvalued outcomes.

It is irresponsible when one does not know how to deal with ambivalence and therefore must treat every situation as if only one value were relevant. Contrary values are then compromised at nearly every turn. What is even more unfortunate (and naive and immature) is when all situations are treated as if the same single value were the only one relevant. But preoccupation with "the bottom line" moves in that direction. If financial considerations dominate in every discourse and every decision, other values and other possibilities tend to be excluded automatically.

The executive who just wants to know the bottom line wants to make his or her job more simple than it is. He or she likely also wants to hear only good news, but such simplistic thinking is apt to produce more bad news (about other, neglected values). Whenever people say, "The bottom line is . . . ," you can be sure they want to cut off consideration of competing possibilities.

2. *"What good is happiness? You can't buy money with it."*
Every human endeavor has its costs, and almost always those
costs can be expressed in dollar terms. Therefore, every prospective project can be subjected to a financial analysis, however
crude the estimates of projected costs and projected gains. In
a sense, then, every other value can be expressed in the currency
(no pun intended) of profit and loss: Other values can be treated,
for analytic purposes, in terms of dollar equivalents.

Cost-benefit analysis has become increasingly popular in
recent years, and the technology for conducting it has improved.
When done casually (or callously), it results in a reduction or
conversion of nonfinancial values to financial terms; *the original
value loses its special potency*. When it is done seriously, one eventually comes to imponderable questions. How much is a human
life worth? Who should receive treatment for life-threatening
disease? What is an acceptable casualty rate for conducting
business when there is risk to life and limb?

Part of the problem is that we have refined measures and
analytical methods for financial values but not for a great many
other values that we may hold even more dear. What measuring rods can be used for gauging happiness or peace or beauty?
What calculus can be used in their analysis? If the currency we
have for evaluating things is the dollar, we should use it, so the
thinking goes. Everything then is brought down to finances, and
the bottom-line mentality reaches its apex. When executives conduct financial analyses to see whether it is preferable to abide
by the law or to break it and pay a fine, integrity is already
seriously compromised.

The point is that cost-benefit analysis, cost-effectiveness
measures, and so forth *are* helpful in making financial decisions
but *not* in making other kinds of value choices. And when all
the numbers and all the analytical rigor are stacked up against
the fuzziness of other values, the numbers tend to carry the day.
They are seen as providing the rationality and the decisiveness.
If there is already a strong prominence of economic values and
a preference for simplicity, a serious consideration of other values
to strive for is less likely.

3. *The push for a quick fix.* The bottom-line mentality tends

to think in the near term. Goals are set for the year or even for three to five years down the road. But the measurements that seem to count are monthly or quarterly. The term *the out years* has gained popularity, at least in Washington. They are indeed very, very "out," because what's "in" is *this* year, this month, this period of time that we're being held accountable for *now*.

The difficulty is that many of the really important problems call for complex courses of action pursued over long time periods. There *are* no quick fixes. But when the dominant press is to look good this month or this quarter, one doesn't want to wait for the outcomes of long-range strategies. The out years become the stuff of promises, which can be broken more or less with apparent immunity. The action that gets real attention tends to be that which serves the organization now. The press is to make the numbers come out right for the current period.

Just as the future is treated (in the bottom-line mentality) as remote and therefore not very important, so is the past. Agreements reached and commitments made long ago lose their potency. The buzzword becomes "What have you done for me *lately?*"

4. *"It's not my job!"* One of the ways organizations manage complexity is through a division of labor and role specialization. Large corporations have many staff departments, each with its special function, responsibility, and guiding values. Specialists can pursue their limited objectives with something like single-mindedness, counting on others to accomplish other organizational goals. When interdepartmental conflicts arise, boundaries between them harden, and specialists become even more isolated and entrenched in their specialization.

Corporate responsibilities regulated by law are often assigned to specialists in staff departments. The assumption is that they will keep the organization clean with respect to that regulation, and others will not have to be distracted from their other responsibilities. This, unfortunately, invites others (including top management) to go about business as usual—that is, to focus on their own functions without needing to understand, much less take action, in service of that regulation. General Dynamics has even created a position called Director of Corporate Ethics.

The simplification of organizational multivalence through specialization will not ensure organizational integrity, especially if there is an aversion to conflict—as there is in most organizations. If key managers are preoccupied with bottom-line thinking, it is unlikely that they will give strong backing to specialists whose responsibilities may be detrimental to the profit motive. But most important: Ethics and integrity are *everyone's* job. They cannot be delegated and they cannot be disowned, not if they are going to have any meaning at all.

5. *"It's all a game."* Many managers dealing with finances are in touch with abstract symbolic instruments—accounts, proposals, contracts, and so on—but they are far removed from the actual people, resources, and activities that those instruments represent. This is especially true of Wall Street, where companies are bought and sold and mergers and divestitures worked out with little need for knowledge of the people whose lives are altered by those transactions or even of the products and services performed by those companies. Decision making is inevitably limited to financial matters. Past financial performance, current intention, and future probabilities of profit are the key considerations. Huge profits are to be made in brokering such transactions.

It is very difficult for brokers, stockholders, and financiers *not* to see it as just a game—a very serious game, to be sure, because there are big winners and big losers, but a game nonetheless that seems to have little to do with real people, real communities, or real consequences other than wealth.

Corporate boards and top executives live in a similarly rarefied atmosphere. They, too, are often far removed from many of the consequences of their decisions. They, too, deal in symbols without real comprehension of local circumstances or awareness of who is likely to be helped or hurt. And they, too, are apt to address things primarily in financial terms.

One of the difficult problems when business is seen as just a game is that it's easy to see just about anyone as your opponent. Moving up the corporate ladder gets to be a game in lots of places. The significant rivalry is not with competing firms but with other people or other departments in your own organization. If you do well in the eyes of superiors, you feel as if you are winning. But if others do well, you must be losing. If it's all a game, one thinks there have to be winners and losers. It is a short step from wanting others to fail (so you can win) to actually helping them fail by undermining their efforts, withholding information, or making them look bad. But then, where goes collaboration? Where goes the integrity of the organization?

The gamelike quality that often creeps into the bottom-line mentality thus undermines integrity in three ways. First, it leads the players into thinking that their actions have only limited consequences—that the nonpaper realities represented by the paper aren't really there. Second, winning and losing—not integrity—is what's at stake. And third, everyone is a potential opponent, a rival who may be playing the game more craftily and whose efforts must therefore be countered.

To sum up, what I have called the bottom-line mentality is a threat to integrity in several ways. It involves simplistic thinking in which financial success is treated as the only value to be considered or as the value to which all others can be reduced. Through role specialization it leads to disowning of other system values in favor of those that are one's own assigned bottom line. It promotes short-term, quick-fix efforts rather than genuine problem solving and progress. It fosters adversarial relations through its gamelike qualities. And, finally, it creates a sense of unreality and a tunnel vision with respect to values when business transactions are treated as just a game. In a mentality that makes a god of money, everything else is to be bought or sold, exploited, or sacrificed in the name of the bottom line.

The Exploitative Mentality. In an earlier time, humankind was at the mercy of powerful natural forces and limited by the availability of natural resources needed for survival. With ingenuity and a capacity for social organization, we have mastered many of those forces and tapped into those resources to the point that we now dominate the planet. We are now no less dependent on the forces and resources of nature, but we have learned to manage and exploit them to our own purposes.

What has really changed during the last two or three centuries is the impact we have on the ecosystem. Huge forests have been depleted. Our efforts cause the extinction of other species daily. We have altered the natural replenishment of fresh water in many places through pollution and overuse. We destroy the very atmosphere we breathe. Whereas we have always been dependent on the ecosystem, it is now increasingly dependent on us. Whereas we are now less threatened by the vagaries of nature, it is more threatened by the follies of humans. As Pogo says, "We have met the enemy, and he is us!"

The exploitation of resources is a deep and essential characteristic in human life. That is our strength. That cannot be changed, nor can our organized efforts to do it more effectively and efficiently. But as we learn more and more about the cumulative effects of our exploitations, we also recognize a growing responsibility for ecological maintenance. The license to exploit at will is running out. We have to tend the garden that feeds us. Executives must be concerned about not only their own or their organizations' integrity but also the integrity of the planet as a living system.

The exploitative mentality, unfortunately, also has been applied as rampantly to our fellow human beings. Persons are thought of as utilities, as tools to be used or not used as business requires. We face a paradox here. We find it very desirable to be *useful* to others, and we hate being treated as useless. Look at the miseries of the unemployed or prematurely retired! But we also hate just being *used,* being a tool for others' purposes, without recognition of our own aspirations, sensibilities, and capacities for living fully.

What integrity is there in the executive who views himself or herself as a full person—an active agent, a decision maker of consequence to the world—but who treats other human beings as things to be manipulated, used, and discarded? How much more tragic when that same executive comes to view himself or herself as only a tool of the system!

The problem derives in part from our mode of abstracting and generalizing. We can and do abstract anything and any process we can see or imagine. And, of course, we do the same with persons. We can thus talk of customers or machine operators or government agents or executives or professors, disregarding variations in personality and in the circumstances of their lives. Through abstraction we can set policies about how various classes of people are to be treated. Although the policies may be intended as guidelines for judicious decision making, they are often used at the choice point as substitutes for any thinking at all.

Some abstractions—for example, the stereotypes that give rise to racism, sexism, and ageism—are prejudicial and fallacious, resulting in unfair treatment of people. This is a serious problem for organizational integrity, one that needs to be worked on throughout our society.

Abstractions applied to people by their very nature depersonalize. Individuality is glossed over. Many of them also dehumanize—that is, distort or deny the human qualities of the persons to whom they refer. They make objects of persons. Thus, while abstractions and categorizations help us manage the complexity of organizational life, they also make relationships more impersonal and mechanistic. The standardization of parts and equipment and of processes for handling recurrent problems, all very rational and fruitful for efficient productivity, carries over into standardization and objectification of persons.

This has two consequences that go beyond the obvious problems of stereotyping and prejudice. First, it undermines the general quality of work life. Individuals lack recognition and meaningful relationships. They become invisible—except when they fail to perform in the standard way. This invisibility, in turn, increases anxiety about making mistakes or not fitting in. And it undermines motivation for excellence or creativity. "Objects" don't create—they just fit into the machinery, put in their time.

Second, the process of abstracting and standardization of people undermines empathy and compassion in the person doing the abstracting. "Objects," roles, categories, and the like are not seen as having feelings or sensitivity or even the capacity for pain or joy. Empathy and compassion are directed toward fellow human beings in one's own group, "people like us," but not toward a faceless one of "them." When people are viewed only as tools or parts or functions, it is hard to imagine them in other than utilitarian terms.

Now, the issue is *not* whether to deal in abstractions or whether to place people in categories relevant to organizational purposes. We cannot avoid doing that, and even if we could, we wouldn't be better off for it. The question is, are we aware of the consequences for those so categorized and of the consequences for our own humanity? Are those the right abstractions to use in reference to human beings? Does one's use of them result in dehumanization either in the other or in self? And when it does, does one at least engage in other processes to counteract the damages—to remind self and other that one is dealing with the lives of real human beings?

When the dominant mode of relationships is exploitative, it breeds an exploitative response. Employees who feel objectified and used by their superiors are more likely to look for ways to rip off the system—or at least to do no more than is absolutely required. Commitment *has* to be only to oneself if the social context is blatantly exploitative.

Behavioral scientists have become part of the problem here. The exchange theory of human relationships, though highly descriptive of much of organizational life, is morally bankrupt. It, too, depersonalizes and dehumanizes. The equity theory of motivation falls into the same trap. Both theories teach that one's fellows are to be thought of in utilitarian terms. What can I get out of them, and how little can I give in return? We are right back to the Brass Rule—hardly the basis for meaningful interpersonal relationships.

The exploitative mentality has become so pervasive, and the impact of organizational practices so potent, that organizations cannot be trusted to ensure the commonweal—to protect the environment, to provide fair and humane treatment for employees, to protect the safety and security of clients and customers, to refrain from misappropriating public funds, and the like. The radical interdependence of the organization and its larger sociocultural and physical environment has been so ignored or denied that the last few decades have seen a virtual epidemic of regulatory statutes. If organizations would not see their self-interest and their social responsibility as linked to that interdependence and thus incorporate these concerns into their own value matrix, they would be governed by law.

A more enlightened organization recognizes its own vital stake in the conditions of its community, its people, its economy, and its ecosystem. It is not unreasonable to expect executives to attend to the social and ecological consequences of their organizations' actions as well as to the economic consequences. Integrity involves the whole, not just one part, one function, one objective.

The Madison Avenue Mentality. Integrity is inseparably tied to making the right choices in multivalent situations, to tracking the secondary consequences of our actions, and to correcting any damage to ourselves, to others, or to the ecosystem. But we also have a stake in our *image* in the eyes of others. We would like to be seen as persons of integrity and associated with enterprises of integrity. We have an investment in managing our public identities, our shortcomings notwithstanding.

What we learn in childhood and adolescence about this is, first of all, to hide our dirty linen and dastardly deeds and cast the blame elsewhere. Along with this we learn to present our best sides—our strengths and virtues—so others will think well of us. Organizations seek to do the same things. A whole industry has developed to serve this purpose, to build good public relations.

The problem with this concern for image, and the reason for including it in this discourse, is that increasingly public image management is replacing integrity. If you have a good PR agent, you don't have to clean up your act. You only have to sell it—or so the thinking goes. But all the selling in the world doesn't turn a junky product into one worth having, a selfish bastard into a saint. Justifications also do not produce justice; nor do rationalizations make ill-conceived actions either rational or ethical.

The basic axiom of the Madison Avenue mentality is that anything is right if it goes over with the public. It is not so different from what psychologists sometimes call the "sphincter morals" of preschool children.

In this mentality there are two ways to make questionable activities come out "right." First, one can hide the activity, cover it up, deny that it is going on. Disposing toxic wastes under cover of darkness or mislabeling contents of a package so that risks will not be apparent are blatant examples. Many other deals made in secret serve the same purpose. All kinds of "covers" are used in many organizations to keep people in the dark about what is going on. This does not make those goings-on right— and it certainly does not make for trust building.

The other strategy is to convince others of the propriety of one's actions or decisions. Let's sell them on the virtues, necessity, or acceptability of our conduct. Let's change their minds, not our actions. Let's demonstrate in other ways what good and noble people we are, and then we'll get away with whatever we want to do that may be questionable.

This mentality involves a curious and troublesome figure/ ground reversal. The focus of ethical concern shifts from the decision or action itself (or from its consequences) to the image-building process. One doesn't have to struggle with questions of right and wrong; one has only to hire an effective PR agent. Integrity is no longer an issue, only popularity, only the image of acceptability.

In business meetings, less and less time is spent on whether a course of action is proper or might have unintended destructive consequences as more is spent on how to put it across, how to make it look right, how to conceal its flaws, how to come out smelling clean. Once the short-term personal gain is fixed in mind, all the rest becomes a matter of manipulative strategy.

If other managers and groups in the organization are operating in this mentality as well—with its deception and manipulation—soon nobody knows when he or she is on solid ground and dealing with real people. Nor do organization members know whether the information they are given is valid or even whether they are solving real problems.

The Madison Avenue mentality is self-deceptive as well as manipulative of others. Executives start to believe their own PR, paying more attention to looking the part than to attaining competence or performing effectively. Success is measured in appearance and life-style, not in genuine accomplishments. Not only do customers and clients become "marks," but colleagues become "dupes" and business transactions become "scams."

As this mentality spreads, authenticity doesn't just lose its hold, it loses its meaning and its relevance. Integrity isn't even a concept or a desired state in this mentality—unless, of course, the *image* of integrity is fashionable, in which case it can be feigned or purchased through PR.

Multivalence and Synergy

The challenges to integrity are grave, and it is time to address what can be done about them. I think we have to start by recognizing the complexity that the executive (or any other responsible citizen) faces. It is not just that we are more aware of interdependencies —there *is* more interdependence to deal with. As we learn more and more about extended chains of cause and effect, both social and ecological, not only does our world become more complex, it also becomes more multivalent. The vortex of relevant values becomes more complex and more subtle.

Primary and Secondary Adaptation. One of our field's most creative founding fathers, Herbert Shepard (1965) produced a masterful piece of social and organizational analysis that is relevant to a deeper understanding of integrity in organizations. He begins by distinguishing mechanistic and organic systems and illustrates the folly of viewing either persons or organizations in mechanistic terms—common as this folly is in economics, sociology, psychology, organizational theory, and management. Persons and organizations must be viewed in organic terms.

A fundamental process in any living system is adaptation. Shepard identifies two orientations or objectives of adaptation in any species—primary and secondary adaptation. Primary adaptation is oriented to the survival and well-being of the individual organism. This involves tracking of both internal states and environmental conditions so as to ensure both the acquisition of resources from the environment to meet the individual's needs and the taking of appropriate action to protect it from harm.

Secondary adaptation is oriented toward survival and well-being of the group, the colony, the species, and one's offspring, even at risk to individual survival. The social insects have highly elaborated secondary adaptive processes, with a rich division of labor, highly effective communication, and instant and persistent readiness of individuals to sacrifice for the welfare of the colony.

In lower animals, most of the adaptive behaviors at both the primary and secondary levels are instinctual, derived genetically through evolution. They are unable to define the problem, much less to pose an intellectual model for improving adaptability. Humans also engage in both primary and secondary adaptive behavior, but a great deal of it is learned and is spread through cultural processes. We, too, are invested both in individual well-being and in the welfare and survival of family, community, nation, and our species. We, too, will sacrifice ourselves for the welfare of others and can develop elaborate strategies for doing so.

For any organism or any species, the basic issue is the degree to which it is able to control the conditions of its own existence. In primary adaptation only the individual counts. An adequate secondary adaptive process must meet the needs of both the individual and the society. The need for such processes is easy to recognize but not nearly so easy to design and create—especially as the threats to well-being are more and more the product of our species' own striving.

We all learn a "primary mentality" based, according to Shepard (p. 1118), on the primary adaptive model. That is, each of us sees himself "as separated from the rest of the world by his skin." Internal needs, both biological and psychological (including needs for safety and security), are to be met through appropriate exchanges with the environment. One must compete with other individuals for scarce resources for meeting those needs. In Western societies, particularly in America with its emphasis on individualism, the primary mentality is highly developed. Many of our institutions and modes of organizing are predicated on it.

There is, of course, a place for cooperative effort in the primary mentality. When individuals are faced with a common enemy or a natural disaster, their survival is enhanced by banding together. Moreover, others often have control over resources one needs, so that a workable framework for bargaining and exchange is often essential. It is quite within the primary mentality to work for an organization in exchange for a livelihood. One turns over to the organization (often grudgingly) control of many of the conditions of one's existence. But at heart, in the primary mentality, everyone is self-interested, "looking out for number one."

Shepard identifies a variety of dynamics in organizations predicated on primary mentality principles:

1. The basic sources of order are coercion and compromise.
2. Solidarity, where it exists, is based either on bargaining—an exchange of favors—or on joining together in the face of a common enemy (who frequently also is part of the organization).
3. More commonly, relationships are basically competitive and marked by a series of intricate win/lose struggles.
4. Individuals and groups engage in a variety of canceling-out processes—efforts to "control, counteract, and exploit one another."
5. Thus, at best, organizational members are joined in "antagonistic cooperation."
6. A pyramid of formal power is established to contain the antagonism and direct effort toward management's goals.
7. Canceling-out processes are used (paradoxically) to prevent canceling-out processes. Great energy is devoted to policing behavior through "approval, checking, reporting, evaluation, accounting, control, supervisory, and disciplinary systems" (p. 1122).
8. A vigilant administration of all these systems imposes a limited span of control, requiring many intermediate levels of management and hence a tall hierarchy.

9. The primary mentality pattern is self-reinforcing, as administrative controls underscore the need to protect oneself and look out for one's own well-being. Defensive or exploitative responses of subordinates are met with intensified control measures. A vicious cycle ensues.
10. This cycle generates a need for risk reduction because of the preoccupation with the many threats engendered. Creativity and innovation are squelched in favor of modest, incremental improvements.
11. These fundamental organizational dynamics are alienating. People are distanced from one another through antagonistic, competitive, and defensive relationships.
12. They are also estranged from themselves and from their potential for growth and development.

It is quite apparent that the three orientations discussed earlier—the bottom-line, exploitative, and Madison Avenue mentalities—are special cases of the more generic primary mentality. They represent strategic maneuvers geared to "successful" operations in primary mentality organizations. These maneuvers are also regenerative; when executives use them to manipulate peers and subordinates, those peers and subordinates, in turn, learn to use them on still others, if not on the executives themselves.

In one sense, integrity in the primary mentality is to be measured in terms of survival and well-being of the individual. However, inasmuch as individuals are pitted against one another, one person's well-being is at the expense of others. This approach to integrity can never come to grips with the need for secondary adaptation.

Primary mentality organizations are an attempt, however misguided, to effect limited secondary adaptive goals through primary adaptive processes. Primary adaptive processes (and the organizational dynamics associated with them) produce other requirements for integrity, namely: (1) compliance with laws, rules, and regulations, (2) living up to one's bargain, and (3) subordination of self to the organization. Beyond limited self-interest, conformity processes are relied on (and enforced) as the major approach to integrity.

Organizations in the Secondary Mentality. Shepard addresses the needs for secondary adaptation more directly and recognizes in the human spirit a corresponding "secondary mentality," which is concerned with the well-being of both the individual and society. The secondary mentality involves an identification of self with overarching societal values—such as Maslow's (1971) "being-values," found in highly self-actualizing persons. It also involves an identification with others akin to and incorporated within the self, an identification with the human species, and a capacity for being-love not based in need/exchange approaches to relationships: "The secondary mentality assumes that individuals can have more than instrumental meaning for one another . . . that personal development, well-being, self-actualization are the products of authentic, non-exploitative relations . . . of trust and openness . . . characterized by authenticity, valid communication, genuineness" (Shepard, 1965, p. 1127).

The secondary mentality recognizes that one's own growth and well-being depend on the insight, effectiveness, and caring of others. One has a commitment to their growth as well as one's own. Solidarity—a sense of "we-ness"—is sought not as a source of power to counteract threat but as a source of knowledge and resources for solving problems and accomplishing agreed-upon goals. It is also sought, at least from others with secondary mentality, for the intrinsic fulfillment that comes with authentic social interaction.

Organizational dynamics based on the secondary mentality are quite different from those sketched out above. Objectives are established through consensus, and they garner personal commitment, not just grudging acquiescence. Relationships are collaborative, mutually supportive, and rich with feedback so that colleagues will function with strength based on valid information.

Individual differences are prized for the diversity of insights, talents, and resources they bring to common problems or enterprises. Conflicts are surfaced and worked through rather than suppressed, denied, or isolated. Management becomes everybody's business through greater reliance on self-management and valid communication among functions. Hence, tall hierarchies are unnecessary and distracting from collaboration. Integrity in collaboration-consensus systems is more directly tied to mutual confidence and trust (for this is the cement that holds such systems together) and thus is not so dependent on bureaucratic rules and authority-obedience relationships. Since many of the forces that promote disintegrity in coercion-compromise systems are not present in organizations governed by the secondary mentality, less energy is needed for policing and more is therefore available for problem solving and planning.

Although the antagonistic atmosphere is less prevalent and canceling-out processes rare, conflict still arises in secondary mentality organizations—as in all of life. But the approach to conflict is to face up to it and to recognize the value of hearing out all sides. There is less likelihood of attributing malevolence or ill will to opposing parties and more confidence that feelings generated will be worked through.

Potential win/lose situations are converted to collaborative problem solving. Consequently, competing values can be viewed as parts of a puzzle and thus as challenges requiring invention and innovation. The goal in such situations, as in all planning, is to search for or create synergies—action sequences that promote multiple values.

Another name for organizations based on the secondary mentality or collaboration-consensus might well be *synergic systems*. As organizational members become more accustomed to and skilled at working in teams—building confidence and trust, communicating openly and validly, confronting and working through conflicts, and inventing synergic solutions to problems—they are also more prepared to face conflicts that may arise with other organizations and with other societal values.

As more attention is devoted to the growth and self-actualization of all, more members will see their own fates as inextricably linked to the well-being of society and the ecosystem. Creating synergy between, as well as within, organizations and institutions becomes an essential part of the agenda: ''The question of individualism versus collectivism is not an issue for the secondary mentality. Freedom and responsibility are identities. . . . Man lives most fully and freely when he lives responsibly. His growth to freedom is through expansion of self to include others, so that his concern for them is also his concern for himself. To the primary mentality this proposition is Utopian and absurd. But to the authoritarian, democracy is absurd; and to alienated man, love is absurd" (Shepard, 1965, p. 1128).

Shepard presents the coercion-compromise and collaboration-consensus models as ideal types and recognizes that living organizations contain a mix of both dynamics. Clearly coercion-compromise tends to dominate in most organizations today. If significant advances in executive integrity are to occur, there will have to be a substantial increase in the growth-promoting qualities of collaboration-consensus and the secondary mentality and a dramatic increase in synergy.

Adult Development and the Maturation of Integrity

> "It was wrong to do this," said the Angel.
> "You should live like a flower,
> Holding malice like a puppy,
> Waging war like a lambkin."
>
> "Not so," quoth the man
> Who had no fear of spirits;
> "It is only wrong for angels
> Who can live like flowers,
> Holding malice like the puppies,
> Waging war like the lambkins" [Stephen Crane].

One of the binds that almost all pronouncements on integrity or ethics face is that many who are exposed to them have neither the depth of experience nor the personal maturity to truly understand them and hence to own them as personal values and abide by them as a matter of reasoned choice. If one has neither the comprehension nor the skill to make them an essential part of living, those pronouncements become at best pie-in-the-sky ideals to be wished for but never attained. More often they are viewed as unreasonable constraints to be complied with when necessary in order to avoid punishment or castigation, but generally to be maneuvered around when self-interest dictates.

Laws, rules, regulations, manners, and the like generally start out as external shoulds and oughts—owned by and serving the interests of others and enforced by superior power. Even when internalized through typical modes of enculturation, they are driven by guilt and shame, which may be as dictatorial as any authority figure. Philosophical treatises on ethics are gobbledygook and codes of ethics mere moralisms unless one is ready to grapple with why, in personal terms, some modes of conduct are preferable to others. That is why so many of the really wise learnings about ethical social living are told in parables.

Socially acceptable conduct in children must rest, to a considerable extent, on conformity processes. Limits must be set even when the reasoning behind them cannot yet be understood. But it is equally important for adults to question why, to consider possibilities that go beyond the "thou shalts" and "thou shalt nots." Undigested incorporations of moral codes are not an adequate basis for mature social living, and they certainly are not up to the wise management of the dilemmas that emerge as we learn more about the complexity of ecological forces and the potential destructiveness of large-scale human effort abetted by technological potency.

If anything, we should rejoice in the counterdependence of youth in spite of the affronts to adult sensibilities and to time-tested standards. It is through such challenges that people begin to wrestle with what they can believe in and commit to. It is also their way of bringing external authority figures down to life size and hence of beginning to take genuine responsibility in the world. This is not to say, of course, that every constraint they rebel against is wrong or that every new maxim they espouse is right and true. Often it is quite to the contrary. Nonetheless, the counterdependence reflects a process of growth from which most people emerge more mature and responsible.

In like vein, those who function more fully in the secondary mentality recognize the primary mentality as a more primitive and retarded state of development. They also are aware of the many social and situational forces that push for preoccupation with self and reinforce the primary mentality. Many of the things that are seen as strengths in coercion-compromise systems are recognized as weaknesses from a more mature perspective. They may be *au courant* in many organizations, but wise men and women have known for ages that might does not make right.

The question is, are people steeped in the primary mentality educable? Can they outgrow their current shortsightedness and self-centeredness? If so, how, and under what conditions? Let us turn to some of the personal strengths required for effective leadership in synergic organizations. We will find that such organizations call for *more,* not less, genuine toughness (both intellectual and interpersonal) than is required in coercion-compromise systems.

1. *Active engagement.* As organizations try to move toward participative management, managers generally recognize quickly that they have to squelch their dictatorial ways. Their first efforts usually involve considerable abdication—neither participating nor managing. This is not entirely bad, since it makes space for others to participate and take responsibility. In fact, though, it denies the group the leader's knowledge and insights, and it models the wrong kind of behavior for collaboration-consensus—almost as bad as being overbearing.

What is called for is a moderately high level of participation and active attention to what is there for the group to manage. Participation is needed, but of a quite different, less controlling kind: openly expressive, encouraging contributions from others, building trust, surfacing and utilizing differences, and centering both task and interpersonal problems to be dealt with.

2. *Cognitive complexity and flexibility.* Simple-minded and routinized solutions just won't do for many of the problems that organizations face today. They certainly won't do in the management of change. What is required is creative problem solving, and this calls for a capacity for looking at issues and situations from many perspectives.

Comprehending the inherent complexity is important, of course, but one also has to do something with that understanding—to look for the *lively possibilities* in the situation. That often means figure/ground reversals, looking at things upside down, creating alternative models of the situation. This requires basic intelligence and an active, playful mind. But these are also things that can be practiced, exercised, extended through interaction with other lively minds.

3. *A spirit of inquiry.* One does not automatically know all the complexities and potentials in a situation as it emerges. One has to find out, explore, discover. Creative problem solving and anticipating unintended consequences call for active learning processes. What really gets you ahead is neither what you know nor whom you know but how you learn.

Much of what one is exposed to in many organizational settings will be opaque and distorted, given the prevalence of gamesmanship, the Madison Avenue mentality and all the rest. Valid information will have to be sought out and uncovered. Much can be done to increase the flow of open communication through trust building, leveling, rewarding openness, and the like. If one recognizes the kinds of distortions (including one's own tendencies toward self-deception), inquiry will be enriched. The real task, though, is not just looking for what is incorrect—in excess, that builds mistrust, too—but searching for what is right.

4. *Autonomous interdependence.* This term is paradoxical, for we often assume that autonomy implies separateness, independence. Real collaboration, indeed, requires the temporary joining of distinct, mature identities, not dependence or confluence. Each person, each mind must be able to function in its own right.

In one of our studies in adult development (Wolfe and Kolb, 1980) we noted the change from outer- to inner-directedness as people matured from early adulthood to midlife. We also explored (Schott, 1981) how that transition is made. Outer-directedness is a very fruitful mode of adaptation in early adulthood; it promotes the learning of many organizational facts of life and facilitates the process of joining the adult world and entering a career in it. But outer-directedness also supports conformity and living out the agendas of other persons and organizations. Lo, the organization man.

To become more inner-directed, one first has to let go of some of that outer-directedness—the dependency on others for guidance and maintenance of self and the attribution of power to authority figures and organizational structures. It is then that one can appreciate one's own power and competence and can more fully initiate in one's own behalf. One becomes one's own person. One begins to set directions for oneself as an autonomous being.

Many people at this stage are egotistical and self-absorbed. They have little interest in collaboration. They want to show what they can do and are preoccupied with how much they can acquire. The rugged individualist, the big-time operator, the driver of men—this is where one often sees the bottom-line mentality and the exploitative mentality in full swing.

But this is not the end of the developmental sequence. Having established a personal center from which to function, one can then return to the integration of inner- and outer-directedness. Now the outer-directedness takes on a different meaning based on a different dynamic. Others are not a source of power to be coped with in dread or awe but a source of strength and creativity to be joined in common effort. They are also not objects to be manipulated (as one was once manipulated) but separate beings who can also contribute their intellects and problem-solving capacities.

Most of all, from this new autonomous perspective, others are persons to be appreciated and enjoyed, to be respected for who they are and encouraged to grow. Now interdependence can take on real meaning and collaboration becomes a win/win process.

5. *Coming to grips with personal multivalence.* Treating oneself simplistically is even worse than treating others or organizational matters simplistically. It is paradoxical that so many mature, wise, self-actualizing people choose simple life-styles and simple pleasures. It is certainly not because they fail to see the complexities in social living or in themselves. Rather, it is in recognition that excessive striving in all directions seldom produces results of excellence. Trying to be in control of all things does not result in control, only in wasted energy. Real influence goes up as other people are allowed to join in that influence. And there is wisdom in accepting and making peace with things one cannot change.

An additional reason that unusually mature people seek

simplicity and solitude is that this choice represents one healthy response to sick organizations. So many others in coercion-compromise systems are caught up in exploitation and Madison Avenue dynamics that they are certainly no joy to be around. If one cannot engage them in more human, more growthful ways, they can only destroy or distort one's own creativity and vitality. But that kind of maturity, much less one that would be a force for change in organizations, cannot be purchased without a recognition of one's own manifold nature.

Personal integrity starts with awareness of one's own multivalence. The more insight one has into one's own dynamics and complex motivations, the more likely one is to be appropriately choiceful and to anticipate probable outcomes. This awareness includes some recognition of likely blind spots and antisocial impulses. Anyone who knows himself well owns up to some capacity for anger, meanness, pettiness, and destructiveness. Seeing this darker side for what it is makes it less likely to dominate behavior unforeseen.

Jung (1971) has written extensively on the individuation process and on the need, particularly in midlife, to come to grips with one's unconscious—to attend to the "shadow self" and to one's underdeveloped functions. An earlier paper (Wolfe and Kolb, 1980) speaks to the same process.

Much in one's unconscious is not vile or reprehensible. It can, in fact, be quite delightful. Having access to it can be a source of much play and creativity. But some of what is there got there through suppression or repression because self or others found it base and unworthy.

It seems strange, but owning up to one's demonic tendencies in fact promotes integrity in at least two ways. First, those tendencies are there anyway, and acting on them without awareness causes real trouble. When we are aware of them, we can choose. Second, when one tunes in to petty or cruel feelings or impulses, one can often find what insult, hurt, injustice, or deprivation lies behind them and thus generate a more effective and less hurtful way of dealing with it.

Awareness of personal multivalence also implies a capacity for facing up to and integrating ambivalence, for working through inner conflicts with a minimum of denial or distortion. If one cannot manage one's own occasionally conflicting motives (without undue anxiety, defensiveness, or immobilization), one is not likely to do justice to anyone else's either.

6. *Detecting and managing conflict.* Just as it is important to manage one's internal ambivalence, integrity also involves a recognition of the existence of competing values both within the organization and in the larger society. I have already decried the folly of a one-dimensional value system. A mature approach is one that accepts the legitimacy of divergent interests, values, and stakes in organizational affairs. Synergistic integrity requires that one not be too quick to polarize situations into we/they, win/lose struggles.

A capacity to see the world from many points of view and to empathize with others who may be working from quite different, equally legitimate agendas is a great asset for protecting and promoting organizational integrity. It does not mean that one never takes sides but, rather, that one understands where various sides are coming from. One is then more likely to anticipate reasonably well what trade-offs are involved and what unintended consequences will have to be rectified.

A sensitivity to emergent conflict makes it more likely that it will be surfaced and dealt with. This requires, of course, some degree of tolerance for the tension that often accompanies interpersonal or intergroup conflict—squelching it or running away won't help. Having the various parties in contention express their objectives *and* the values or purposes underlying them is the first step to creative resolution. Then those involved can begin whatever problem solving and inventing of synergic strategies may be possible. At least, then, one can see where the conflict is apt to lead and can begin cleaning up the debris.

Effective conflict management is certainly not easy. Not every conflict can be resolved nor every war headed off. But these are learnable skills and are quite essential for organizational integrity. The primitive methods most commonly in use today are generally just not up to the job.

7. *Appreciation of ambiguity and of differences.* Clarity and certitude are wonderful conditions. It is almost always better to

know where you stand and where you are going. But real life in complex social systems always involves ambiguity. Those who would be consequential in organizations must have a reasonably high tolerance for ambiguity. Otherwise they fall prey to simplistic thinking or lose their creativity in vain efforts to keep everything under control.

But tolerating ambiguity is not enough—one must positively welcome it. Premature efforts at standardization and routinization produce much of the stagnation and futility in many modern organizations. Structures constrain and rigid structures stultify, and so some degree of ambiguity is a blessing.

Ambiguity connotes opportunity; thus anyone with creativity appreciates it and seeks it out, not for tolerance's sake, but to make new sense of it and tap into its inherent possibilities. Ambiguity is the stimulus to inquiry and the challenge to cognitive complexity and flexibility. It is the ground for creative problem solving, for synergistic planning, and for change. One should not give it up too quickly—it is too hard to get things unfrozen again when better ways of working are found.

Among the sources of ambiguity with which managers often have difficulty is individual differences. For many, difference begins to look like conflict or at least like resistance to managerial control. Hence the move to standardize and routinize people into overdefined roles and control them with tight regulations and close supervision. Any adult finds that depersonalizing and stagnating.

But the real issue here is that our differences make collaboration constructive. The bringing together of not just more hands but a greater range of talents and insights is what solves complex problems. The presence of difference is an asset to be sought, not a problem to be overcome, for organizational effectiveness.

Even differences in values are to be appreciated rather than disdained if the organization has workable modes of developing consensus. Differences in values make it more likely that diverse and important organizational interests will be recognized and that societal well-being will not be ignored. The secondary mentality thrives on differences because they enhance secondary adaptation. Whatever else integrity means, it means the integration of differences.

8. *Courage.* An old Hasidic prayer goes something like this:

> Lord, help me to know what I feel, to say
> what I mean, and to do as I say.

That is a pretty simple and eloquent request for the kind of integrity I have been discussing. At least it would carry one a long way toward integrity if one could live by it.

But what is especially interesting to me is that those three simple things are posed in a plea for divine intervention—that one needs special help to do them. Indeed, those are three very difficult things to do on a consistent basis. Without doubt we need all the help we can get to live by this prayer. But perhaps what undermines these efforts the most in everyday life is lack of courage. It takes a special kind of courage to stay in tune with your feelings when those feelings conflict and seem to work against you. It takes courage to speak the truth in many situations, especially when that truth is unpopular and may bring down the wrath of others who would rather see the world differently. And it takes courage to live fully by one's beliefs and values—to persist in actions that run the risk of failure or the risk of hostility and rejection from others.

To live with integrity in our highly pluralistic and multivalent society (for that matter, to develop any of the other characteristics sketched out above) takes courage. And we had better not expect it to come easily.

Generativity and Hope

Many readers by now must be saying, "You've got to be kidding! Where are we going to get all those towers of strength and nobility? Who can be that good? Aren't you asking for too much? Wouldn't it be enough if people just stayed within the law, lived up to their contractual agreements, and avoided cruelty to old people, children, and dogs? Why pose ideals that are so far from the realities of most organizations as we know them today? Aren't you, like the angel in Crane's poem, setting the standards too high?''

Believe me, I'm no angel. I know a good deal from personal experience about the difficult struggles toward integrity and about many of the failures along the way. When we lost our absolutes of right and wrong, we also lost our mechanisms for redemption. We have to *work* our way out of the mess we're in.

In my darkest hours I despair of our ever getting on top of the destructive forces we participate in before they do us in altogether. But I'm aware that every age has had its pundits with ample claims that theirs was mankind's darkest hour. I'm also aware that every age has had its share of mature and wise men and women—and ours is perhaps more rich in that than has ever been true in the past.

Where are we going to get the wise, mature, and socially responsible leaders for our organizations of tomorrow? They will have to be grown, as always. And for this they will have to be in touch with the learnings and the *persons* of those exemplars who live today or have lived in the past. Perhaps more important, the conditions for higher levels of personal and professional growth will have to be created. Quite a lot has been learned about that in recent years.

Even if developed, will such people want to work in large-scale organizations? Not if they are like most organizations today. At an increasing rate, highly creative, self-actualizing people either seek no organizational affiliation or seek one that is free of much of the bureaucracy, politics, and narrow-minded constraints of typical organizational life. Who wants to be in the rat race, much less a continual dogfight? No, they want to be more in control of the conditions of their existence, and they want more opportunity to create and innovate. Organizations will have to go through a transformation to be hospitable to many of precisely the kind of executives who could invent and manage such a transformation. And there's the rub.

I have said a good deal about the vicious cycles in coercion-compromise, primary mentality organizations and their bottom-line, exploitative, Madison Avenue thinking. But there are also virtuous cycles—regenerative cycles on the positive side. Mature, growth-oriented people (if not interfered with) create growthful processes and relationships that make the context more hospitable for themselves and others. This, in turn, sows the seeds and prepares the ground for further growth of still others.

The objective is generativity: innovating organizational conditions and processes which can foster growthful mentoring (not just protection for survival or exploitation for personal gain) and which can return the joy to creative collaboration. That's a key objective. And generativity yields the warm glow of being with others in a significant way, participating in their growth and creativity. That's where the hope lies for significant improvement in personal and organizational integrity.

In the framework I've been dealing with here, integrity is not something that one *has*. It is not a trait or an attribute or an acquisition. Rather, it is something one does, something one pursues—a process of reasoning and valuing and creating. And it is a social process of valid communication, mutual accomodation, and synergistic problem solving. Most of all, it is a process of continuing learning and growth. The hope for the future lies in the generativity of the present.

7

Integrity Management:
Learning and Implementing
Ethical Principles
in the Workplace

James A. Waters

"We were giving a discount to a particular customer and selling
the same product at a higher price to [another] company. I asked the
sales manager why and he said, 'Because he didn't ask!' I said, 'Is this
the right thing to do? Do it because it's right.'"

"We offer one standard service where one guy pays $1,100 and
another guy pays $400. It's okay. The guy who is sharp deserves the lower
price."

In this chapter, I focus on one aspect of integrity: adherence to ethical principles. In exploring management integrity,
therefore, I am interested in the extent to which managers' decisions and actions conform with standards of goodness or rightness in human conduct.

Narrowly conceived, integrity refers to *personal integrity* in
the sense that when we raise questions about a manager's integrity, we are asking whether that manager's behavior is consistent with his or her own personal principles of goodness or
rightness. It is this image of personal integrity that allows us
to entertain the notion of "honor among thieves" and acknowledge that behavior of which we and perhaps many others

disapprove may show integrity. In short, as long as we believe that a manager is true to his or her sincerely held ethical principles, we do not question his or her personal integrity.

The views of the two managers quoted at the beginning of this chapter on the propriety of charging very different prices to different customers for the same product are certainly in conflict (examples from Waters, Bird, and Chant, 1986, p. 374). However, accepting at face value what these managers are telling us about their positions on differential pricing (and setting aside any legal considerations), we should not necessarily raise questions about either manager's personal integrity.

However, there is a broader conception of integrity, *social integrity*, that would likely prompt such questions. Social integrity involves not simply consistency between action and principle but also adherence to generally accepted principles or standards of goodness or rightness in human conduct. When we raise questions about a manager's social integrity, we are questioning whether his or her behavior is consistent with moral principles that are reasonable and appropriate—that is, generally accepted principles as we understand them.

Obviously, for some issues that managers face, no generally accepted principles of right behavior will exist. That is, some issues are surrounded by so many competing views of ethics that reasonable people will differ in their judgments of the social integrity of management decisions in these instances. The current debate about investment in South Africa indicates that it may be one of those issues. Right now the debate on this issue is so intense, and attitudes on the question are shifting so rapidly, that in six months it may no longer be one of those issues. This is a vivid example of a certain type of ethically questionable act that I discuss later.

Nevertheless, for many more ethically questionable acts, there will indeed be more or less of a consensus among managers themselves about relevant ethical principles. Whether these principles provide adequate direction for action in most concrete situations is a question to which I will return. At this point, though, I would suggest that most managers would question the social integrity of the person who doesn't see anything wrong in charging one customer $1,100 and another customer $400 for the same service, even while they suspend judgment on his or her personal integrity.

Other examples where there is similar widespread consensus about generally accepted ethical principles might include the practice of bribery in the form of money, drugs, and prostitutes (Burrough, 1985), ''laundering'' cash for criminal organizations (Cohen, 1985), and firing with rifles at Environmental Protection Agency representatives to keep them from taking pictures of toxic waste being dumped into a river (Meier, 1985). Most managers would be quick to assail the social integrity of the managers who engaged in these acts. In fact, most would have to suspend their disbelief in order to accept that, in the examples cited, the participants acted with personal integrity.

But what about the senior managers of the organizations where these acts took place? What questions can be raised about their integrity? Consider, for example, the following case:

Connor Homes Corp., a major mobile home manufacturer, was indicted on criminal charges of defrauding veterans and the Veterans Administration through an invoice padding operation . . . . The indictments accuse Connor Homes of making false statements, conspiracy, and mail fraud to conduct invoice padding. One fourteen-count indictment charged that the company added washing machines, dryers, air conditioners, porches, and other items to inflate the invoice prices it submitted to the VA . . . . Veterans buying the homes never received the items, which, when listed, raised the loan amount guaranteed by the VA, the indictment alleged . . . . ''We've got 115 or 120 sale lots,'' . . . Connor Homes's vice-president, finance, said, denying that the company pads invoices or engages in any of the illegal practices cited in the indictments. ''With that many people out there, someone could have done something they shouldn't have done. But it would have been without corporate sanction, and it's not something we would condone'' [Lublin, 1985, p. 20].

The report is of an indictment, and so, in fairness to the management of Connor Homes Corporation, we cannot assume that the acts cited were actually committed. However, the story is almost prototypical of corporate response to revelations of wrongdoing by middle- and lower-level managers. Disclosure of illegal or unethical behavior by a company's employees typically brings forth from a company spokesperson a response of the following general form: "We're shocked. This is certainly the responsibility of a few isolated individuals and will be thoroughly investigated. This is obviously against company policy and is not something condoned by senior management."

Given the enormous size and complexity of many corporations, it is not difficult to accept the truth of this typical response in most cases. However, given the frequent disclosure of failures of management integrity (in 1985 the *Wall Street Journal* published roughly 400 stories about illegal or unethical behavior), the typical response seems increasingly unsatisfactory.

Despite the size and complexity of many major corporations, it is well accepted that chief executive officers and their senior management teams take responsibility for the financial performance of the firm. It is humorous to think of a CEO explaining poor quarterly results to security analysts by saying, "It's a big company with a lot of people, and some of them didn't do what they should have done; we certainly don't condone their performance." Yet we seem to accept explanations of that sort for poor ethical performance. Why?

I suggest that the major reason for our limited expectations and demands in this regard is that failure of managerial integrity is typically viewed as an individual problem, a character flaw. Many a senior manager has been heard to say that he or she has to rely on the basic integrity of the firm's people as it was developed over their lifetimes before they joined the firm. However, I believe that this preoccupation with questions of individual integrity is a perspective with serious limitations.

One major purpose of this chapter is to explore those limitations by developing the notion of integrity management. By this phrase I mean to direct attention to the managerial decisions and actions which determine the premises of others' decision making when that has an ethical character—that is, which influence the process of integrating ethical judgment into particular decisions and actions. Whether we speak in terms of corporate policies (Andrews, 1971), social architecture (Bennis and

Nanus, 1985), or organizational culture (Ouchi, 1981), there is a sense in which we think of senior managers guiding (more directly or less directly) and taking responsibility for the behavior of all other managers in the organization. Managers in an organization may be said to act with greater or lesser integrity, and integrity management is the process by which senior managers influence the tendencies in either direction.

A second major purpose of this chapter is to show how little attention this kind of integrity management receives in most corporations. I will suggest that the kinds of ethically questionable acts that attract the most attention from senior managers are the kinds that are the least troublesome for most managers and that, ironically, the real problem areas get ignored. I will consider the question whether the failure of senior managers to provide systematic and continuing attention to integrity management in their own organizations is a failure of personal integrity.

My third purpose is to explore how integrity might be better managed in large, complex organizations. Using the metaphor of ''good conversation,'' I will describe how senior managers can stimulate discussion of ethical questions so as to facilitate informed and responsible action. The final part of the chapter addresses the normative character of both management integrity and integrity management. I will consider whether integrity is most usefully viewed as a constraint on or a goal of management action and will draw attention to the special responsibility of senior managers for integrity management.

The Meaning and Importance of Integrity Management

Earlier, I mentioned the common tendency to regard failure of management integrity as an individual problem, that is, as evidence of either a lack of personal integrity or a lack of sensitivity to common ethical standards—a lack of social integrity—in the individual manager. Reflection on the moral milieu of management, on the conflicting and ambiguous demands that managers routinely experience in organizations, indicates that this view is misleadingly simplistic.

In interviews conducted with managers about the ethical questions that come up in the course of their work lives (Waters, Bird, and Chant, 1986), we observed that many managers make implicit or explicit reference to some common ethical assumptions or standards. The ethical standards were identified as (1) honesty in communication, (2) fair treatment, (3) special consideration (in special circumstances), (4) fair competition, (5) organizational responsibility, (6) corporate social responsibility, and (7) respect for law (Bird and Waters, 1987). Note the inclusion of "organizational responsibility" in the list. Managers take their work seriously and regard pursuit of organizational objectives and fulfillment of their own specific duties as ethical obligations. As one respondent said, "It is hard to fire a man [for stealing] when you know his wife and children and the financial need of the family; I've done it, though, because the organization must survive" (Bird and Waters, 1987, p. 9).

The fact that managers do agree somewhat on ethical standards might be cited to support the position that senior managers are reasonable in their complete reliance on the integrity of individuals in their organization. The reality, however, is that these standards provide only very general guidance and, in fact, are frequently in conflict. Analyzing the results of the interviews, we observed that:

When the managers' implicit statements about moral standards are viewed as a composite, the picture that emerges is one of ambiguity and competing principles. Managers talk about the need to deceive as well as the need for truth. They talk about the need to show special consideration for special circumstances as well as the need to treat all others fairly and impartially. They discuss the need to compete aggressively, seeking every possible advantage vis-à-vis customers, suppliers, and competitors, as well as the need to observe and conform to standards of fair competition. Moreover, even these competing or bivalent principles are exceedingly general in that, by themselves, they do not always clearly point toward specific forms of appropriate action. When does legitimate bluffing or concealment of a basic position in negotiations with a customer or supplier or employee become inappropriate dishonesty in communications? When does legitimate preferential treatment for special classes of customers, suppliers, or employees become unfairly discriminatory to others? When does avoid-

ance of certain widespread yet questionable selling practices become a
breach of moral obligations to the stockholders? . . . The competing moral
standards can be said to serve the function only of alerting the manager
in a given situation that a moral issue is involved. The same standards
are less useful in providing concrete direction on how to act in that specific
situation [Waters and Bird, 1987, pp. 16–17].

These conditions—the inherent abstractness of the standards and their frequently conflicting nature—produce a situation that subjects managers to moral stress. Contributing to this
stress is the ambiguity of the expectations suggested by the standards. Are they lofty ideals that should be pursued even though
they may never be fully realized, or are they compelling obligations with higher priority than immediate economic goals?

Most important, the stress of coping with these judgments
is exacerbated by a sense of isolation: "A key source of moral
stress for individual managers is the general absence of institutionalized structures which accord a public character to moral
concerns. Very seldom in the interviews did we get a sense that
managers talked with others about moral questions, in the same
way that they might discuss questions of marketing, production, or finance. Morality is a live topic for individual managers,
but it is close to a nontopic among groups of managers. Because
managers do not feel able to discuss moral questions with peers
and superiors, they often experience the stress of being morally
on their own" (Waters and Bird, 1987, p. 18).

This sense of isolation, this feeling that it is difficult to
discuss ethical questions within the organization, is a critical
issue to consider in thinking about integrity management. Managers seldom make reference to religious beliefs or formal codes
of ethics, nor do they often engage in philosophical ethical analysis of the issues they confront. Rather, the ethical standards
to which they refer usually take the form of cultural conventions—that is, "culturally shared normative standards that are
often viewed as taken-for-granted common-sense ideas, honored
and justified by customary practices and conventional wisdom"
(Bird and Waters, 1987, p. 12). In other words, the "rules of
good behavior" for managers are nowhere written or synthe-

sized. Codes of ethics are often considered too general to be of much help, and philosophical analysis is generally experienced as not very useful. Rather, managers regulate their behavior by applying loosely held conventions about how managers should handle various situations. Because of the isolation they experience, however, managers invoke these conventions uncertainly and tentatively.

Clear and compelling ethical positions on particular questions can come about only through debate and dialogue, through what one observer labels simply "good conversation" (King, personal communication, 1986). Good conversation can have three main effects. First, it can legitimize ethical concern as an important dimension of managerial life (and probably allow many managers to discover how similar their views on moral standards are). Second, it is probably the only way managers can seek guidance and gain clarity about what to do in a particular situation. Ethical standards will always be general and abstract, and managers must always make judgments in response to concrete situations. Finally, it is out of public discussion and agreement that feelings of obligation ultimately arise; "conventions are not made by fiat; they grow and develop initially as individuals openly or tacitly agree to be guided by specific standards, as they act in keeping with these standards, and as they renew this agreement by their willing deference to them" (Waters and Bird, 1987, p. 19).

In summary, integrity management is the planned facilitation of open discussion and decision making about the ethical questions that managers face in the normal course of organizational operations. It is an explicit recognition that the interests of both shareholders and the larger society are best served when managers and organizations act with a sense of social integrity. Attention to integrity management is an acknowledgment that management integrity is not simply a question of individual character and that because general ethical standards often conflict and often provide little guidance in a particular situation, being unable to openly discuss questions and concerns may place an individual manager in an untenable position of moral stress. Finally, integrity management has as its purpose informed and

responsible action—that is, action which reflects the best information and thinking available and for which members of the
organization are willing to take responsibility.

In the absence of conscious attention by senior managers
to integrity management, it has been argued, it should not be
surprising that, despite the good intentions of those senior managers, organization members continue to commit ethically questionable acts. In most organizations there is very overt (and
legitimate!) pressure for economic performance. When this pressure is coupled with an absence of overt attention to (much less
pressure for) ethical sensitivity, managers cannot help experiencing moral stress, an experience that tests, rather than supports,
their convictions.

Senior Management Attention to
Different Kinds of Ethically Questionable Acts

In this section, I examine how much attention is typically
given to integrity management or, more broadly, how senior
management attention is divided among the different kinds of
ethically questionable acts that take place in organizations.

Earlier I suggested that senior managers pay most attention to the kinds of ethical questions that least trouble most
managers, and vice versa. To pursue that argument, I will first
introduce a typology of ethically questionable acts (this section
is drawn from Waters and Bird, 1986). I use the cautious label
"ethically questionable acts" in order to avoid imposing my
own judgment on the list, since that is not germane here. Certainly, some of the examples that follow would receive very little
debate and others a great deal, although even that might depend on the audience. That ambiguity, in fact, forms part of
the challenge of integrity management.

In this four-part typology, acts are classified by how the
managerial role is used or observed. In *nonrole* acts, the actor
is acting outside his or her role of manager; they are managerial
only in the sense that they take place in organizations and frequently involve people who happen to be managers. Examples
include embezzlement, stealing supplies, cheating on expense

reports, and investing in suppliers with whom the firm does business. Nonrole acts are also defined in the typology as being committed "against the firm." That is, the acts involve direct gain for the actor, and the costs are borne largely by the organization.

The second category, also of the "against the firm" type, is *role failure*. In this category, the acts are directly related to the managerial role and amount to a failure to perform that role. Examples include failure to confront expense account cheating, failure to conduct candid performance appraisals, "palming off" a poor performer with an inflated recommendation, or inequitably distributing salary increases. Again, these involve direct personal gain for the actor (though often not financial gain) at the expense of the organization (and often at the expense of another person's well-being).

In contrast, the remaining two categories involve ethically questionable acts committed in behalf of the firm, or, in shorthand, "for the firm." It can be argued that in the long run all unethical acts are ultimately against the interests of the firm; and, in a kind of motivational calculus, all acts may be said to serve the interests of the actor. However, the distinction between against-the-firm and for-the-firm is reasonably clear in the short run. In contrast to acts of the "against the firm" type, acts "for the firm" produce direct gain for the organization and only indirect gain for the individual actor; direct costs are borne largely by parties outside the organization.

The third category, *role distortion,* includes such acts as bribery, price fixing, unjustifiable differential pricing, pressuring the low bidder in a closed-bid process to knock an additional 10 percent off the price, or padding insurance claims. The organization gains in the short run, but in most organizations such acts would be viewed with disapproval even though the actor would be seen as involved with tasks properly within his or her role; hence the label "role distortion."

Acts in the fourth category, *role assertion,* have something of a one-of-a-kind quality where there is a lack of authoritative direction from law, precedent, or customary practice and on which the corporate position must be more or less asserted in public debate. It is through role assertion acts that a firm attempts to shape and define societal expectations of the corporation (Waters, 1980).

As noted earlier for the example of investing in South Africa, role assertion acts do not remain so indefinitely. Given sufficiently intense public debate, public attitudes typically solidify in one direction or another; in other words, generally accepted principles of goodness or rightness emerge and, typically, organizations shift their positions to comply. For a contrasting example, consider decisions about whether air bags should be standard equipment in automobiles. Although a case can be (and is) made in this regard, generally accepted principles have not yet coalesced on this question.

Other examples in this category include decisions about using nuclear technology for energy generation, withdrawing a product line in the face of initial allegations of inadequate safety, and cooperating openly and completely with regulatory agencies. As the examples show, role assertion acts typically also differ from role distortion acts in scope (the former are larger and more strategic) and visibility (the former involve senior officials in debate with the media, regulatory agencies, and so on; the latter involve few people and a great deal of secrecy). Table 1 summarizes the four-part typology.

What can we say about the attention that each of these four types of ethically questionable acts receives in organizations? I believe the differences are striking. To begin with, it has been observed that formal auditing and control systems in most organizations are almost exclusively concerned with the first category in Table 1, nonrole acts committed against the firm (Waters and Chant, 1982). That is perhaps predictable, since the technology of auditing and accounting lends itself to acts in this category and is largely inadequate for the other categories: "Conventional accounting controls are designed primarily to detect and prevent acts committed against the organization, such as fraud and theft, and rely heavily on the principle of management authorization and random checks on appropriate documentation of explanations for expenditures. These tests for authorization and documentation, the heart of

Table 1. Types of Ethically Questionable Managerial Acts.

Type	Direct Effect	Examples
1. Nonrole	Against the firm	• Expense account cheating • Embezzlement • Stealing supplies
2. Role failure	Against the firm	• Superficial performance appraisal • Not confronting expense account cheating • Palming off a poor performer
3. Role distortion	For the firm	• Bribery • Price fixing • Manipulation of suppliers
4. Role assertion	For the firm	• Investing in South Africa • Utilizing nuclear technology for energy generation • Failure to cooperate completely with regulatory agencies

internal control, are inadequate. Many illegal and unethical acts will have been duly authorized by managers who feel, however mistakenly, that the transactions are made in the company's best interests'' (Waters and Chant, 1982, p. 62).

Corporate codes of ethics also tend to focus on this category. Reporting on a survey conducted in 1979, the Ethics Resource Center observes that, of firms having formal codes of ethics, 94 percent prohibited conflict-of-interest activities, 97 percent specifically prohibited taking bribes or favors to influence decisions, and 62 percent specifically prohibited abuse of expense accounts, special allowances, and perquisites (Opinion Research Corporation, 1979).

What is most interesting about this survey is the questions that were *not* asked and the topics *not* addressed in the ethics codes (or at least about which no findings were reported). Except for a limited reference to taking bribes, the survey report is preoccupied with what I have described here as nonrole acts; the other three types of morally questionable acts are almost completely ignored. I am not asserting that corporate codes of ethics are concerned exclusively with acts committed against the organization (in fact, on the basis of some limited exposure, I know they are not) but, rather, pointing out that acts in the against-the-firm, nonrole category are a major preoccupation in many organizations. Moreover, I believe that this category has little if anything to do with management integrity as I am interested in that topic; such acts tell us little about the ethical tensions involved in managerial work itself.

What of the other three categories of ethically questionable acts? Almost by definition, the for-the-firm, role assertion category receives significant senior management attention, although that attention frequently has an episodic quality. Because this kind of act is the target of the media and social interest groups, it is front-page news, so to speak, both externally and within the firm. Senior managers and their staffs will be preoccupied with such questions until they are resolved and slip from the front pages, of both the newspapers and the executive committee agenda. Evidence of a more continuing management interest in this kind of issue is found in the establishment by many corporations of staff groups specifically concerned with social issues in management. In addition, numerous stories have appeared about executive training on how to handle oneself in encounters with the media, again evidence that this kind of issue receives ongoing senior management attention.

I have argued to this point that two of the categories of ethically questionable acts, against-the-firm nonrole and for-the-firm role assertion, receive a great deal of management attention in most large organizations. Let me now suggest that, in comparison, the against-the-firm role failure category receives little management attention and the for-the-firm role distortion category even less. I acknowledge that I am on thin empirical ice here; it is a far more challenging task to argue that something doesn't happen frequently than it is to point to its occurrence. Nevertheless, the assertion above is based on evidence from several sources, including my own experience as a manager, informal discussions with many managers over many years, examination of testimony before congressional committees investigating some well-known scandals such as price fixing in the electrical equipment industry, overseas bribery in the aerospace industry, and falsification of test results in the aircraft and drug industries (Waters, 1978), and interviews with managers about the ethical questions they face in their work lives (Waters, Bird, and Chant, 1986).

The picture that emerges from all these sources is that little organizational attention is given to these categories (compared with other concerns), and the little that is is experienced as perfunctory. The personnel department may be active with respect to the role failure category and the legal department with respect to the role distortion category, but (with apologies to personnel officers and corporate lawyers) toward neither category does line management direct vigorous, sustained attention.

The irony of this imbalance in attention is that the kinds of ethically questionable acts that are most salient and troublesome for most managers are the kinds that receive the least attention in the form of proactive management and control. When managers are asked to describe the ethical questions that come up in their professional lives, the issues for which they report the most instances of unethical behavior by managers are overwhelmingly in the two categories of against-the-firm role failure and for-the-firm role distortion (Waters, Bird, and Chant, 1986).

This is not surprising when the two categories that do receive attention are reconsidered. The stark, unambiguous quality of acts in the first category, against-the-firm nonrole, is such that the vast majority of managers view them with repugnance, do not engage in them, and do not experience them as a very salient aspect of their work lives. Acts in the fourth category, for-the-firm role assertion, are viewed with interest by most managers because of the media attention that surrounds them, but except for the most senior managers, questions in this category are not critical in their work lives.

These observations are not made to denigrate the importance of attending to acts in these two categories. People do steal from organizations and leaders must take difficult stands on ill-defined issues, and both kinds of problems warrant attention. Rather, the observations are made to highlight the fact that integrity management does not receive the attention it deserves. Many role failure acts are not extremely obvious, but they are immediately costly to those affected and destructive in the long run for the firm. Role distortion acts are ultimately corrosive for the firm even if undetected publicly. When, as frequently happens, they are reported in the press, they are a source of shame for the organizations involved as well as management in general. It is with respect to these two types of ethically questionable acts that integrity management can make a significant difference. And it is here that senior management effort typically falls short.

To this point, I have made two basic assertions, briefly summarized as follows:

- Integrity management is a critical senior management responsibility. Failure to attend consciously to this process, coupled with normal pressure for results, creates widespread moral stress in the organization; this stress impairs the ability of managers to act with integrity.
- Senior management attention is not directed at the kinds of morally questionable acts about which managers experience the most stress; for the most part it can be said that senior managers typically address little systematic and conscious attention to integrity management.

It can remain a question whether the second assertion is true of most firms, many firms, or only some firms. At the very least, I believe it is true of a sufficient number of firms that it warrants critical attention. In these cases, then, what can we say about the personal integrity of the senior management?

To the extent that these managers claim they are deeply concerned that all managers in their organizations act with high integrity and at the same time do little or nothing to ensure that that will happen—in other words, they ignore the whole area of integrity management—it is hard to avoid being drawn toward raising questions about their personal integrity. However, this judgment may be without basis.

In fact, my experience with senior managers lead me in the reverse direction. Those with whom I have had any dealings strike me as people of the highest personal integrity. The answer to this paradox is, I believe, that they have typically never thought about these issues in this way. If that is the explanation, then the question may be one of social integrity rather than personal integrity. More precisely, perhaps we as a society need to establish some generally accepted expectations for senior managers' involvement in integrity management. It is to that topic that I turn next.

Integrity Management: How and Why

I will sketch out some ideas about how to address the challenge of integrity management by starting with a defense of management practice with respect to role assertion questions. Much of the social criticism directed at senior managers focuses on these large questions pertaining to social responsibility. Firms, and their senior managers, have been and are attacked for decisions about closing plants in economically depressed areas, selling nonunion produce, production of dangerous pesticides, involvement in weapons manufacturing, inadequate support of charities, and the like. Certainly, these criticisms fill an important societal need, since, as discussed earlier, only through debate and discussion of such issues can competing views be subjected to public scrutiny; only through such debate and discussion can generally accepted principles of goodness and rightness take shape and crystallize.

However, in the heat of such debate it is often overlooked that for the most part the managers of the corporations involved are doing just what they should be doing—that is, they are arguing as vigorously and effectively as they can for their position on the issues. To do less would be a failure in their responsibilities to the stockholders and employees.

Given that the substance of these issues is debatable— that is, cogent ethical arguments can be raised in support of competing positions—judgment on the appropriateness of management behavior should be directed at the *process* of debate. To the extent that senior managers engage fully and openly in such debate, responding directly to competing views and explaining and arguing their positions as best they can in an attempt to shape societal expectations of the corporation, I do not see how their integrity can be questioned.

This same attention to the *process* by which ethical questions are addressed within the firm is at the heart of integrity
management. Some issues will not be reasonably debatable; that
is, persuasive ethical arguments in support of a particular practice will not be possible. Examples of such issues would include
the cases noted earlier regarding bribery in the form of drugs
and prostitutes or firing with rifles at Environmental Protection Agency inspectors. If we imagine for the sake of argument
that the senior managers in the organizations involved are well
aware of these practices and condone them (I must add that I
have no reason to believe this is so), then the notion of integrity management would not be relevant. Organization members
would be faced with questions of "exit, voice, and loyalty"
(Hirschman, 1970), and in ordinary circumstances, individual
integrity could be maintained only through exit or voice or both.

Continuing with these same examples, if we make the
more likely assumption that the senior managers in the organizations involved are not aware of the practices and would view
them with repugnance if they were aware of them, then integrity management would be relevant, though in a minimal sense.
This minimal integrity management would be concerned with
facilitating whistle blowing in connection with gross violations
of the law and ethical custom, with ensuring that practices do
not take place that could not and would not be openly defended
by reasonable people.

However, the clear-cut nature of these examples makes
them a limiting case—hence the idea of minimal integrity management. Far more common are situations where managers must
act on the basis of ethical judgments in the face of competing
and ambiguous demands. In these situations, "right answers"
will often not be easy to come by, trade-offs and compromises
may be required, and not everybody will agree with every decision. These situations are the province of a full conception of
integrity management.

The pleasingly familiar image of *good conversation* is a useful
metaphor for integrity management. A good conversation in
this context will involve two or more managers who are struggling to figure out how to do the best job possible in a particular

situation while respecting and strengthening the ethical standards relevant to the situation. Armed more with questions and provisional suggestions for action than with right answers and unalterable positions, the participants in this kind of good conversation will experience it more as a problem-solving effort guided by values of inquiry and cooperation than as a debate guided by values of strategy and competition. They will be struggling sincerely to arrive at a good solution to a problem that concerns them, a solution which they can live with and which they will be willing and able to explain to whoever might legitimately be interested.

The idea that participants will be able to explain organizational decisions involving ethical judgment is central to the notion of good conversation. Since the questions being discussed are by definition open to disagreement among reasonable people, it is not realistic to expect that totally integrative solutions will always or even frequently be possible. However, it is reasonable for organization members to expect that their values and opinions will be heard, understood, and considered on any question of direct concern and that they will understand and be able to explain the ethical reasoning behind trade-offs and compromises made, even if they do not fully agree with them.

I have been describing how concerned managers might effectively handle problems with an ethical dimension, how an organization might look when senior managers successfully respond to the challenge of integrity management. The core outcome of integrity management, good conversation as required, seems quite compatible with current contingency theory and practice with respect to participative decision making. Nevertheless, this kind of good conversation doesn't just happen, as is evidenced by the fact that it just doesn't happen that frequently. In what follows, I will make some suggestions about what a concerned senior manager might do to stimulate such good conversation.

As I have argued elsewhere (Waters, 1978; Waters and Chant, 1982; Waters and Bird, 1987), a logical starting point in this process is that senior management communicate an explicit position on the importance of the moral dimension of management and explain the philosophy and values that are to guide the organization. This can take the form of policy statements, speeches, and the like and can set the stage for more open discussion of ethical questions.

Three suggestions can be made about these communications. First, ambiguity about corporate priorities has to be eliminated. Somebody has to bite the bullet and say straightforwardly that the long-term vitality of the firm rests on the social integrity of its managers, that obeying the law and respecting the ethical standards of society come before and have a higher priority than immediate economic objectives, and that these priorities will be maintained even when the pressure is on for short-term sales and profits.

Second, these communications have to move from the "do good and avoid evil" level of abstraction to open discussion of concrete problems that would be obvious to anyone in the company and in the industry. To avoid mentioning and taking a specific position on the very problems with which managers in the organization are wrestling not only misses an opportunity to deal with those problems but also introduces a note of ambiguity into the communication.

Third, these communications should not only point to the value of "good conversation" but also make demands that it take place routinely and regularly. In getting people to do something, a place to start is to ask them to do it. In considering questions of legality and morality, there is a perverse tendency to focus on the "bad guys" and ignore the "good guys." I believe that a demand for more "good conversation" is a way to unleash an avalanche of energy from good people, who will greatly outnumber the few bad people in any organization.

However, my optimism notwithstanding, there are good reasons to believe that these communications of senior management's ideology are best viewed as necessary but not sufficient. First, there are problems of change and inertia. If an organization has been operating without these "good conversations," it will take some concerted effort to break old patterns and establish new ones. Second, initial conversations will probably be awkward and difficult. Most managers don't have the same vocabulary or language fluency on ethical questions that they have on topics such as accounting or production, and they may be tentative at first in discussing such questions. Third, if these conversations are not to be treated as "time away from the real job," ways must be sought to build them into ongoing job responsibilities. Finally, there may be a period of doubt or uncertainty about what the senior management is about with these communications. Obviously, this can be more or less of a question depending on senior management's prior visibility and activity with respect to issues of integrity.

For all these reasons, the desired "good conversation" might be stimulated and facilitated by using some of the following, more formal devices (from Waters and Chant, 1982, pp. 64–65):

- Managers could be requested to include in their annual plans a statement of the steps they will take to ensure that illegal and unethical acts do not take place in the areas under their responsibility. These activities would then become part of their annual performance review.
- The legal department could be made responsible for periodic, simply written presentations to all departments or business areas about the existing legal requirements most relevant to the corporation's affairs.
- Task forces, composed of managers from different parts of the organization, could be periodically formed to review the legality and ethicality of practices in selected business areas. These reviews might include interviews, not only with employees in the area, but also with major suppliers and customers.
- A staff group could be assigned the responsibility of monitoring newspapers and journals for information about questionable practices in the industry. When examples are disclosed, these can become the subject of planned discussions throughout the organization.
- In a manner analogous to environmental impact statements, new business proposals might be required to include a review of the ethical climate of any new business area for which entry is being considered.

- Managers could be required to hold periodic "deep sensing" sessions in which they would meet informally with employees from lower levels of the organization to encourage sharing of any concerns.
- In each business area, managers could be required to hold periodically what might be called "doomsday sessions." Selected employees would meet to brainstorm about what could be going on in that area that shouldn't be. The ideas generated could inform management directives and make everybody more aware of the possibilities.
- The training of new employees could emphasize the importance of questioning suspected illegal and unethical practices and could introduce them to the proper channels for raising those questions.
- Auditors could be requested to report annually to the audit committee of the board of directors on the appropriateness of the control climate and the system for stimulating examination of ethical issues. In this way, rather than having the impossible task of assessing the propriety of management practices, auditors can be assigned the more realistic task of determining whether it is possible for managers themselves to raise questions about the propriety of management practices.

Using any or all of these approaches must not, however, obscure the real objective of widespread "good conversation." Perhaps the most critical determinant of success in any embryonic integrity management effort will be its reception of the people who first raise moral concerns and express a desire to discuss those concerns with others. Without prejudging the substance of their concerns, it will be of crucial importance to publicly laud and reward the fact that they raised the concern in the first place. If in fact their concerns have validity or if it turns out that they are "blowing the whistle" on some other managers engaged in an unsavory practice, they may not only have to be rewarded, they may also have to be protected from reprisals. Given the problems of doubt and uncertainty noted above, and given the fact that actions do speak louder than words, this need to welcome, praise, reward, and protect early "conversation starters" probably cannot be overemphasized.

Management Integrity: Constraint or Goal?

Clearly the ideas of both management integrity and integrity management have a normative character—that is, they involve prescriptions, assertions about how senior managers should behave. The rationale one adopts in support of these prescriptions will depend largely on whether one views integrity as a constraint on or a goal of management action.

Implicit in conventional images of management integrity is the idea that ethical standards serve as a constraint on managerial actions taken in pursuit of organizational objectives. For example, in his classic discussion of the social responsibility of business, Friedman (1970, p. 33) argued: "In a free-enterprise, private-property system, a corporate executive is an employee of the owners of the business. He has direct responsibility to his employers. That responsibility is to conduct the business in accordance with their desires. Which generally will be to make as much money as possible *while conforming to the basic rules of the society, both those embodied in law and those embodied in ethical custom*" (emphasis added). This perspective—that of management integrity as a constraint—is widely accepted as a bedrock conservative stance toward the social responsibility of managers. It provides a compelling logic and rationale for senior managers' attention to integrity management. Given the competing and ambiguous nature of both the laws and the ethical standards with which their people must cope, senior managers are failing perhaps the most elementary test of their social responsibility if they fail to attend to integrity management.

Integrity management is the particular responsibility of senior managers, since they are the custodians of an organization's basic culture. They are the symbolic interface with the larger society in which the organization is embedded, and they personify the relationship the organization will have with that society. If the legitimate drive among people in their organizations "to make as much money as possible" for the shareholders is to be constrained by conformity to legal and ethical standards of society, they must be personally involved in the struggle to make sure that happens. Senior managers must participate in the good conversations that are at the heart of integrity management and facilitate those discussions among others, since that is the only way to establish the clarity and authority of the legal and ethical standards that are to hold sway in particular situations. Consistent with sound management practice in regard to any task, they may delegate authority in this area but never responsibility.

The "typical response" described earlier that corporate spokespersons provide to revelations of misdeeds by lower-level managers ("We're shocked . . . ") should be considered a threat to the fundamental legitimacy of the corporation in society. The nature of the questions and challenges that make up senior managers' agendas signals what is important and valued in an organization. A claim by senior managers that they didn't know what was going on, far from being a justification, is an admission of their failure to attend to a basic responsibility.

Thus, I have argued that viewing integrity as a constraint on management behavior provides a compelling rationale for the importance of integrity management. Nevertheless, that argument is incomplete. Organizations are also partly value-driven. In keeping with Kant's admonition that we should never treat other people simply as means, all thinking managers realize that they are not simply instruments of the shareholders. Direct responsibility to the owners of the business, in Friedman's terms, does not imply that managers thereby abandon their own humanity. The quality of life in an organization is not simply a means to performance on behalf of the shareholders; it is also an end in itself on behalf of the members of the organization. To the extent that acting with integrity is essential to the quality of managers' lives, it must also be considered a goal in organizations.

If we all can be said to exist on some continuum between saints and sinners, then most of us likely fall somewhere in the middle; for lack of a better label, let's call ourselves regular folks (Waters, 1980). It is neither the saints nor the sinners but, rather, the regular folks who experience moral stress in the complexity of corporate life. It is the regular folks whose integrity is strained by strong pressure for performance when they can't raise their moral concerns for discussion. It is the regular folks who absorb the tension of dealing with ambiguity and conflicting signals when senior managers don't bite the bullet about corporate priorities. It is the regular folks whose integrity gets compromised when they are pressured into doing small things about which they have shame or, at best, little pride. These are real costs, and the quality of life is diminished when our organizations are run in such a way that we can voice our moral concerns only with difficulty.

Viewing integrity as a goal leads us to consider whether organizations are managed in such a way as to allow their members to experience a sense of integration between their private and professional lives. The notion of the citizen-manager as a linking pin between a society and its corporations is an essential element of the integrity-as-constraint perspective. If, however, managers feel forced to leave their citizen selves at home when they go to work, they eventually will become estranged from their work. Consider, for example, these comments by a plant manager: "Rather than incurring costly warehousing costs to smooth the wild swings in consumption of our product, we lay people off in slack time—on and off, on and off. The stress and strain it puts on a man when he is out of work for a month or two weeks bothers me, but that is how the industry works. I've hinted about this problem with my superiors, but that runs the risk that the opinion they will formulate is, This guy doesn't really have the guts to do what a manager needs to do" (Bird and Waters, 1987, p. 9). The purpose in using this example is not to address the substance of the concern this man has raised. Certainly it is not a simple problem and might not even be viewed as a problem by many managers. But it is a valid problem or concern or question for this citizen-manager. And he feels that he cannot even talk about it in his own organization, that he must leave his citizen self outside the plant gates. Eliminating such experiences and feelings among managers is a legitimate objective of integrity management.

It can remain a question whether management integrity is most appropriately viewed as a constraint, as a goal, or as both. However, if management is to be worthy of our continued investment of ourselves, if it is to enhance us as individuals and enhance the quality of our society, if it is to attract the best and brightest of our young people to its ranks, then certainly our organizations must be inspirited with purpose through the strong ethical leadership of the people who head them. The ethical dimension of management must be prominent in the minds, hearts, and actions of the senior managers of our organizations. We can demand no less and no more of them.

8

Reciprocal Integrity: Creating Conditions That Encourage Personal and Organizational Integrity

Chris Argyris
Donald A. Schön

Webster's unabridged dictionary offers as the first meaning of *integrity* (from the Latin *integritas,* "integer") "the quality or state of being complete; wholeness; entireness; unbroken state." Its second meaning is "the quality or state of being of sound moral principle; uprightness, honesty, and sincerity." In the conventional sense, then, a person of integrity is a whole moral person (like the biblical Job, who is described as *tam v'yashar,* "whole and straight"), and a person who lacks integrity is "broken" or "incomplete." But the dictionary does not say whether integrity requires acting on sound moral principles, as distinct from espousing them, and makes no reference to what might be meant by integrity in organizations.

On these issues, there has recently been a great deal of discussion, not only in the literature of organization theory (Goffman, 1968; Bailyn, 1985) but also in organizations themselves, as illustrated by the following vignettes:

1. A scientist rebels against his firm's refusal to recognize what he sees as a serious problem of product safety. When he voices his discontent, his superiors tell him to "cool it" and make

197

himself useful. He protests, couching his protest in terms of professional integrity, and eventually leaves the organization.

2. Is *Challenger* ready to fly safely in the cold of Cape
Canaveral? McDonald, an engineer at Thiokol, says "No!" His
superiors tell him, in the name of loyalty to the firm, to shape
up and sign off. He does so, thinking to himself, "This is the
first time the burden of proof has been on me to show why the
rocket *shouldn't* fly." But he keeps his thoughts to himself until
interrogated by the commission charged with investigating the
disaster.

3. A recent *New York Times* article quotes former White
House Chief of Staff Donald Regan as follows: "In the nervous
silence, Donald Regan proceeds to review the president's sched-
ule for that day. 'What upsets me is inefficiency, stupidity, and
unexpectedness,' he says later. 'If someone knows of a problem and conceals it from me, I get more upset from that than
from the problem itself. I tell our people time and time again:
Bad news first. Never a surprise. Please! Particularly an unpleasant surprise'" (Weinraub, 1986, p. 12). For a subordinate to
present "bad news first," especially when he has reason to fear
Regan's (or Reagan's) reaction, requires integrity in the conventional sense: a willingness to speak up even at the risk of
threat or embarrassment. And Regan's need to warn his staff
"time and time again" suggests a history of sad experience with
individuals who fail, in this sense, to demonstrate integrity.

Examples like these raise the question of what it means
to be a member of an organization.[1] Organizations may make
demands or exert pressures on their members to behave in ways
that violate members' moral or professional principles[2] or their

---

[1]The authors have benefited from the thinking of Gidon Kunda, whose doctoral
thesis deals with the idea of organization membership.

[2]It is not surprising that discussions of integrity, in the prevailing mode, focus
on *professionals* in organizations, for in their case ordinary moral codes are sup-
plemented by codes of professional behavior. And professional integrity is associated with professional autonomy, as Bailyn (1985) and others have pointed out.
According to the professional's bargain with society (Hughes, 1959), society grants
professionals—in return for their esoteric knowledge in matters of great human
import—extraordinary freedoms of action, mandates for social control in the areas
of their expertise, and license to determine who shall enter the profession. In the

sense of their personal rights or freedoms. Or, as in the White House case, an organization may make contradictory demands of its members, advocating a kind of behavior for which members believe they will be punished. In all such examples, individuals are seen as expressing integrity when they speak up or stick to their guns in the face of organizational pressures to do otherwise. In terms made famous by Albert Hirschman in *Exit, Voice and Loyalty* (1970), individuals in organizations express their integrity through voice or exit. When an individual's interests come into conflict with organizational policy or practice, Hirschman points out, three options are available: remain loyal to the organization, try to influence the organization by giving voice to discontent, or leave the organization. In these terms we can redescribe integrity, in its conventional usage, as a social virtue through which an individual dissents from organizational policy or practice by means of voice or exit, thereby upholding individual interests against organizational ones.

In conventional usage, individuals are said to express integrity when their dissent is based on moral or professional *principles*. This usage is shared by many contemporary writers on identity, autonomy, or integrity of individuals in organizations. Hirschman (1970), on the contrary, makes few references to principles, confining himself to the language of *interests*. But this language seems to derive from his wish to integrate theories of economics and political science in a unified theory of organizational effectiveness. He points out that just as individuals in the role of customer act from an interest in consumption, so individuals in the role of organization member act from a political interest. Exit is the quintessential market mechanism; voice, the quintessential political one. Both mechanisms serve individual interests. In this spirit Hirschman argues that voice is "nothing but a basic portion and function of any political system, known sometimes as 'interest articulation'" (p. 30). Individuals may

---

context of life in organizations, professionals may find their freedom of action abridged and pay a high price for their efforts to adhere to professional principles in the face of organizational demands.

at times act from principle; but when they do, their action still serves the interest inherent in the principle. A special case of individual integrity arises when the individual's interest is of the particular sort that derives from principle.

Hirschman uses exit, voice, and loyalty, and the conditions under which these choices are likely to be made, to explain organizational "lapses from efficient, rational, law-abiding, virtuous, or otherwise functional behavior" (p. 1). Voice and exit on the part of an organization's members or customers are "mechanisms of recuperation" that serve to prevent or correct organizational deterioration. Here, Hirschman's thinking anticipates other contemporary writers who link the expression of individual integrity to organizational effectiveness, beneficence, or morality (see, for example, Bailyn, 1985). In cases like the one involving *Challenger*, for example, failures of individual integrity may be seen as contributing to an organization's callous disregard for human lives. When individuals fail to speak up, they may contribute to an organization's self-inflicted injury, as in Du Pont's decision to proceed with a new product in spite of an intractable technical problem of which production people were well aware (Argyris and Schön, 1978). Failures of individual integrity may contribute to an organization's sluggish response to threat, as in the American automotive industry's inattention to increasingly dangerous competition from foreign imports in the 1970s.

Hirschman also shares with much of the contemporary literature a particular way of framing relations between individuals and their organizations. He treats exit and voice as measures by which individuals may resist organizational tyranny (Hirschman, 1970, p. 8) and exert a corrective back-pressure on organizations. In this respect, he resembles Erving Goffman (1968), who sees organizations as sources of coercion and threat to individuals, for whom personal identity can be maintained only "in the cracks" between mechanisms of organizational control.

A close look at examples like the ones described above, however, suggests that the corrective/coercive relation between individual and organization is reversible. Individuals may exert coercive pressure on organizations, and organizations may exert a corrective influence on individual behavior. Managers may use voice, or even exit, to bring unresponsive or recalcitrant individuals into line with organizationally sanctioned principles.

In the product safety case, for example, managers argued with the laboratory scientist by appeal to principles of cooperative organizational practice. In the Thiokol case, McDonald, having had his say, was asked to conform to established principles of organizational decision making. And it would not be difficult to imagine Regan arguing that subordinates should, as a matter of principle, protect their superiors from unpleasant surprises.

A fuller interpretation of our examples suggests that they involve *conflicting* conceptions of integrity. *Individual integrity* consists in holding fast to individual interests—including an interest in acting from principle—in the face of organizational pressures to do otherwise. *Organizational integrity* consists in holding fast to organizational interests—including an interest in acting from organizational principle—in the face of individuals' resistance to doing so. This more complex view of integrity pits individual ''wholeness'' against organizational ''wholeness'' and loyalty to self against loyalty to organization. A recurrent drama of organizational life takes the form of contention between those who speak for the first sort of integrity and those who speak for the second.

As such conflicts have become increasingly visible, certain measures have been advanced to encourage the expression of integrity, individual or organizational:

1. Managers exhort their subordinates to show integrity or threaten them with the consequences of failing to do so.
2. Governments introduce ''whistle blowing'' and ''sunshine'' legislation in order to make it easier for individuals to take a stand against official policy or to make it more difficult for organizations to cast a veil of secrecy over actions that warrant public scrutiny.

3. Managers introduce high-performance work systems so that individuals will be strongly reinforced in their commitment to organizational purposes and principles.

4. Managers institute procedures, sometimes called "organizational dialectics," to promote open debates in which conflicting views about important organizational decisions are surfaced and brought into confrontation with each other.

The Paradoxical Consequences of Integrity

Measures like the four above are intended to correct a corrective—that is, to foster expression of integrity in its role as corrective for organizational deterioration. Paradoxically, however, expression of integrity may actually contribute to organizational deterioration. Organizational situations arise in which everyone diligently strives to express integrity, with results that all parties see as contrary in the long run to the interests and principles they are trying to promote and to the further expression of integrity.

Such events tend to follow a characteristic pattern. First of all, an issue surfaces around which individuals or groups come into contention. Participants in the ensuing organizational drama experience threat or challenge to their interests, including their interests in strongly held principles. All parties become aware of a potential for embarrassment or threat to individuals and/or the organization as a whole.

All parties may then frame the issue in terms of their several conceptions of integrity, give voice to their views, and stick to their principles. But as different meanings are assigned to principles and associated procedures or codes of conduct, expressions of integrity may inhibit one another. All sides may then contribute to escalating interactions of the type that Gregory Bateson (1972) calls "schismogenetic: the more, the more." The consequence is a polarization of the organization, often perceived as unmanageable.

Polarization may trigger the exit of one or more participants. The sequence of events—voice, contention, exit—may be seen as good or bad, depending on one's view of the values at stake in the conflict. One may see the dissenting individual as a moral hero or as sand in the gears of the organization. In a variation on this scenario, polarization may be followed by stalemate. No one exits. Each party feels helpless and hopeless about changing the others. There is a prevailing cynicism about the other side's wish to change and a fear that the situation may blow up again.

In a second scenario, also triggered by the surfacing of a divisive and threatening issue, participants who have learned from their experience of the first kind of scenario fear its recurrence in the present instance. They strive to avoid setting off schismogenetic loops that carry a threat of unmanageable polarization. Top managers may try to reduce the likelihood of polarization, for example, by formally sanctioning the public expression of dissent while communicating informally that subordinates would be well advised, when stakes are high, to keep their negative opinions to themselves. Subordinates also design actions aimed at preventing blowup while maintaining an appearance of self-respect and do not exit. They restrict their most dangerous opinions to corridor conversations and employ other devices to ensure their self-protection. Thus, the two sides use similar behavioral strategies, contributing to the production of a manifest behavioral world of peace, cooperation, and concern, along with a latent behavioral world of cynicism, helplessness, hostility, and distancing. Organizational and personal routines used to avoid blowup and to keep everyone at the table require that individuals learn to monitor and control their feelings of indignation or despair triggered by threats to self-respect. Eventually individuals may so internalize the organization's defenses against the threat of polarization as to become unaware of their own defenses and their attempts to camouflage their defenses.

Over the long run, the two scenarios are likely to converge. The unmanageable polarization resulting from the first scenario usually leads to the second scenario, with its organizational distancing, its undiscussability, and its residue of unreliable information, or "noise," available to infiltrate the next threatening situation (Argyris and Schön, 1978; Argyris, 1985; Schön, 1983). Thus, the unvarnished pursuit of integrity, a social virtue, yields consequences one might expect from a vice.

How are we to explain such paradoxical outcomes?

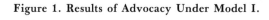

Figure 1. Results of Advocacy Under Model I.

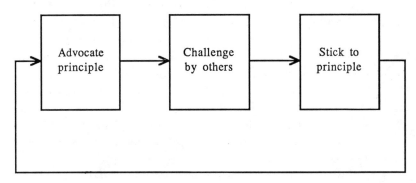

Explaining the Paradox. Figure 1 illustrates the idea that when parties to organizational conflict conform to the prevailing conception of integrity, they are likely to become closed to inquiry into the principles they advocate. The paradox inherent in this sequence of actions is that if A shows integrity in the prevailing sense, and if B, who disagrees with A's principle, also shows the same sort of integrity, then A and B are likely to come into a kind of conflict whose predictable outcome is unmanageable polarization or stalemate.

Sometimes such an outcome is justifiable. If A's principle is compelling enough, polarization or stalemate may be preferable to compliance or compromise with B's demands. A may be justified in defending his interests or sticking to his principles when he sees that B is irrevocably bent on harming him or involving him in an evil action. It would have been preferable, for example, for Eichmann to refuse to ship Jews to the gas chambers.

But such examples as this one are persuasive only when there is clear agreement that A's principle is right and B's is wrong. Most situations of organizational contention fail this test. Disagreements of principle are frequently ambiguous or relativistic. Although each party *sees* his or her position as the right one, there is no clear, consensual, objective standard by which to judge who has the greater weight of argument on his side. Under these more usual circumstances, the unvarnished pursuit of integrity may be as damaging to individuals and organizations as the abandonment of integrity.

When individuals display integrity in the prevailing sense, they speak up and stick to their principles according to a theory of action we call Model I. Theories of action are systems of values, strategies of action, and assumptions used to guide behavior. "Espoused theories" are theories of action used to explain or justify one's actions; "theories-in-use" are theories of action embedded in actual patterns of behavior. A Model I theory of action leads individuals to advocate positions so as to win and not lose, remain in unilateral control of the situation, and at the same time avoid expressing negative feelings and maintain an appearance of cool rationality (Argyris and Schön, 1974).

When individuals express integrity according to a Model I theory-in-use, they advocate their interests and principles in such a way as to try to gain control of the situation and "win." Other individuals, submissive to the organization, would allow themselves to be controlled. But individuals who are targets of Model I integrity also hold a Model I theory-in-use. If they respond to the originators through confrontation, then they act consistently with Model I. But, as we have pointed out, this is not tolerable to the originators, because it limits the expression of *their* Model I integrity. And so on, schismogenetically, the more, the more.

If the originator has more power in the situation, she is likely to win, but also to mask her victory. The fear that winning may trigger negative feelings or disturb the appearance of rational discourse activates another type of Model I strategy. So, for example, a boss may give lip service to respect for her subordinates' point of view, and the latter may in part comply with the boss's expression of her Model I integrity, covering up the anger and frustration they feel, drawing on these feelings, perhaps, to fuel small acts of subversion. They bypass the expression of their own integrity and act as if they were not doing so.

Such automatic, face-saving reactions are examples of *organizational defensive routines* (Argyris, 1985). These routines prevent human beings from experiencing negative surprises, embarrassments, or threats and simultaneously prevent organizations from reducing their causes. They are organizational in the sense that they persist in spite of turnover in membership and they are shared by individuals whose personalities are otherwise very different.

A prominent example of an organizational defensive routine is the mixed message. Here, the sender designs a message that is clearly ambiguous and precisely imprecise, acts as if his message were not inconsistent, makes the ambiguity and inconsistency in the message undiscussable, and makes that undiscussability undiscussable. A superior may tell his subordinate, for example, "Be innovative and take risks, but be careful about upsetting others"—a message that says, in effect, "Don't get into trouble!" But the designer is careful not to specify just what will and what will not upset others, both because he finds it difficult to be precise ahead of time and because he wants to cover himself. The ambiguity and imprecision of his message, however, are likely to be clearly and precisely understood by those who receive it, just as the individuals grasp and honor the speaker's intention to keep the inconsistency of his message undiscussable.

Defensive routines are designed to bypass threat and embarrassment of the sorts that often follow from the conflicts generated by expressions of Model I integrity. In the name of avoiding organizational blowup, they work in an automatic and camouflaged way to effect organizational censorship. Often they avoid embarrassment and threat but also trigger such unintended outcomes as organizational noise and distancing. Endemic in the Model I behavioral worlds of most organizations, they are critically important components of the causal systems that link expressions of integrity to such paradoxical outcomes as the muted polarization, hopelessness, and cynicism described in the previous section.

A Fresh Start: Reciprocal Integrity. What way of expressing integrity would be likely to achieve its manifest purposes while also reducing its unintended, paradoxical outcomes? The schismogenetic interactions that follow Model I expressions of integrity are notable, as we have pointed out, because originators and targets employ similar behavioral strategies. *Both* parties speak up, stick to their guns, and struggle for unilateral control of the situation; both parties collaborate in attempts to mute and camouflage the unbridled polarization they fear. Distancing, hopelessness, and cynicism are consequences of the mirroring, or contagion, of the theories-in-use that individuals bring to expressions of individual and organizational integrity.

If expressions of integrity are to contribute to an organizational world conducive both to principled action and to inquiry— processes essential to effective mechanisms of recuperation, in Hirschman's phrase—then one individual's expression of integrity must increase, rather than decrease, the likelihood that other individuals will be able and willing to express integrity. Integrity must be such that its mirroring, or contagion, will enhance the further expression of integrity. But this means that individual expressions of integrity must couple advocacy with inquiry. As in Figure 2, advocacy of principle coupled with inquiry into principle invites an inquiring challenge that provokes further advocacy and inquiry as a result. This process depends on individuals who can enact a theory-in-use conducive to the *reciprocal* expression of integrity, a theory-in-use we call Model II (Argyris and Schön, 1974). The values of this theory-in-use are valid information, informed freedom of choice, and personal causal responsibility for action. Its action strategies include advocating one's position so as to encourage inquiry into it, public

Figure 2. Results of Advocacy and Inquiry Under Model II.

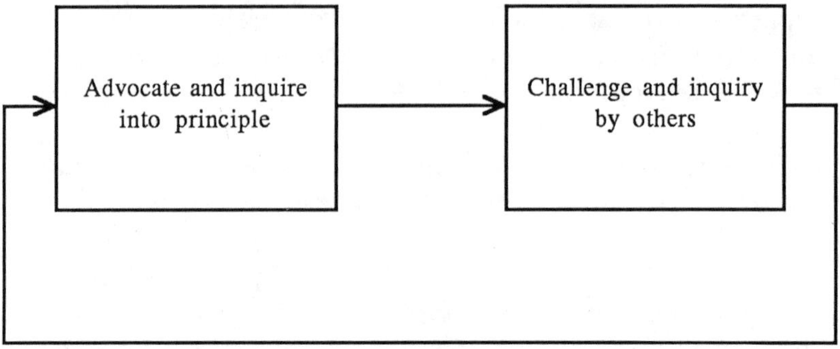

testing of one's private attributions, and minimizing unilateral protection of self and others.

A Model II expression of individual integrity would include publicly advocating one's position, for example, but would also include making public the reasoning that led to it, inviting its confrontation, and eliciting both the expression and public testing of other individuals' conflicting positions. Reciprocal integrity informed by such a theory-in-use would increase the likelihood that rights and values inherent in conflicting organizational positions would be surfaced, explored, integrated, and enacted.

The idea of reciprocal integrity leads to a reconsideration of exit, voice, and loyalty. Hirschman wrote very little about the *ways* individuals carry out these strategies; he was mainly interested in the consequences of carrying them out at all. But from our perspective, ways are crucially important. A person may express voice, for example, in such a way as to communicate loyalty to a person; she might speak up for an embattled scientist so that other individuals, following her lead, will speak up for individuals on the other side of the issue to whom *they* are loyal. Or her use of voice may communicate loyalty to a principle, so that other individuals following her lead will communicate their loyalty to countervailing principles. Only if her use of voice communicated both advocacy of a principle or person and loyalty to a process of inquiry into her own and others' views would her actions express reciprocal integrity and increase the likelihood that other individuals would do the same.

Those who frame the issue of integrity in terms of individual resistance to organizational pressure tend to blame failures of integrity on organizations, tacitly assuming that individuals free of organizational pressures would be capable of expressing integrity. Sometimes they also claim, as Goffman did, that individuals are most likely to express integrity by distancing themselves from their organizations. If our analysis is correct, however, these assumptions and claims are false. It is true that reducing organizational pressures or increasing one's distance from the organization may enhance the expression of integrity in the prevailing Model I sense. But, as we have argued, Model I expressions of individual integrity tend, paradoxically, to *foster* organizational ineffectiveness and immorality and to lead in the long run to reduced expression of integrity. It is reciprocal integrity that tends to promote recuperation from organizational deterioration. But this sort of integrity demands a kind of competence most of us are unable to display, even under conditions of minimal organizational pressure: an ability to make our theories-in-use congruent with the theories of action we espouse through a kind of inquiry in which we both advocate our beliefs and open them to confrontation. Moreover, the competence to express reciprocal integrity is more likely to be gained by actively engaging organizational pressures than by withdrawal and distancing.

In normal organizational life, however, reciprocal integrity is more often espoused than practiced. Human beings in organizations are more likely to face the reality of potent Model I theories-in-use and their associated defensive routines. It may be attractive, for example, to espouse a principle like "We will not permit a space shuttle to fly unless we have conducted reliable inquiries that lead us to believe it is safe to do so." But acting consistently with such a rule can be difficult when organizational pressures to fly are combined with genuine differences about criteria for adequate safety. The *Challenger* disaster illustrates both how individuals with power were able to impose their views and how those who lost avoided embarrassment by switching from advocacy of their dissident judgments to compliance with formal decision procedures. As one of the engineers testified, "I must emphasize, I had my say, and I never [would] take [away] any management right to take the input of an engineer and . . . reach their own conclusion" ("Presidential Commission . . . ," 1986, p. 93).

In order to break through the barriers to reciprocal integrity, individuals would have to deal with defensive routines that discourage the expression of relevant, valid information because it is potentially threatening or embarrassing. For example, some engineers opposed to the launching began to believe that their superiors were closed to further inquiry because, for the first time, these engineers were made to assume the burden of proving that the shuttle should not fly. Although they felt this difference very strongly, they never discussed it. Indeed, some of them never became explicitly aware of the difference in the stance they were being asked to take until the investigating commission called it to their attention.

Illustrating and Testing Our View

If our analysis is correct, then the remedial actions proposed by managers and legislators to stimulate individual or organizational integrity—measures such as the four listed on pages 201-202—should fail in the long run to achieve their purposes, for they would leave untouched the underlying, Model I dynamics we have described.

More specifically, we predict that when such remedies are introduced into settings where organization members use Model I theories-in-use and associated defensive routines,

1. Reciprocal inquiry aimed at learning from the contending perspectives will not occur.
2. Management will deal with the issues in a manner that may

be caring and supportive but ultimately falls back on unilateral control.

3. Subordinates will see managers' responses as evidence of inconsistency and distance themselves appropriately.

4. Subordinates will maintain their state of compliance coupled with distancing, even though they may act as if they were not doing so.

In this section we describe examples of attempts to implement remedial measures of the four kinds mentioned earlier. In each case we will report what has occurred, or what we believe will occur, in relation to our predictions. We will then describe how the remedy in question might be redesigned in Model II terms and suggest the likely consequences of doing so.

Exhortation. Here, a superior usually combines a plea for risktaking and speaking one's mind with advocacy of excellence and hard work ("Never be satisfied with very good; seek the best!"). The superior may also promise subordinates that they will not be punished for speaking up. For example, Donald Regan's subordinates described him as tough and decisive, at times even cold. Nevertheless, they went on to say, when someone made an honest error, he would often say to the subordinate, "'Forget it, let's get on with it.' He was understanding and forgiving" (Weinraub, 1986, p. 31).

Regan acted in a supportive and caring manner but, when upset, left little doubt whose point of view would prevail. His subordinates, in turn, sensed his caring, dominance, request for candor, and unilateral control of discussion. Not surprisingly, they were "scared stiff of him," noting that he expressed anger with "a look that would stop a locomotive in its tracks." Hence, they spent an inordinate amount of time designing their roles for particular meetings, explaining their posturing by their view of Regan as a "complex man" (p. 36).

Although Regan may have espoused something like reciprocal inquiry, his theory-in-use was consistent with Model I. Consequently, his subordinates spoke their minds up to the point they considered safe and designed their presentations in ways that made them appear candid without betraying whatever they were covering up. All this is consistent with our view.

We would not expect to find, and we did not in the *New York Times* article quoted earlier, that subordinates routinely confronted Regan on actions of his that made reciprocal integrity impossible. For example, a subordinate would not be heard saying, "I appreciate your intent to be supportive, but rather than forget it and get on with it, I would like to examine what happened in order to see what you and I said that prevented full exploration of the issues." Nor would we expect to find a discussion between Regan and his subordinates in which they explored how subordinates used the "complex man" image to rationalize some of their fears as well as their cover-ups. And we would not expect to read that Regan took the initiative to say something like "To what extent did what I say and the way I said it make it less likely for others of you to say what is on your minds?" or "There may be times when my impact on you is to make it less likely that you feel free to be candid, and I appear unaware of that impact. That is the time when I especially want to hear from you." Nor would we expect to read that Regan modeled how others might confront his views not only by asking for their reactions but also by suggesting things they might be thinking but be unwilling to say.

Such an approach is possible in an organization where executives try to foster reciprocal integrity. For example, the CEO of a growing consulting firm, who wanted to obtain more information about his employees' treatment of their clients, devised a reporting form for them to fill out. It contained a list of questions that all of them should cover. He then identified some of the ways such information could be used as a negative control system. He identified fears his subordinates might have and asked whether they had had negative experiences with similar reporting systems elsewhere. His subordinates offered many such examples. The CEO then suggested that a group of his subordinates should meet by themselves to design ways to overcome these dangers. He also identified several negative behaviors of his own, spontaneous and sometimes tacit, that might have to be dealt with. His strategy was not one of exhortation but one of commitment to inquiry, where he took the initiative to identify possible factors that could be counterproductive, beginning with his own behavior, and asked his subordinates to help him design ways to deal with them. His strategy was to show strength through vulnerability combined with inquiry.

Sunshine Laws. "Whistle blowing" and "sunshine" laws are intended to enhance two social values: the free expression of individual views, especially those at odds with formal organizational policy, and the public's right to know what goes on in organizations whose actions affect a public interest. Whistle-blowing laws are more explicitly aimed at the first of these values; sunshine laws, at the second. Underlying both, however, is a concern to enhance public accountability (and reduce the likelihood of harm to the public) by increasing the openness with which organizations conduct their business.

On the basis of the theory proposed in the previous section, we would expect both of these legislative remedies to have paradoxical consequences. In effect, we would expect both individuals and organizations to adapt to their new regulatory environments in terms of the governing variables of their Model I theories-in-use and behavioral worlds. We would expect individuals to learn to mute their public expression of private views when they believe the consequences of open expression would be threatening or embarrassing. We would expect them, nonetheless, to go through the motions of living with the laws, distance themselves from the situations in which they do so, become increasingly cynical about the laws, and perhaps ultimately become unaware of the self-protective strategies they employ.

An interesting study of the effects of sunshine laws on the process of selecting a university president (McLaughlin and Riesman, 1985) provides one instance of outcomes consistent with our predictions. On the basis of their study of the impact of sunshine laws on a recent search process in a state system of higher education, McLaughlin and Riesman conclude: "Unfortunately, the effect of the sunshine law has been the promotion of the value of access to information to the neglect of the ultimate purpose for which sunshine laws were enacted—good government and good decisions" (p. 27).

In the story they tell, a state board of regents established a large selection committee, consisting of campus representatives, community leaders, and students. Sessions of the committee were rigorously kept open to visitors and members of the press, according to a state sunshine law that had recently been enacted.

The committee sought a leader "of national stature" and therefore added to the long list of individuals who had applied for the nationally advertised position some forty or fifty names of prominent persons. They then proceeded through phases in which they sounded out individuals' willingness to be considered for the job, discussed the merits and disadvantages of those who became candidates, telephoned about 100 persons to invite them to be interviewed, conducted a vote to establish a short list of candidates, held on-campus forums for several finalists, and eventually elected one candidate president.

McLaughlin and Riesman point out the following effects of the extraordinary "openness" of the process induced by the sunshine law:

• Most prominent individuals refused to become candidates, at least in part because they did not want their candidacy to become publicly known.

• Committee members were "reluctant to evaluate candidates in any detail in the public setting" and couched their negative views in "vague language" (McLaughlin and Riesman, p. 7). Moreover, candidates were dropped from consideration whenever some committee member—presumed to have special knowledge—hinted vaguely that the candidate might be undesirable. Discussions were marked by an absence of argument and debate, so pervasive that when a committee member said of one candidate, "I don't think he's qualified for dogcatcher, never mind university president!," other members said they found it "refreshing to hear an honest statement" (p. 8).

• At one meeting, an unplanned vote was held to pare the long list of candidates down to a short list. The stated intention was to include only those candidates who received a majority of the votes. After the meeting, individuals privately wondered whether the vote had been a good idea, since only two candidates had received an actual majority of the votes. Later the chairman decided to discard the vote because it had had the unwanted effect of rank-ordering the candidates. But there was no public discussion of the issues raised by the vote. Moreover, the results of the vote—published in the next day's newspapers—revealed that neither of the inside candidates had been supported by on-campus members of the committee, an outcome profoundly embarrassing to all parties.

 • When the list was finally narrowed to two front runners—a sitting university president from another state and a local lawyer active in higher education affairs—a local newspaper announced that the lawyer "had the job secured." Although committee members denied this, the resulting media publicity created the presumption of a front runner. And when a vote was finally taken, the lawyer was unanimously selected. More than a few members of the board of regents had expressed negative views about the lawyer in private conversations with members of the committee. But when the vote was taken, individuals were unwilling to put themselves on record as opposing someone they saw as likely to become the next president.

So the regulated openness intended to foster free expression of personal views and public accountability for decisions had the unintended effect of suppressing the open expression of negative views and squelching debate. Members of the committee stated, when they were interviewed, that they did not want to risk "losing a friend," "provoking litigation," or "making an enemy of the next president." McLaughlin and Riesman observe that the members of the committee, "unable to talk candidly in public, . . . avoid controversy altogether, or talk privately, outside of committee sessions, despite the fact that such conversations are illegal" (p. 26).

Sunshine laws raise a dilemma of openness. In view of the perceived dangers of secrecy, with its potential for the formation of cabals and the exercise of illegitimate pressures on individuals, legislators enact laws that *mandate* decision-making processes open to the public. But openness to public inspection creates threats and pressures of its own. And in the face of these, individuals enact the normal, Model I scenario of suppressing "integrity," in the Model I sense, and muting contention—with results that lead to skepticism about the quality of the decision process and the effectiveness of the law. After the search, McLaughlin and Riesman state, "members of the . . . advisory committee agreed, almost unanimously, that the sunshine law had inhibited open and frank discussion of vital issues" (p. 21). And when the lawyer was named president, "many observers of the search shrugged their shoulders and said, 'But of course.' They assumed that the selection was predetermined; as one person commented cynically, 'As soon as [the winner's] name emerged on the list of candidates, I knew that "the fix" was in.'"

Interestingly, the authors end their paper by proposing an alternative model of decision making: "In our experience, the best searches are those in which search committee members, who may have entered on the process regarding themselves as representatives of particular interests, learn in the course of joint effort to become less defensive about their special interests and more appreciative of each other's contributions" (p. 28). The kind of "learning" suggested here, we believe, implicitly requires reciprocal integrity. For how can individuals "learn" to become more appreciative of each other's contributions and less defensive about their own unless they learn to combine advocacy of their own views with inquiry into the views of their colleagues?

Espousing a New Philosophy of Management. Recently, executives have focused on enhancing organizational effectiveness by making individual integrity more compatible with organizational needs. The vehicle is a new philosophy of management aimed at gaining employees' commitment, in contrast to familiar approaches to management through unilateral control over employees (Lawler, 1986; Walton and Lawrence, 1985). The new philosophy of management requires that employees be given a significant role in designing their tasks, team activities, and structures of governance. It is based not on exhortations to loyalty or pressure for excellence but on providing structural opportunities for employees to control their work life.

Although there is growing literature on the successes (and few failures) of the new philosophy, there are very few detailed accounts of the actual processes and behaviors required to move from unilateral control to high involvement. Perry (1984) has published the most extensive study to date, a case study of Digital Equipment Corporation's Enfield plant project. According to Perry, Digital's top management was initially so committed to the experiment that it delayed opening the new plant for nearly a year in order to make certain that employees received adequate training and that designs produced by employee teams could be implemented.

In this case, where top management espoused the new philosophy but had not yet learned a new theory-in-use to go with it, we would predict that reciprocal inquiry should occur only in relation to nonthreatening issues where no one's integrity was challenged; management would act in a caring and supportive manner until something unexpected and threatening occurred and would fall back on unilateral control; and employees would then see managers' responses as inconsistent and eventually distance themselves appropriately, complying while hiding their distancing.

Perry's account of the Enfield story shows that unexpected consequences did occur, as they often do in pioneering experiments. For example, employees and local management got so involved in managing their work that they overestimated what they could produce. Once top managers saw that the goals defined by the employees were not reached, they began to doubt the credibility of the entire idea. Top managers reacted with strategies of unilateral control and exhortation, revealing their loyalty to principles they were presumably abandoning. Their reactions tended to upset employees and managers at the local level who saw the return to old principles as proof that the entire Enfield project was actually based on principles of control.

Interestingly, Perry's data show that when pressure from the top increased, the firm's inside and outside consultants also returned to principles of unilateral control. Perry provides many examples of employee bewilderment, distancing, and intergroup rivalry that consultants dealt with through exhortation and admonition, almost to the point of being menacing.

An alternative scenario of reciprocal integrity might begin with the consultants' reeducation. They might be educated to help line managers explore unrecognized negative consequences of their new programs. The consultants reacted so negatively and apparently blindly, we believe, because they too had sold their ideas to the managers during their training programs with the same zeal and through the same strategies that line managers used to sell their ideas to employees.

Seminars in which participants were introduced to the new ideas might emphasize possible threats to the program's credibility as much as its possible payoffs. Employees would be encouraged to find ways to disconfirm the new philosophy of management. If they succeeded, they would be given an opportunity either to redesign a more effective program or redefine conditions under which the new rules of management would *not* be used.

Organizational "Dialectic." This term refers to an institutional procedure employed in some business firms to encourage public expression of individual views that may run counter to perceived organizational policy. One firm (the one in the first vignette in this chapter) uses a version of organizational dialectic to make sure that conflicts inherent in the development of new products surface in the form of productive, public debate. Managers responsible for new product development provide special forums in which representatives of research and development, engineering, and marketing groups can air the disagreements that inevitably arise in the career of a new product. In this firm, a division manager observed, "You work like mad to make sure the conflicts surface; it breaks your heart if you find people are protecting you from them."

In another firm, top management has instituted a devil's advocate role, to which individuals are assigned whenever an important policy decision must be made. Managers give the name "dialectic" to the debates that ensue when proponents of a policy proposal—investment in a new business, for example—encounter the arguments advanced by the devil's advocate.

In both cases, managers seek to increase the likelihood that negative information will be assessed, risks fully discussed, and alternative possibilities considered. Their "dialectics" are intended to foster "speaking up," on the several sides of an issue—those against prevailing corporate policy as well as those in favor of it.

The theory described in the previous section leads us to predict the following long-term consequences of these procedures:

- In the first instance, the procedure may work as intended. Individual members of the organization are likely to try acting in the spirit of the procedure, especially when it is reinforced by top management. But their compliance has, at least in part, the meaning of a test: They will be very attentive to management's responses when the chips are down.
- In some situation of stress, where a great deal is at stake in a decision, top management or high-level managers invested in a proposal are likely to deviate from the spirit of the dialectic by resorting to negative sanctions against individuals who speak out against a decision that management favors.
- Under these conditions, individuals learn to treat the dialectic as a mixed message: a procedure to be followed in spirit under conditions of low threat but only to the letter, and not the spirit, when stakes are high.
- So, over time, the dialectic will lose its effectiveness in just those situations where it might be most productive. And, as one consequence of this shift, members of the organization will learn to be cynical about the procedure—and keep their cynicism from public view.

An approximation to this scenario occurred in the company mentioned in the first vignette. Here, after large amounts of money had already been invested in a new product and costly mistakes had been detected and corrected, with resulting delays and further expense, a scientist from the main research laboratory tried to call management's attention to a new issue of product safety. Then informal processes, quite apart from the formal dialectic, took over. Members of the product team responded to the scientist by saying, "Whose side are you on?," "Why don't you do something useful?" And upper management took the scientist to task because he had failed to behave like a team player.

Eventually, as we have already noted, the scientist exited, giving as his principal reason the corporation's insult to his professional integrity. Other laboratory scientists grumbled but camouflaged their grumbling. And the subsequent hero of the story was a product development man who engineered what he called a political solution to the product safety issue, incorporating ideas from the several R&D groups that were in contention over the best way to fix the problem and retain the product's effectiveness. Members of the organization adjusted their understandings of the real significance of the dialectic: Express your criticisms openly, except when the stakes are high.

How might the dialectic have been carried out so as to reduce the likelihood of such outcomes as these? High-level managers might try to model reciprocal integrity as they prepared the ground for the dialectic. They might anticipate, for example, how their own behavior, under stress, could revert to unilateral control of the product development process. They might ask others to design with them a way of monitoring and reviewing actual behavior in the dialectic—managers' and subordinates'—so as to test its congruence with the desired values of surfacing conflict and opening up debate. Managers might seek to make themselves publicly accountable for congruence. These actions would be unlikely to work, however, unless managers had the capacity to demonstrate the reciprocal integrity they wanted from their subordinates and the willingness and competence to inquire with others into their own deviations from the espoused norms of the dialectic.

Summary and Conclusions

According to prevailing conceptions of integrity in organizations, individuals express integrity when they uphold their interests, especially their interests in professional or moral principles, in the face of organizational pressures to do otherwise. Integrity is seen, in this view, as a social virtue essential to the maintenance of moral wholeness and professional identity *and* as a corrective to organizational deterioration.

We have argued that organizational situations in which

questions of integrity arise typically involve conflicting conceptions of integrity, derived from the divergent interests and principles of individuals and organizations. The corrective functions of integrity flow from organization to individual as well as from individual to organization.

In either case, however, expressions of integrity yield long-run consequences opposite to those intended. When all parties express integrity in the prevailing sense, they tend, paradoxically, to contribute to organizational deterioration and reduce the likelihood of further expressions of integrity.

We have explained these paradoxical outcomes by reference to the Model I theories-in-use, behavioral worlds, and defensive routines in which prevailing conceptions of integrity are embedded. These phenomena explain why individuals, acting as agents or organizations or in their own interests, express integrity in such a way as to close off inquiry, polarize organizations, and ultimately create an organizational climate of distancing, hopelessness, and cynicism.

We have proposed an alternative conception, reciprocal integrity, which requires that individuals both advocate their views and encourage inquiry into them, in such a way that other individuals are likely to do the same. Reciprocal integrity requires that individuals behave according to a theory-in-use that we call Model II, whose governing variables are valid information, free and informed choice, and personal causal responsibility for action. We have argued that reciprocal integrity is more likely to reduce the use of defensive routines and promote organizational recuperation from deterioration. But the capacity for reciprocal integrity is unlikely to be created merely by relief from organizational pressures; it demands a fundamental reeducation of individuals with respect to the theories-in-use they bring to their lives in organizations.

Managers and legislators, aware of dangers to organizations and society that arise when the corrective force of integrity declines, have instituted several types of measures to enhance the expression of integrity in organizations. These range from managers' exhortations and policies of high-performance management to organizational dialectics and laws designed to protect or mandate integrity. As a test of our explanatory model, we have predicted likely outcomes of the introduction of these measures. Because they neglect the Model I processes in which prevailing conceptions of integrity are embedded, we have argued, such measures tend, over the long run, to reinforce the very phenomena they are designed to correct—polarization, distancing, and cynicism about change. We have also described and in some cases illustrated how these measures might be redesigned in Model II terms to foster reciprocal integrity.

Our analysis suggests that the larger class of social virtues to which integrity belongs, a class that includes strength, courage, support, caring, and respect, may have very different meanings and organizational consequences depending on the theories of action in which those virtues are embedded.

9

Organizational Alignments, Schisms, and High-Integrity Managerial Behavior

Samuel A. Culbert
John J. McDonough

Managers want power, and they want trust; but rarely
  do they know how to get both.
Without power, they can't get today's job done.
Without trust, they can't get tomorrow's job done.
Faced with a choice, most managers choose power.
However, without both trust and power, there is no
  integrity for the manager.
And without both trust and power, there is no long-term
  effectiveness for the organization.
This forces managers to act schismatically; they espouse
  trust and practice power.

Organizational life is fraught with schisms. Thoughts,
words, and deeds are disconnected. People think one thing and
say another. People say they are doing one thing while they are
doing something else. What is said and done in one moment
is often at odds with what is said and done in the next.

The motives behind these schisms are not necessarily bad.
People set out to achieve goals that they sincerely believe will
benefit their organization. They have tasks to accomplish, responsibilities to exercise, priorities to protect. However, when

223

encountering opposition, they often find no other way to proceed than to bend the truth. Sometimes the bending is done to hide the truth, as the individual knows it, from others; sometimes it is done to hide the truth from oneself. What's more, people don't want others to recognize that deception is involved. Often they don't want to recognize that they themselves are deceiving others.

People reason that, by its very nature, organizational life is a compromise, and as long as what is compromised is not essential to their fundamental personal values or to their basic organizational commitments, then bending the truth is an acceptable thing to do. Thus, the issue that every practical-minded manager and professional struggles with is how to avoid crossing the fine line that separates doing what is necessary to maintain one's organizational power and personal credibility from performing the type of self-serving, organizationally disoriented deception which constitutes dishonesty and deceitful manipulation and which signifies a lack of personal integrity.

In an organization, then, integrity involves far more than merely a congruence of thoughts, words, and deeds or an accuracy of perceptions and an honest portrayal of those perceptions. Integrity also has a great deal to do with the goals an individual sets out to accomplish, the personal and organizational constructiveness of those goals, and whether the individual is acting consistently with his or her priorities for action. Integrity cannot be judged solely by whether or not an individual operates openly, congruently, and without the intent to manipulate. Misrepresentations, self-convenient omissions, politically timed disclosures, self-interested shadings of the truth, and other acts of manipulation and expedience often constitute the organizational skills required for an individual to maintain an empowered course. However, there is a point of excess where one loses integrity and the capacity to engender trust.

What causes people to take great liberties in their representations of the "truth," and what determines when the line separating organizationally valid actions from deceitful, trust-breaking manipulations is crossed? What are the circumstances under which deception is an organizationally constructive skill? These are issues of high interest to us, and they form the subject matter of this chapter.

Alignment

For us the construct alignment is the key to thinking about most facets of an individual's behavior at work and to considering whether they are personally and organizationally constructive. By *alignment* we mean the orientation an individual devises in balancing his or her self-interested pursuits with the production needs of the organization (Culbert and McDonough, 1980). Alignments represent the basic strategy an individual uses in achieving personal and organizational effectiveness (Culbert and McDonough, 1985a), in achieving an empowered organizational course (Culbert and McDonough, 1985b).

Alignments are orientations one develops in response to the need to perform work with many considerations in mind at once. At the same moment, one is concerned with structuring one's job to require skills one possesses in abundance, to not require skills one doesn't possess (or lacks confidence that one can perform with excellence), to feature activities that one finds personally interesting, to require ways of operating that are congruent with one's personal values, to utilize logics and thought processes that are personally relevant, and to make the daily flow of work activities compatible with the rest of one's life commitments. What's more, all these personal considerations take place with a concern for performing functions and producing work that the organization needs and expects to receive from one in a professional role and position.

With considerations as extensive and complex as the above, as well as others too numerous to list, there is no way that an individual can give checklist-conscious attention to each and perform spontaneously with the appearance of competence. In order to perform competently, and appear that way, an individual needs an orientation, what we call an alignment, not a checklist of concerns. An alignment allows a person to focus on each situation or organizational event and immediately react to it in ways that simultaneously are personally, professionally, and organizationally relevant.

Alignments, then, are the orientations and participation strategies that an individual works out for being personally and organizationally effective. They determine an individual's basic predisposition to organizational events—how an individual sees and interprets the situations he or she finds him- or herself in and the actions other people take. When a person lacks an alignment—say, at the start of a new job, when he or she has not been able to comprehend the circumstances sufficiently to see what opportunities for expression and contribution exist—the person's actions tend to be disjunctive and uncertain, and the individual appears to operate as if he or she were in "structure shock." After the person has worked out an alignment, he or she reacts spontaneously in a way that instantaneously decodes the opportunities and threats each situation holds. "Instinctively" he or she knows the conditions that need to be present in order to operate with personal power and is sensitive to the presence of conditions that work against his or her effectiveness.

We see three categories of alignments: effective, ineffective, and organizationally powerful. We say an individual has an effective alignment when that individual has worked out a way of orienting him- or herself that is, in that individual's mind, both personally meaningful and organizationally productive. We say that an individual has an ineffective alignment when that person operates in a personally meaningful way without producing an organizational product that he or she can value. We also say an individual has an ineffective alignment when that person orients to a set of productivity goals in a way that is self-depriving and perhaps even self-alienating.

We see an individual's orientation, or alignment, as organizationally powerful when there is external acceptance and credibility for how that individual is operating and what he or she is trying to produce in the way of organizational product. The alignment is organizationally powerful because the context that others use in relating to organizational events makes it so. Their ways of framing organizational events causes the individual's perceptions, actions, and orientations to work events to be seen as relevant and organizationally valuable.

Being seen in a context that values one's alignment allows an individual to operate with feelings of personal empowerment, knowing that his or her every spontaneous action will evoke an organizationally creditable response even when specific others, with different alignments, feel the need to oppose what her or she advocates. This contrasts with having an alignment that lacks context, one that lacks widespread understanding and support and requires that an individual constantly elaborate and justify his or her actions or suffer nonacceptance. With context, the organizational effectiveness reasons behind someone's actions are usually apparent. Without context, one constantly has to provide others with a rationale that links what one is doing to an organizational imperative for it.

A person with an effective alignment who has context, what one might call organizational power, has a personally empowered position where doing for one's self and doing for the organization are interrelated. In such a position a person knows that his or her perceptions and actions will be viewed as credible by those whose support is crucial to gaining organizational acceptance for what he or she is attempting and how he or she is going about it.

However, effective alignments are not always organizationally powerful. An individual's orientation may be personally and organizationally productive but be resisted by others in the organization. The resistance may be for "valid" or "invalid" organizational reasons. On the invalid side, others may perceive the context needs of the individual to be competitive with their own needs for context and for that reason be reluctant to make a response that might support or endorse the picture of reality on which the first individual's actions are based. They fear supporting any view of reality that makes it more difficult for them, with their own needs for context, to succeed.

On the valid side, others may believe that an individual's effective alignment entails an orientation that is out of focus with the dominant orientation of their work team or even their organization. They may see the press of daily operations as too urgent to take time out to search for a mutually empowered organization fit, or they may have actually spent time searching and discovered that the empowerment needs of the individual and the stability needs of the organization would be most efficiently served if the individual went somewhere else. In such situations, the most efficient solution is for the individual and his or her superiors to effect a no-fault separation. We say "no-fault" because the separation is based on a lack of fit rather than an attack on the departing person's abilities.

Alignments and Executive Integrity

As mentioned above, an individual's alignment encompasses skills, nonskills, interests, and life-beyond-work commitments; it includes what the individual is committed to accomplishing in the way of living a personally meaningful life in and out of the organization. In encompassing values, an alignment includes the types of relationships an individual pursues and the tactics he or she entertains in his or her drive to be effective. In encompassing organizational productivity, an alignment includes what the individual is committed to producing for the benefit and productivity of the organization. Thus, when the topic is executive integrity, one begins by scrutinizing the private commitments that compose an individual's alignment and then examines how well what an individual is working toward personally matches up with the goals and values of the organization.

An individual's alignment, then, is the crucial frame of reference to use in judging whether that person is on course with self-beliefs and organizational priorities. It is what one needs to know in determining whether any action an individual takes can have self-integrity or organizational integrity. If a person's alignment—one's basic orientation to work events—fails to express his or her fundamental priorities, then any action that individual takes, no matter how well it conforms to formally stated organizational priorities, lacks integrity. Thus, as part of considering the integrity issues entailed in an individual's organizational actions, one must examine that person's alignment and determine how well the orientation he or she is pursuing embodies the higher-order interests of both that individual and the system. By *system* we refer to an ever-enlarging circle of social groupings, beginning with one's immediate organizational unit and, depending on the viewer, expanding to include the interests of one's department, the entire organization, and perhaps even the society as a whole.

Of course, different people with unique alignments apply organizational standards differently in evaluating one another's orientations. The reason is that each individual's interpretation of organizational standards is as much associated with that person's own empowerment needs as with broad organizational rules and ethics. In organizations, as in any social setting, absolute standards for ethical and social conduct do exist. However, what we want to emphasize is that each person's interpretations and applications of these standards are relativistic. They are as much a function of that individual's own alignment as of organizational imperatives and philosophical absolutes.

In our model, it is possible for an individual with an ineffective alignment to operate with integrity, but only for a short while. An individual whose alignment is ineffective, who sacrifices personal meaning in order to produce what he or she thinks the organization requires, can initially operate with integrity. However, we expect that the focus this individual brings to his or her organizational activities will gradually lose its contemporary relevance. Without a meaningful self-interested focus, one's contributions become stale. The individual lacks the internal cues necessary to upgrade the character of his or her contributions and becomes overly dependent on what other people think is organizationally correct. In our minds, such a situation is devoid of integrity.

Conversely, an individual whose alignment is ineffective because that person orients primarily in terms of self-interest, without producing what that person believes the organization requires of him or her, will eventually suffer from a lack of self-respect and come to doubt the integrity of what formerly had self-meaning. We believe that everyone's self-esteem is connected to feelings of organizational productivity and that one's feelings of integrity suffer when one believes one is not returning the proper value in exchange for one's organizational pay.

Only after an individual's alignment has been scrutinized for personal meaning and organizational productivity is it possible to meaningfully examine the integrity of that individual's actual behavior. That is, an individual's goals and inner commitments may have high integrity, but the behavior that he or she takes to implement those goals and commitments may lack integrity. Of course, if examination of an individual's alignment reveals a lack of integrity, whether the standards used to judge integrity are universal to the culture or idiographic to the person reviewing the first individual's commitments, then it is meaningless to examine further.

To summarize what we have presented thus far: In an organization, the minimal condition that must be satisfied before an individual can be considered to function with *self-integrity* is for that individual to possess a self-meaningful set of personal and organizational commitments and strategies for accomplishing them—an effective alignment. And the minimal condition necessary for that individual to function with *organizational integrity* is to have the commitments contained within that effective alignment generally viewed to be in conformance with the dominant values and production standards of the organization.

Thus, for most people, most of the time, having an effective alignment is not enough. Organizational acceptance for that effective alignment is also required. People need to feel empowered, and usually this requires the support of a harmonious relationship between their alignment and the dominant reality of their organization. Occasionally people lacking a harmonious relationship with the dominant reality can tough it out without compromising their self-integrity, but usually not for long. Eventually something has to give. Either the organization must change to incorporate the insights contained in their "disenfranchised" orientations, or they will shift to a schism-ridden, deceptive course in a last-ditch effort to achieve a sense of personal empowerment.

Schisms

Now we are ready to extend beyond the integrity issues involved in an individual's alignment to examine the integrity issues involved in an individual's actual behavior. We are particularly interested in how an individual deals with the schisms of organizational life, because this is a weak point in most people's behavior. Most people relate to schisms with schisms of their own, justifying their deceptions on the grounds that they are merely doing what is necessary to protect the integrity of their commitments in an organizational world where others are deceiving them. Hence, we are particularly interested in examining whether an intentionally deceptive communication in the service of protecting a high-integrity orientation represents a lack of integrity in the person making it. In thinking this through with us, keep in mind that for most people, most of the time, there is little organizational integrity without a strong sense of personal empowerment.

In our model three relationships are crucial to examining the integrity of an individual's behavior: the individual in relation to himself or herself, the individual in relation to the particular others with whom he or she is transacting, and the individual in relation to the organization (or institution) and the system.

The Individual in Relation to Him- or Herself. Whether a person possesses an effective alignment is the beginning point for examining that person's integrity, not the end. An effective alignment must be maintained, implemented, and upgraded. Maintaining an effective alignment requires that an individual possess a strong sense of self and a strong inner orientation. Implementing an effective alignment requires that an individual have an impact on others and establish an accepting organizational context in which his or her thoughts and contributions get valued. And upgrading an effective alignment requires that an individual learn from the responses his or her thoughts and actions elicit and, where relevant, modify his or her alignment to incorporate this feedback.

Even with an effective alignment, the problems of living in a schism-ridden organizational world are considerable. Others are on their own alignment-oriented course, self-conveniently characterizing organizational events in ways that differ from one's own perceptions and conflict with the interpretations and framing of events that satisfy one's own needs for context and empowerment. One walks a tightrope between self-alienation and alienation from those others. An individual who accepts other people's portrayals of organizational events and acts as if they were correct risks alienation from his or her own perceptions and alignment-determined interpretations; an individual who acts as if other people's portrayals of organizational events were incorrect encounters aggressiveness and often hostility and finds him- or herself alienated from others. Thus, at issue is how to accept and learn from feedback in an environment where few people understand that one has an alignment-determined view of organizational events, where almost no one knows what one's alignment is, and where almost everyone is inclined to view the presence of differences in viewpoints as threatening to his or her own ends.

In our experience we find that individuals who are not sufficiently conscious of their alignments have a difficult time achieving an empowered course and insulating themselves from external distractions. They have difficulty discriminating between battles that must be fought, to establish and ensure the conditions that preserve their personal integrity, and battles that are better overlooked, because nothing essential to important self and organizational priorities is at stake. They have trouble discriminating between reactions and feedback that should be taken at face value and those that are contaminated by other people's agendas. Everyone recognizes that working in an organization involves some compromise, and everyone knows that integrity in an organization involves not compromising on certain essentials. However, without a good sense of one's alignment, one runs the risk that conflicts engaged in to preserve the integrity of one's orientation will become ends in themselves. In the absence of understanding exactly what one must protect, one mistakenly reasons that because one is involved in a fight to protect integrity, one has integrity.

As we have been describing, alignment needs and the desire to operate with empowerment provide people with the motive and propensity to see organizational events self-conveniently. To us, a high-integrity response entails that the individual operate with an openness to external data and feedback that might disconfirm self-convenient and empowering portrayals of organizational events. That is, the individual will be open to reality portrayals that are more "objectively" consistent with the facts.

Thus, a key dimension in evaluating someone's commitment to high-integrity behavior encompasses whether that person recognizes that he or she views events in biased ways, recognizes what many of those biases are, and actively seeks data and facts that might alert him or her to when and how personal biases are dominating the way organizational reality is being construed. In short, high-integrity behavior requires that a person understand that he or she has adopted an alignment and be committed both to learning what that alignment is and to making modifications that result in upgraded personal and organizational effectiveness. This is the self-knowledge necessary for an individual to pursue an empowered organizational course.

The Individual in Relation to Others. How does someone who recognizes that he or she functions with an alignment-centered picture of organizational events and who wants to make a high-integrity response deal with others who similarly view all organizational events self-conveniently but who have little consciousness that they do? We find this a particularly challenging question, since each individual's needs for context and feelings of empowerment depend on others' modifying their alignment-centered views of organizational events to better value what that individual is trying to achieve. However, in observing how most "others" operate, we find a set of responses that can readily block a high-integrity-oriented individual from accepting responsibility for his or her alignment-centered view of organizational events. An integrity-oriented person will find:

- That most people are but minimally sensitive to how their own sentiments, subjective attachments, and personal biases affect their work style and orientation.
- That most people are very sensitive to how another individual's sentiments, subjective attachments, and personal biases affect that other person's work style and orientation.
- That most people readily see how another individual's sentiments, subjective attachments, and personal biases can

detract from the quality of that other individual's participation.

• That most people do not accurately comprehend how another
  individual's sentiments, subjective attachments, and personal
  biases can enhance the quality of that person's participation.
• That most people are only minimally sensitive to how their
  own sentiments, subjective attachments, and personal biases
  compete with or block the quality of another individual's
  participation.
• That most people hold others, and the system, responsible
  for the shortfall in their performance—that is, for structuring relationships and situations in ways that prevent them
  from efficiently producing what they have to contribute of
  value.

This set of observations paints a picture of other people pursuing their self-interests, seeking out empowerment, blocking the
empowerment of others, and taking little, if any, responsibility
for the role they might play in helping others to operate more
effectively. It portrays a competitive organizational environment
in which one person's integrity—that person's effective, empowered alignment—is pursued at the expense of other people's
integrity. It raises the question whether respect and active consideration for the alignment needs of those who hold divergent
and competing views should be included as a necessary dimension of an individual's integrity. Certainly the needs of the
organization are best served if as many people as possible achieve
effective and empowered alignments. But can one be expected
to support the empowerment needs of others at the expense oɪ
one's own empowerment?

　　　Years of consulting and alerting managers and professionals to opportunities to enhance the empowerment of others
has taught us that supporting the empowerment needs of the
people with whom one is competing entails more vulnerability
and open-ended responsibility than most people are inclined to
take. It involves spreading out one's focus so broadly that one
fears losing the capacity to pursue one's own alignment-centered
view of organizational events. Practical issues of maintaining
one's own power and the organization's power are involved.

We find that even people possessing what appears to be the highest integrity eventually snap back to taking the most limited, or even no, responsibility for others once they feel their own power compromised. Nevertheless, the possibility of extending oneself to actively support the empowerment needs of another person does not exist until one is familiar with that person's specific alignment and the context needs that the person attempts to meet in achieving an empowered course. To us, at a minimum, a high-integrity response entails maintaining a sensitivity to and active inquiry into the alignments of others and the organizational perspectives that might afford them context. Whether or not one can openly acknowledge and empathize with the context needs of others is a practical matter that depends on the politics of the moment.

To our way of seeing things, high-integrity performance includes concern for the empowerment needs of others and the empowerment needs of the team as a whole, but not at the expense of integrity for oneself. If one cannot afford to take responsibility for the context and empowerment needs of key others, we think one must, at least, be sensitive to their alignment needs and the conditions for their empowerment and be amenable to making a supportive response should the politics of the situation eventually permit it.

The Individual in Relation to the Organization. Professionals and especially managers have responsibility that extends beyond the integrity of their own participation: responsibility for preserving the integrity of the organization. There are systems to create, to install, to maintain. Each managerial action must be evaluated both on its own merits and against the criterion of how it affects the system. Potentially, every managerial response can set a system precedent and cause people to modify the participation parameters and constraints they take as givens.

Once an individual interprets his or her managerial or professional role to include the integrity of the system, that individual usually finds him- or herself on the receiving end of countless schisms. One interacts with people directed primarily by self-serving, alignment-centered perceptions and logics acting with little, if any, immediate concern for how their actions affect the system. Of course, no one with any political savvy admits to being unconcerned with the well-being of the system, and most, in fact, disguise their self-centered advocacies by asserting that what they are doing or proposing is motivated primarily by concern for the productivity and strength of the system.

As we noted in the previous section, most managers are skilled in decoding self-serving advocacies and in identifying the personal motives and negative biases contained in the actions and words of others. The question, of course, is what to do about it. Does one directly confront the other person on the schism, or does one try to compensate for the schism covertly? We find that most people are inclined to avoid confrontation, fearing that a direct encounter will only result in the other person's denial, which is a second schism. So they deal with matters covertly. This tactic, by definition, entails meeting a schism with a schism. What one appears to be doing is not at all what one is actually doing. What one is doing is not motivated primarily by the reason one gives for doing it. The person one is dealing with may not even be the main person that one is trying to affect.

We find that few people defending the system against the self-serving advocacies of others interpret their use of schisms as a breach of integrity. Most see their use as doing what the job requires in the way of looking out for the welfare of the system as a whole. For us this is a topic of considerable deliberation, since a large percentage of our consulting time is spent in behind-the-scenes discussions, helping managers decode the needs of the system and the behavior and motives of others in contemplating what type of managerial response will ensure preservation of the system and its integrity. However, the process of helping managers contain the alignment-centered strivings of others periodically confronts us with the fact that most of the schismatic acts managers take in the service of protecting the system conveniently protect themselves as well. "Inadvertently" managers find self-indulgent ways to protect the system from the indulgences of those they see as neglecting it.

Accordingly, we think high-integrity behavior includes a commitment to decoding the self-serving aspects of the stands one takes when acting in behalf of the system. It entails considering the extent to which one's own self-interested and empowerment pursuits are competitive with the productivity needs of the organization and limiting self-indulgences. It entails respect for the self-interested pursuits and empowerment motives of others, particularly when one judges their productivity to be contributory to the system. It entails an active desire to produce what we call "win/win/*win* outcomes," in which an individual tries to frame reality in ways that simultaneously attend to his or her own needs, the needs of the system, and the needs of someone else. It entails some self-sacrifice, in that the needs of the system and the needs of another are occasionally pursued to the neglect or detriment of one's own self-interested pursuits. It entails occasionally settling for win/win outcomes, in which one's own needs and the needs of the system are pursued in a reality framework that excludes the possibility of meeting the needs of someone else. However, in the latter instance, high-integrity behavior entails an inclination to rectify the neglect of others when the means for doing so, without abandoning one's responsibilities to the organization and to oneself, become apparent.

High-Integrity Managerial Behavior

To this point our analysis of high-integrity managerial behavior reveals few absolutes. Before the fact, before one performs any act or makes any managerial response, one can and should have a set of high-integrity commitments both to oneself and to the organization. Our model calls this an "effective alignment." However, whether or not an individual subsequently is able to operate with high integrity, by avoiding the intentional use of schisms, or whether the conscious use of schisms in a particular situation—say, to defend the integrity and effectiveness of the system—constitutes a lack of integrity are matters for further deliberation.

Most basically there is the question whether any intentional use of schisms constitutes a breach in an individual's integrity. For our parts, we find it difficult to discriminate between a conscious misrepresentation to accomplish a self-convenient end, commonly called a lie, and (1) a self-convenient portrayal of the ''truth'' as the individual knows it or (2) a partial and calculatedly timed representation of it or (3) an intentional omission aimed at tricking others into thinking one's beliefs or behaviors are different than they are, which respectively we call ''framing,'' ''fragmenting,'' and ''playing it both ways'' (Culbert and McDonough, 1980). All these are universally used ways of furthering one's own ends by attempting to modify other people's beliefs about organizational events and reality, albeit often with the needs and interests of the organization in mind. In this way, organizational life is inherently political. People with different self-interests, alignments, and needs for context vie with one another to get the dominant reality reconceptualized consistently with their pursuits. Certainly participation in these political processes, to ensure one's empowerment, does not automatically disqualify an individual from having his or her behavior seen as high-integrity. If it did, no person possessing organizational power would be seen as functioning with high integrity.

Emotionally our sentiments parallel the conclusions reached by Sissela Bok (1978, 1982), who took up these issues in a slightly different social context. Consistently with Kant, she concludes that telling the truth is the unconditional duty of the individual and that to do otherwise denigrates the integrity of that individual. However, she also concludes that *withholding* the truth—secrecy and concealment—is indispensable to the workings of a modern society and therefore is not in itself good or bad. As mentioned above, distinguishing among conscious misrepresentations to accomplish a self-convenient end, lying, and calculated and selective sharing to accomplish a self-convenient end is not a separation that we can logically make.

In our use of the term *alignment,* by definition, all statements of the truth are relative and biased by one's needs for context and empowerment. We do not think people can function with high integrity toward others without internalizing and taking responsibility for this fact. Emotionally, dishonesty is abhorrent to us, but logically, we recognize that all organizational behavior is calculated. People are ever negotiating and renegotiating facets of the dominant organizational reality in an effort to get context for their self- and organizational pursuits. Not accepting this fact is, for us, the ultimate schism.

As we see things, the main obstacle blocking the integrity strivings of the practical manager in contemporary organizations is the managerial environment itself. Despite considerable rhetoric to the contrary, today's environment does not emphasize each individual's need for alignment or promote choices that are good for both the individual and the organization (Culbert and McDonough, 1985a). This is a blatant oversight, given that people are focused mainly on their self-interested pursuits and needs for empowerment and, for the most part, possess the means to modify and distort the formulation of organizational events in conformance to their own needs and interests. Organizations insist on defining the function and role to be performed before they select the individual to fill them and, except in rare instances, refuse to redefine or significantly modify them after the individual is recruited. Instead, organizations attempt to socialize and reshape the individual and install excessive controls to this end (Culbert, 1974).

To us, creating an environment in which people can upgrade the integrity of their behavior is relatively straightforward. It is implied in everything we have written to this point. People need effective alignments, they need to feel empowered, and their management has to accept these as legitimate needs requiring active organizational acknowledgment and support. At its core, an organization is a highly subjective entity, and the life each individual leads there is determined as much by internal forces, and by self-centered and biased characterizations of external forces, as by any dominant or "objective" reality that it meets management's convenience to impose on the individual. Elsewhere (Culbert and McDonough, 1985a, 1985c) we have made a careful point of emphasizing our beliefs that, in organizations, people live two realities simultaneously—their own and that of the dominant organizational culture—and that for most people the two realities are distinct and competing. Although the individual who is on an empowered course attempts to achieve as much overlap as possible between his or her own reality and the reality of the dominant organizational culture, we believe that his or her self-integrity and independence of personal identity depend on keeping these realities separate. Ignoring differences between the two creates too much confusion, for oneself as well as for others, to the detriment of both one's self-interests and the credibility of one's actions in the organization. Management needs to accept this as a given.

We believe that the question of integrity in one's operations—how one acts after one has an effective alignment—comes down to whether an individual's self-convenient framing of reality leaves other people with the freedom and choice to see organizational events differently and to frame reality self-conveniently for themselves. Optimally, we see the symbols of high-integrity behavior as honesty in searching out the truth for oneself; commitment to sensitizing oneself to the alignments of those with whom one interacts; diligence in presenting facets of truth that, in one's sensitivity to the alignments of particular others, one knows matter significantly to a particular other; and perseverance in working toward reformulations of the dominant reality that empower oneself and others as well. However, today's managerial culture lacks widespread and committed acceptance of a model that links self-interested behavior to every organizational act and perception, such as what we offer in our construct of alignment, thereby rendering people vulnerable to discreditation whenever the connection between the organizational actions they take and their self-interests is made.

Thus, we concede that, in today's managerial environment, schisms are an inevitability on which the practical-minded professional must rely. For the time being we must submerge our Kantian emotions and settle for a morality that is sensitive to the political situations people face when they seek empowerment in organizational settings that do not recognize as legitimate the ingrained and ever-present pursuit of such interests. Instead of seeking rules for enforcing a set of rationally conceived moral principles that create expectations of impartial, unbiased, and objective behaviors from people whose viewpoints are subjectively determined, we find ourselves seeking frameworks for comprehending high-integrity, personally and organizationally effective efforts that respect other people's subjective interests along with one's own.

In today's management environment, honesty, truth seeking, and totally aboveboard performances are desired but cannot be delivered irrespective of practical considerations for achieving organizational empowerment. However, we believe there is no integrity when the goal becomes maintenance of one's organizational empowerment irrespective of the means one uses and of one's impact on those who similarly have a right to empowerment. Because other people have their own alignments that cause them to see organizational events differently, because the dominant reality that governs the formal framing of organizational events is more the result of political compromise than of any individual's actual perceptions, and because organizational participation is, by definition, a compromise, one cannot tell the truth in absolute terms (or withhold it) without concern for the impact that the truth (or the lack of it) will have on others. Thus, as much as telling the truth has the capacity to signify the presence of integrity, to us neglecting the impact that one's words, perceptions, and activities hold for those whose actions also contribute to the organization's productivity signifies a lack of integrity.

In conclusion, we see the character of the managerial environment as far more critical in determining the presence of high-integrity behavior than we see the character and heroics of any individual manager. In organizations, morality is relative, and the best thing that executives with high-integrity ideals can do is to create the conditions under which others can achieve personally effective alignments, can operate with responsibility for facilitating the alignment-determined behavior of others as well as themselves, and can organizationally succeed. Along these lines, we see three levels of insights that, when institutionalized, can create the conditions for high-integrity behavior:

- First, there needs to be widespread understanding and acceptance of the fact that each individual operates with a unique alignment.

- Second, there needs to be widespread empathy for the fact that each individual seeks a slightly different brand of personal and organizational empowerment.
- Third, there need to be widespread caring and involvement in the framing of organizational events so that people with different alignments and different needs for empowerment can simultaneously succeed.

Embracing these insights will not do away with organizational politics. Politics are inevitable—they occur whenever two or more persons with different alignment-centered orientations see the same organizational situation differently. But when insights such as those above are made part of the dominant organizational culture, we expect that the politics will be carried out in a way that promotes high-integrity self-reflective and organizationally effective behavior.

10

International Dimensions of Executive Integrity: Who Is Responsible for the World

Nancy J. Adler
Frederick B. Bird

As we focus our attention on society's problems, will our "solution" reflect [our] inability to see the forest for the trees? Will we solve racism by eliminating race? Will we deal with hazardous factors in the workplace by identifying and removing people whose genotypes render them more sensitive to the factors rather than cleaning up the workplace? Will we handle environmental toxics by engineering people to tolerate higher levels of contaminant? Will the ultimate military tool for global skirmishes be weapons with complete ethnic specificity? Unless we confront the profound *limitations* to the insights and impact of science and technology, we will never gain any hope of controlling this powerful way of knowing [David Suzuki, 1986].

Daily our ears are assaulted by global crises: famine in Ethiopia; the AIDS epidemic; recurrent terrorist attacks leveled against Tylenol users, airline passengers, and Lebanon-based journalists; continued international, interracial, and interreligious violence, equally visible between Iran and Iraq, Afghanistan and Pakistan, North Ireland's warring factions, and the blacks, whites, and coloureds within South Africa's apartheid system; the insubstantial progress on arms control; the growth of addiction to drugs and of drug-related crime; poverty; over-population—and the list goes on.

With growing frequency, questionable corporate conduct accompanied by predictably unfortunate consequences confronts us: the Chernobyl meltdown, bank failures within an increasingly fragile worldwide financial system combined with the simultaneous emergence of superbanks, Wall Street's bout with insider trading, hazardous nuclear and toxic waste disposal, the specter of national insolvency, negligent quality control, questionable safety practices causing such disasters as South Africa's latest mine fire, Union Carbide's Bhopal tragedy, and NASA's *Challenger* explosion.

With equal intensity and frequency, we hear of increasing global competition across markets, industries, technologies, and organizations: a global imperative. The critical importance of international competition to the future of business has become self-evident. Even in the United States, with the largest single domestic market, "imports and exports as a percentage of GNP doubled between 1970 and 1980; 70 percent of all [American] domestic markets now face competition" (Vogel, 1986, p. 145). To succeed, many formerly domestic managers must work outside their own cultural and national environment. These trends toward the globalization of business are no longer novel; their impacts will continue to be felt throughout the coming decades. As management has expanded from its previous domestic base to an international, and now a global, scope, our approach to managerial integrity must also expand.

How should we respond to the global trends and world crises? To date, we have had too few opportunities to question, let alone applaud, corporations' responses to the global environment. Is the explanation that corporations are remiss, or that governments, rather than corporations, bear the responsibility for global governance? Have the models for structuring our understanding of global dynamics failed to guide us toward identifying effective approaches, let alone "answers," at both the corporate and the governmental levels?

Paradoxically, to date, people in international business appear not to have considered integrity very important. As shown in Table 1, studies across eleven Asian, European, and

Table 1. International Negotiators' Perceptions.

	$Nation^a$										
	J	K	PRC	T	F	E	G	C/E	C/F	M	B	US
Negotiator Sees Counterpart As[b]												
Exploitative (versus accommodating)	2.6	2.2	3.6	2.5	3.0	2.6	2.9	2.7	3.0	2.8	3.1	2.7
Honest (versus deceptive)	3.7	3.9	4.2	3.9	3.5	3.3	3.5	3.6	3.7	3.8	4.2	3.7
Unbiased (versus biased)	N.A.	3.6	3.8	3.4	3.2	2.9	3.5	2.9	2.6	3.7	3.8	2.8
Negotiator Sees Self As[b]												
Exploitative (versus accommodating)	2.7	2.5	4.3	2.7	3.3	3.2	3.2	2.9	3.0	3.2	3.3	3.0
Honest (versus deceptive)	3.6	3.7	4.3	3.6	3.2	2.8	3.6	3.4	3.5	3.8	4.0	3.3
Unbiased (versus biased)	N.A.	3.4	4.2	3.7	3.0	2.6	3.7	2.8	2.5	3.6	4.0	2.6
Importance of Nego-tiator Traits[c]												
Trusting temperament	4.5	2.4	2.5	4.7	5.2	5.3	3.3	5.9	4.0	3.6	3.3	6.1
Integrity	2.6	4.6	2.9	4.1	2.8	3.4	4.5	3.2	3.9	3.6	3.1	2.7
Ethics	5.1	3.4	4.9	4.3	2.7	4.3	5.2	4.8	4.5	5.1	3.8	4.9

[a] Legend: J, Japan; K, Korea; PRC, People's Republic of China; T, Taiwan; F, France; E, England; G, Germany; C/E, Canada/English; C/F, Canada/French; M, Mexico; B, Brazil; US, United States.

[b] Five-point scale from 1 (first characteristic listed) to 5 (second characteristic, in parentheses).

[c] Eight-point scale of importance from 1 (most important) to 8 (least important).

Source: John L. Graham, School of Business, University of Southern California.

North and South American countries revealed that business negotiators in each country rated themselves as less honest and more
exploitative than their counterparts.[1] They saw integrity as a fairly
important trait in negotiators but not as one of the most important traits (rating it from 2.6 to 4.6, across the eleven countries,
on an 8-point scale of importance), and the same negotiators rated
business ethics as even less important than integrity. Moreover, informal interviews with thirty-one European and North
American international executives by the senior author produced
similar results. The executives' most common response to the
question "To you, what is the meaning and importance of
managerial integrity in your work and in your company?" was
"It is not a problem for us." Although we could easily interpret
their response as defensive or attribute it to the phrasing of the
question, the results clearly fail to support the belief that international businesspeople perceive business ethics and integrity
to be critical and central to their own or their organization's success. Why? Perhaps integrity is thought to be unrealizable or
an exercise in personal heroics. Perhaps, though well aware of
the meaning of integrity, executives are unaware of the personal
and organizational costs of managing without integrity.

In this chapter we take the perspective that integrity is
achievable and that acting without integrity has severe personal
and organizational costs. We address the question of executive
integrity from a global perspective. We recognize that the comparative issues of morality and integrity are essential, but our
focus goes beyond comparison to intercultural interaction and
integration. The chapter proposes a practical and relevant way
of viewing integrity for international executives who daily must
resolve numerous transnational dilemmas. Although our ap-

---

[1]John L. Graham, of the School of Business, University of Southern
California, has conducted research on within-culture negotiating partners across
eleven cultures on four continents: Asia (Japan, Korea, Taiwan, and the People's Republic of China), North America (English- and French-speaking Canada
and the United States), South America (Brazil and Mexico), and Europe (England,
France, and Germany). One of the authors (Adler) has been involved with the
Canadian and the PRC Chinese studies and is currently investigating the issue
of perceived integrity across the eleven cultures.

proach may well be useful for those working within culturally homogeneous domestic environments, our focus is on multinational and multicultural contexts. In no way is this chapter audacious enough to give solutions; we hope it is cogent enough to suggest new approaches.

Integrity

Ethical behavior is on some levels universal and on many others culture-specific. Evaluations of morally correct and incorrect business behavior vary across cultures. For example, "Thou shalt not kill" is universal and, luckily, not an issue most managers face. Unfortunately, primarily as a result of unintended consequences of corporate action, it is faced. By contrast, definitions of honesty are not universal—they are strongly colored by particular cultures' evaluations. For example, is *caveat emptor* ("buyer beware") dishonest, as many American consumer protection laws imply, or good business, as is Hong Kong's implicit and explicit reality? It all depends on the culture. Managers working internationally continually face culturally contingent definitions of correct and incorrect behavior.

Integrity is one of a number of moral virtues relevant for managers, including industry, reliability, justice, a sense of social responsibility, empathy, and courage. Although it is impossible to arrive at a purely objective, amoral definition of integrity, we can begin to indicate the meaning of integrity by recognizing that having integrity and being moral are not identical. This lack of identity often becomes particularly apparent when working internationally. Foreign colleagues may possess a high degree of integrity but in relation to moral standards that differ considerably from our own. Other foreigners may act in keeping with similar moral standards to ours but possess little integrity. Working across cultures often involves working with people whose definitions of morality and integrity neither coincide with our own nor are fully recognizable or easily understood by us.

A Definition. Integrity is associated with several traits, including the following:

Self-integration, or centeredness—a clear sense of identity and focus for action; the ability to incorporate various activities within an identifiable sense of purpose.

Principled consistency, entailing the capacity to operate with self-consistency in various roles and settings (for example, at home, at work, at civic occasions, and at societal occasions; with workers, managers, consumers, investors, officials, and so on), based on the same fundamental principles or ways of interacting.

Self-candor—the absence of self-deception; personal honesty, at least with respect to oneself and generally apparent in relation to others.

Integrity implies having more than simply a clear sense of identity. It involves a morally defined sense of self. Those who have integrity are characteristically presumed to have two additional traits: the capacity to resist attractive alternative actions that compromise matters of principle and the capacity to assume risks in defense of these principles.

Consequences of Acting Without Integrity. We can gain a better understanding of the particular nature of integrity by approaching it indirectly—that is, by examining how managers with little or no integrity act. First, since to possess integrity is to act consistently, managers lacking a clear sense of integrity are likely to act in inconsistent and seemingly inexplicable ways. For example, managers lacking integrity might insist in impersonal relations with suppliers in one setting while in another being quite willing to give and accept personal favors. Executives with low integrity might provide workers in one country with generous wages and pension programs while providing neither in a neighboring country. Such inconsistencies confuse those with whom managers regularly interact by creating uncertainty and changing expectations.

By definition, to possess integrity is to act with consistency; the real issue is how we define and gauge this consistency. Frequently, we define it mechanistically in relation to some set of rules or codes that allows little discretion in its application (Durkheim, 1893/1933). What we expect is similarity of overt behavior. Clearly, organizations find such consistency very difficult to achieve, especially when operating across different nations and cultures. Organizations cannot establish exactly the same wage guidelines, retirement programs, and incentive plans for societies in which the standard of living varies markedly. Such consistency, beyond being difficult to achieve in the face of public pension programs ranging from ample to nonexistent and definitions of social life varying from highly individualistic to collective, becomes irrational. To aim at achieving consistency through "likeness of overt behavior" is to ignore variations in context—specifically, in international operations, the cultural context of each foreign location.

Hence, integrity should not be identified with consistency of behavior with respect to particular social rules but, rather, with the ability to adhere to universal moral principles (not rules) that can be followed consistently. Such principles provide guidelines for determining local social rules. For instance, an organization might identify general principles with respect to equity in wages and benefits. Local rules could then be established based on those principles.

Identifying general principles usually is not easy. Historically, people have used two different, but complementary, strategies to identify general moral principles, one deductive and the other inductive. In the first strategy, principles are defined abstractly in relation to particular moral assumptions. For example, employers might define their responsibility for fair wages and pensions as contingent on the prevailing governmental practices and economic conditions. In the second strategy, moral principles are identified empirically, in the same way that Roman jurists defined the *ius gentium,* the natural law of people—by observing different local practices and identifying commonalities that transcend them. The two strategies may be combined—as they were, in fact, by the aforementioned Roman jurists, who used the abstract principles of Stoic ethics for guidance in identifying commonalities with respect to standards, for example, for inheritance, property transfers, credit, and commercial transactions.

Second, in addition to acting inconsistently, managers lacking strong integrity lack a grounded sense of identity and purpose. Consequently, they often act without firm priorities and focus. They therefore behave reactively rather than proactively, responding now to this environmental issue and now to that internal issue without any clear direction. Managers lacking a strong sense of integrity often act without a clear understanding of the relationship between intermediate and long-range goals. Often such people miss opportunities. They fail to see how to respond to new information and demands because they fail to perceive them as related to their current activities. In contrast, managers with strong integrity have a clear, centered sense of identity and purpose, grounded in consciously selected priorities that allow them to adapt to new challenges with initiative.

Integrity should not be viewed as a constant. Managers may possess integrity to a greater or lesser degree. Those with much integrity are able to act with principled consistency across many settings, while those with little integrity act consistently only in small, well-defined areas, those in which divergent circumstances do not really test them. Unfortunately, given the diversity of the circumstances in which they work, international managers rarely have this second option. They must either intentionally attempt to achieve high degrees of integrity in relation to identifiable principles or blatantly act inconsistently, often falsely excusing such inconsistencies by pointing to the variations in the national contexts in which they work.

Whether weak or strong, integrity implies centeredness. The difference lies in the amount and variety of experience and information that each individual can connect with his or her conscious sense of identity and purpose. Thus, strength of integrity is not measured simply by consistency of commitment but more especially by the firmness of commitment and scope of purpose. That is precisely why the virtue of integrity is associated with the capacity to take risks. Those whose integrity is strong are able to act when they are not completely certain of the consequences. Their commitment allows them to respond proactively even when facing uncertainty.

Many people associate integrity with the capacity to adopt

or incorporate opposing tendencies within a larger, more integrated sense of self. Those with strong integrity seem able to respond to present exigencies and yet act with a steady grasp of long-range objectives, to honor particular rules and yet act on the basis of loyalties, to balance programmatic considerations with firm moral commitments (Weber, 1946/1961, p. 142). This flexibility results from a centered sense of identity that is not narrowly defined but quite large and full.

Third, along with consistency and centeredness, those possessing integrity must act and speak in such a way that verbal profession matches actual practice and vice versa. They must act consistently with their value commitments and articulate value commitments in ways that are consistent with their conduct. Those having little integrity make no real attempt to make their behavior correspond to their verbal expressions of morality or to alter their expressions to make them correspond to their behavior.

This discrepancy between moral profession and practice may assume several forms. One form is blatant hypocrisy and cynicism. Since others cheat, violate conventional understandings and laws, and deceive consumers, the individual assumes such behavior to be acceptable or at least excusable. In addition, the discrepancy often takes the form of self-deception (Fingarette, 1965). Individuals simply do not allow themselves to become aware of the divergence between their expressed value commitments and their conduct. When confronted, they frequently blame the discrepancies on others or on passing circumstances.

The virtue of integrity calls for continual attempts to correlate conduct with verbal expression of moral standards. Hence, integrity requires both an earnest endeavor to act in keeping with moral standards and the candor to acknowledge actual discrepancies. Candor, in this sense, has two meanings. Candor implies the honest recognition of failings in relation to professed standards. Moreover, candor requires that people articulate precisely those standards that they do in fact honor and treat as authoritative, rather than professing more idealistic standards that might appear more moral or fitting.

Integrity: An Expanded Definition. First, integrity is a *standard of excellence,* not defined by minimally acceptable or obligatory conduct. In fact, the standard to which one aspires defines integrity. For an organization, promoting a healthy environment is a standard of excellence; simply adhering to legally set standards is not. Significantly, from the perspective of the United States, "the two most extensively studied topics in business ethics, namely corporate involvement in South Africa and the marketing practices of the manufacturers of infant formulas overseas, both represent areas in which corporate conduct is *not* constrained by American law" (Vogel, 1986, p. 143). The notion of integrity is less culturally relative than the "set of moral commitments," or standard of excellence, that underlies it. To what standard do I aspire? How similar is it to that of my foreign colleagues and clients?

From this perspective, the centeredness, principled consistency, and self-candor that are the marks of integrity represent standards of excellence. We may argue that international executives act with integrity insofar as they can openly defend their actions in relation to identifiable moral principles. Defined in these terms, the notion of integrity is probably less culturally relative than a number of other moral standards, such as justice, filial piety, civility, caste propriety, industriousness, and patriotism, to name a few.

A second characteristic of integrity is that it is a *relational* phenomenon: Individuals do not develop integrity by themselves. To be sure, individuals demonstrate integrity when they withstand pressure from others while taking risks in defense of behavior they conscientiously consider to be right. However, this strength of character, whether in acting alone or in concert, is cultivated through interaction with others, particularly parents and mentors who expect and demand principled behavior, as well as peers and colleagues who support and reward it. Correspondingly, individuals who develop personal integrity generally expect and demand similar consistency, honesty, and centeredness from those with whom they regularly interact. Thus, integrity is developed and practiced in relation to other people and situations.

Several examples illustrate the relational character of integrity. In sports, for instance, players expect competitors to abide by the principles and rules of the game as defined by some relevant notion of honesty (which, in many cases, allows some forms of bluffing). Similarly, intimate friends and close colleagues characteristically raise expectations of each other. As they personally seek to act with integrity, they demand that their close associates do so as well. Thus, even though integrity is a uniquely individual virtue—that of acting with principled self-consistency and without deception—it is a moral character trait that both is cultivated by others and seeks the company of others.

Similarly, for executives, social factors foster integrity. Executives find it easier to act with integrity when such action is supported by colleagues who themselves act with honesty and principled consistency, even when those colleagues' principles differ from the executive's own. Within domestic settings, national legislation and professional societies often cultivate integrity by setting standards of performance and demanding open disclosure of conduct. Corresponding pressure on international executives is less developed and therefore more haphazard. Moreover, identical legislation and similar professional norms rarely bind international executives.

Issues in Individual Integrity for Executives

Executive integrity can be viewed as having two components: individual integrity and organizational integrity. One can examine the integrity of individual managers in interaction with other individuals and of the organization as a whole interacting with its internal and external environment. Although these overlap in reality, for purposes of clarity we will discuss them separately.

Individual integrity has been defined as a moral virtue associated with the traits of centeredness, self-candor, and principled consistency. Implied in that definition is the assumption that integrity is a relational phenomenon, being based on principles, not rules, and articulated as a standard of moral excellence. Therefore, at its simplest level, the question of integrity

Executive Integrity

in both domestic and international business is "Do I, in dealing with people and situations internal and external to the firm, act as honestly and consistently as possible?"

Though difficult and important enough for executives to achieve within a national context, integrity becomes even more difficult and important in working across national and cultural boundaries. Markedly different expectations and local customs make it hard for people of dissimilar cultures to act with easy and obvious consistency. Similarly, under varying conventions about full and partial disclosure, privacy, and privileged information, acting with self-evident candor across cultures is far from easy. Any form of limited or parochial integrity becomes inappropriate when transactions cross national and cultural boundaries. Let's examine "bribery" as an international case in point.

Bribery, it would appear, is the preeminent individual integrity issue for American businesspeople working abroad, at least as discussed in the international business literature.[2] "American integrity" is pitted against the demands of "evil foreigners"; the complaint is "They force us to do bad things." U.S. businesspeople have praised the Foreign Corrupt Practices Act of 1977 for upholding American corporate ethical standards and have simultaneously condemned it for its ethnocentrism and consequent strangling of U.S. business abroad.[3] From the perspective of ethical behavior, it is important to note that (1) definitions of unfair practices (such as bribery) vary markedly across cultures and (2) using one culture's definition to operate in another culture often results in inappropriate behavior as well as in negative economic consequences. This is not to argue for economic expediency but, rather, to indicate one consequence

[2]Examples of discussion of bribery include Adams and Rosenthal (1976), Alabanese (1982), Baumhart (1968), Beeman and Timmins (1982), Clinard and Yeager (1980), Clinard and others (1979), Feinschreiber (1982), Gladwin and Walter (1980, pp. 297–329), Jacoby, Nehemkis, and Eells (1977, pp. 125–207), Johnson (1985), Kirk (1981), Lane and Simpson (1984), Leitko and Kowalewski (1985), Noonan (1984, pp. 425–683), and Richman (1979), among many others.
[3]For discussion of the U.S. Foreign Corrupt Practices Act, see Benjamin, Dascher, and Morgan (1979), Brennan (1984), Graham (1983), Ittig (1982), Kim (1981), McQueary and Risden (1979), Rauch (1981), Reisman (1979, pp. 151–173), Romaneski (1982), and Siedel (1981), among many others.

of a set rule—"no bribery"—when followed outside its indigenous context.

Interestingly, in the United States, individual international managers, not the organization as a whole, often must bridge the multiple and frequently conflicting definitions of ethical and effective behavior. All too often, U.S. corporations espouse American ethical standards and legislation in their formal codes of conduct while admonishing their managers to "get the business." Companies leave the resolution of this contradiction—the seeming impossibility of acting effectively in the foreign environment while using home country ethical standards—to the discretion of each manager. Not surprisingly, individual managers frequently feel that they must choose between acting ethically (and consequently failing to get the business) and violating home country ethical standards in order to get the business. They fear being passed over for promotion if they select the first option (and fail to get enough business) or being fired for choosing the second option (violating the company's code of conduct). At the organizational level, this form of "ostrich integrity"—"Get the business, but don't tell me how you did it"—reveals a disturbing selective blindness. Although the perceived contradiction between ethical and profitable behavior with respect to bribery may not, in fact, accurately describe reality (see Graham, 1983), the choice is neither easy for the corporation nor altogether appropriate for the individual.

Issues in Organizational Integrity

Individual integrity focuses on a person's interaction with other people, while organizational integrity addresses the firm's interaction with its internal and external environment. The definitions of integrity for the individual and for the firm are similar; only the domain, level of aggregation, and process differ. Like individual integrity, organizational integrity involves acting in consistency with principles and objectives, not simply with rules or across tasks. Even more pronounced for organizations than for individuals, consistency with respect to rules guarantees inflexibility, not integrity. To foster integrity, the organization's

principles and objectives must form a standard of excellence for
organization members to aspire to, not simply a minimal or
obligatory standard for them to adhere to. Hence, while the
organization's principles can span the globe, specific interpretations in the form of behavioral guides or rules can remain culturally and contextually specific. As a standard of excellence, principles allow for both consistency and flexibility.

For executives, the issue of personal integrity cannot be
isolated from that of organizational integrity. Executives necessarily assume responsibility for the overall well-being of their
organization. Whether expressed implicitly in the dynamics of
the organization's culture or explicitly in corporate policy statements, whether defined narrowly vis-à-vis shareholders or more
broadly in terms of stakeholders, the responsibility is theirs.

In moral terms, executives bear responsibility for providing effective leadership in creating and sustaining an organization ethos defined in relation to particular principles and objectives—or, in Selznick's (1957) terms, for creating and sustaining
the organization's mission and identity. In our judgment, default
of moral leadership adversely affects corporate performance in
the same way as default in providing adequate leadership to
manage production, finance, marketing, or the human resources
system, although perhaps not in so immediately visible a fashion.
Hence, since executives implicitly, if not explicitly, assume
responsibility for the moral leadership of their firm, any discussion of executive integrity must include a focus on the creation
and maintenance of the integrity of the organization as a whole.
Executives' integrity is measured not simply with reference to
their personal conduct, but also with respect to their role in
creating and maintaining organizational integrity.

We have noted that it is more challenging for individuals
to operate with self-evident and principled consistency of behavior across cultures. It is equally difficult, if not more so, for
an organization. As captured in the maxim ''When in Rome,
do as the Romans do,'' common wisdom expresses respect for
the host culture but leads to legitimate charges of inconsistency.
How can I purport to act with moral consistency when following Islamic strictures in Iran, Buddhist principles in Thailand,

socialist dictates in Eastern Europe, and Common Market rules in the European Economic Community? In addition to the charge of inconsistency, many local customs explicitly violate home country legal or moral traditions. A Canadian business-man described a particularly pointed example: "We respect the local culture. As international managers, we leave the manag-ing of local personnel to host nationals. In one African country I worked in, this meant allowing tribal members to punish co-workers who broke company rules 'in the traditional manner': by putting errant workers in the back of a truck and pushing them out along the roadway as the truck sped on. They always suffered injuries, often severe."

Organizations cannot purport to act with moral consis-tency when adhering at home to seemingly impersonal bureau-cratic guidelines while overseas following a mixture of local customs, highly personal practices, and laws that vary from one nation to the next. Similarly, organizations cannot view their behavior as moral if they consistently fail to follow moral prin-ciples worldwide. Although integrity is certainly more complex at an organizational than an individual level, we will try to show that taking an organizational perspective not only illuminates many of the issues of personal integrity that international ex-ecutives face but also provides operationally practical ways to address both levels of integrity.

Integrity and the Internal Environment: Organizational Culture. What type of organizational culture must a firm create to encourage self-aware behavior consistent with its principles? First, for employees to act with integrity, the organization's principles must be intelligible, openly acknowledged, and mean-ingful for all organization members. Second, to ensure shared meanings, the organization must facilitate two-way communi-cation, including accepting and encouraging public discussion of difficult situations and their possible resolutions. Third, if the organizational culture is to encourage integrity, it must not punish participants, formally or informally, either for voic-ing concerns that lie outside currently accepted norms or for using discretion in interpreting the principles. However, the organization can, and in most cases must, punish behavior that violates that implied by the principles.

When clearly stated and communicated, the organization's principles should become a source of identity and purpose for all employees. Moreover, by stating its standards of excellence at a level of principles rather than rules, the organization will create a culture that will allow, if not encourage, innovation, adaptation, learning, and risktaking.

Clearly, organizational integrity cannot be achieved by executive fiat or by developing eloquent policy statements and distributing them throughout the organization. Rather, employees and managers establish viable ethical principles by openly discussing difficult situations until they reach a consensus on appropriate resolution. Consensus, however, does not occur simply as a result of such discussions. Executive leadership is needed to allow, stimulate, guide, and complete such discussions. The organization eventually realizes integrity not simply through the principles that emerge but through the sense of direction and trust such discussions engender. Organizational integrity never becomes a static orientation aimed at setting forth hard and fast positions that must not be violated. It always remains a standard of excellence for organization members to approximate as they continually aspire to both consistency and flexibility. This pursuit necessarily is ongoing, as the organization constantly responds to new stimuli from both within and outside the organization. Integrity is realized best when an organization constantly pursues it, and it is lost, or at least diminished, when the organization thinks, because of its prior achievements, that the pursuit of integrity can be relinquished.

The organization's pursuit of integrity thus involves several complementary strategies. Within the organization, executives must seek to gain clarity and consensus on normative standards for all business relations, including those with personnel (for example, nondiscrimination, merit promotion, and full employment), suppliers and consumers (for example, product excellence and some notion of fair competition), and other stakeholders (see Bird and Waters, 1987). The organization achieves this clarity and consensus more through establishing norms and structures encouraging full discussion of difficult issues than through articulating principles, although the latter is necessary to disseminate the conclusions of the former.

The organization's pursuit of integrity is even more influenced by relationships than the individual's. Organizations seeking to achieve integrity necessarily must seek others' cooperation and support—including that of other businesses, governments, trade associations, consumer groups, and trade unions. Organizations are more likely to act with integrity when other organizations pressure them to do so. They are more likely, for example, to trade fairly, to hire, promote, and fire employees without racial, gender, ethnic, or age discrimination, and to reinvest proportional amounts of nationally generated profits within the local economy if collective norms foster such behavior. The adoption of the "Sullivan principles" by a number of firms doing business in South Africa exemplifies what can be achieved when organizations cooperate to act with integrity and hence to operate with similar nondiscrimination standards worldwide. General Motors, at the initiative of the Reverend Leon Sullivan, one of its board members, not only instituted the "Sullivan principles" in its own operations but also sought to gain other firms' agreement. As a result, many multinationals changed their employment practices in South Africa, while General Motors was able to act with greater consistency in principle throughout its worldwide organization.

Creation and maintenance of an organizational culture that sustains integrity is considerably more challenging in multinational organizations. In creating and sustaining integrity, multinational organizations must include in their discussions employees and managers from all cultures represented. Yet, for example, relevant norms vary markedly across cultures. Most Occidental cultures, for instance, value openness and directness. This is particularly true in the United States. By contrast, many Oriental cultures do not. In Japan, for example, harmony— maintained in part through face-saving behaviors—takes precedence over openness. Many Japanese believe some things to be best left unsaid, or said very indirectly. An American, for example, might, in all openness and honesty, say, "Hiring the untrained father of an employee for a professional position is impossible," while a Japanese might communicate the same information by saying, "That would be very difficult." By the American's definition, the Japanese is being neither open nor direct. Similarly, many Moslems believe that discussing a hypothetical situation increases the likelihood that the event discussed will occur. Many Moslems therefore try to avoid discussing possible negative outcomes of present and future actions. By contrast, most people with European backgrounds do not believe that thoughts influence external events. Their beliefs render them freer than their Moslem colleagues to discuss comfortably the possible negative consequences of corporate actions. These divergent beliefs have very different implications for corporate openness and two-way communication patterns.

When viewed from an organizational perspective, issues of executive integrity, especially in international business, seem less intractable than when viewed only on the level of individual behavior. Ultimately, individual managers and employees need intelligible and organizationally supported guidelines for actions. However, effective guidelines are never produced by individuals' stoic resoluteness to act with mechanical sameness in settings that are ambiguous and changing or by high-minded company policies or national legislation. Organizations cultivate real integrity by fostering a greater sense of accountability to others within the organization—and, as discussed in the next section, outside it—as well as encouraging more candid and full communication among these people. Within such discussions, difficulties and bad decisions can be acknowledged and can provide the basis for learning and for building a consensus on standards that are both workable and responsible—standards that insist on consistency in principle and allow for flexibility in practice.

Integrity and the External Environment: Social Responsibility. Organizational integrity sets standards of excellence for the firm's interaction with both its internal and its external environment. What are "society's legitimate expectations of business [when] extended beyond the making of profits" (Vogel, 1986, p. 142)? To what constituencies is the corporation responsible? The traditional economic answer has been shareholders; the expanded answer has been all stakeholders, or constituencies—that is, consumers, employees, community members, suppliers, and, of course, owners. More frequently today, the list of stakeholders indirectly includes "the nation." National "patriotism" demands a sensitivity toward protecting home country employment, production, markets, and distinctive cultural traditions. Though praiseworthy from a national perspective, these forms of national patriotism may become detrimental to the very nature of international business and societal integrity. The interdependence of today's world and the transnational nature of today's corporate affairs may, in fact, render nation-bound definitions of responsibility, and therefore integrity, necessarily limited and partial.

From the perspective of corporate integrity, global business implicitly raises the question of an additional constituency: the world. Do global corporations have a responsibility for the well-being of the world? The appropriateness of this additional constituency can be addressed from at least two perspectives: that of a global mandate and that of a reactive environment.

A Global Mandate. The issue of a global mandate raises the question "Who is responsible for the world?" Traditionally, governments, not private corporations, have assumed responsibility for their citizens' welfare and for maintaining the common good (in economic jargon, for managing externalities), by providing such services as health care, education, transportation, adequate environmental quality, and national defense. However, by definition, the primary mandate of national governments has been the nation-state, not the world. Yet, many, if not most, of today's most pressing societal problems cross national boundaries. Review, for example, the global problems listed in the opening of this chapter.

Governments generally choose to respect national sovereignty, the notable exception being war. They tend to manage border-spanning problems either by ignoring the multinational causes of those problems and artificially treating their multinational consequences as nationally delimited or by seeking redress through bilateral and multilateral agreements. Even when such agreements are reached, their solutions most commonly outline minimally acceptable, legally defined behavior, not standards of excellence. A current example is the debate over acid rain in which Canada is attempting to outlaw certain levels of sulfur emission downwind from the U.S./Canadian border. If signed, such an international agreement would legislate minimum performance standards but would provide no incentive for the companies involved to perform beyond the legally set minimum (that is, to emit lower levels of pollutant than what the law would allow). In this sense the agreement would be legalistic rather than systemic. An example of a systemic agreement, in the case of sulfur emission, would be a tax on pollution. If appropriately set and enforced, such a tax would economically encourage polluters to minimize emissions rather than simply reducing them to some legally acceptable standard. Such a tax would encourage striving for a standard of excellence to minimize pollution rather than meeting an obligatory standard. Because many international, governmental agreements fail to encourage the parties involved both to aspire to standards of excellence and to take responsibility for stakeholders beyond their own borders, they rarely encourage integrity. The mandate of national governments has been to take care of their citizens, including protecting them from invasion—whether economic or militaristic. Their primary mandate has not been to take care of the world.

Unlike governments, private corporations are not limited by national borders or mandates (except that they are required to register and incorporate under national laws and pay national taxes). This is true in two senses. First, geography does not limit corporate boundaries. Corporations can, and frequently do, span multiple boundaries. Second, the mandate of corporations, unlike that of governments, has not been to protect the general welfare. As discussed earlier, corporations have a responsibility to their shareholders or, more broadly, their stakeholders. Yet, few, if any, corporations have included the world as a stakeholder. The contradiction is apparent. Although global corporations have the appropriate structures to address global issues, most lack a clear mandate to do so.

Multinational corporations do use "their economic resources to change other countries' political [and economic] systems [to] more closely reflect their vision of a decent and just society" (Vogel, 1986, p. 147). However, our lack of consensus on the appropriateness of such interventions highlights the ambiguity of the corporate mandate. For example, evaluations of corporate decisions to provide funds to the rebel forces in Nicaragua and to remain in South Africa while enforcing alternative personnel practices have been less than unanimously laudatory. Unfortunately, there is no consensus on what constitutes responsible or irresponsible corporate behavior.

Is it surprising that global issues tend to come to our attention only after reaching crisis proportions? Can it be that our "zones of indifference" (Barnard, 1938) have become so large that only crises capture our attention (as in the classic television-news saturation hypothesis)? We doubt it. The question has become one of appropriately responsive structures, not merely general public awareness. In terms of corporate integrity, fault may lie more on the side of omission than commission. Corporations fail to do what they could do to "take care of the world" because they do not see such behavior as within their mandate.

A Reactive Environment. Even with its global structures, why would a corporation choose to take care of the world? If we take history as precedent we are highly unlikely to predict that corporations will choose to expand their mandate to include global social responsibility. To date, the evidence makes such a suggestion more laughable than laudable. However, it is highly probable that corporations will continue to act in their own self-interest. Therefore, one intriguing question becomes: Might "taking care of the world" emerge as an issue of self-interest for global corporations rather than one of narrowly defined social responsibility? It is conceivable that global social responsibility could become more consistent with corporations' economic mandate and self-interest. Surprisingly, the answer may be yes.

Emery and Trist (1965) proposed a paradigm of organizations' interaction with their external environment. Their four models range from the "placid, randomized environment" (analogous to the classical free-market economy), in which neither other firms nor the environment itself reacts to any one organization's actions, to the "turbulent field," in which not only do other firms (for example, competitors) react to a single firm's actions, but the field itself reacts. In a turbulent field, "dynamic properties arise not simply from the interaction of component organizations, but from the field itself [with] . . . deepening interdependence between economic and other facets of the society. This means that economic organizations are increasingly enmeshed in legislation and public regulation. In these environments, individual organizations, however large, cannot expect to adapt successfully simply through their own direct actions. . . . A solution . . . may . . . be the emergence of values that have overriding significance for all members of the field" (pp. 20, 22). International firms today face the equivalent of Emery and Trist's turbulent field. Each firm's actions cause reactions not only from other firms, but also from, among others, host governments, labor unions, environmental action groups, and financial markets. International firms create the environment in which they work: By definition, they create the global environment in which they operate.

More recently, Maruyama (1980) proposed a similar paradigm describing four metatypes of causality. The most complex of his four models, the "morphogenetic causal loop model," views causal relations (among elements both internal and external to the organization) as forming loops. Heterogeneity of all types, including the international dimensions of geographical dispersion and cultural diversity, is seen as capable of generating new patterns of mutually beneficial relations among the parts, thus raising the level of sophistication of the whole system. Hence, systems can evolve on their own. Diversity is thus seen as basic, indispensable, and desirable, whereas homogeneity is viewed as the source of conflict and competition. The organization constantly seeks new patterns of harmony among dissimilar elements and demands. In no way does the organization have the luxury of enduring stability, separateness from its external environment, or recourse into explanations that rely on environmental determinism.

From the perspective of integrity, the importance of these two models lies in their power to explain organizations' actual and potential behavior in the most complex and highly interactive environments—those most similar to today's global business environment (corresponding to Emery and Trist's turbulent field and Maruyama's morphogenetic causal loop model).

As we move toward a world in which organizations implicitly and explicitly *create* their external environment as much as responding to it, we move toward a world in which the firm's best interest is served by creating (rather than simply reacting to) a positive external environment. For global corporations, this means creating a positive global environment. From the perspective of stakeholders, it means that the world becomes a constituency. From the perspective of integrity, it means that it will become incumbent on global corporations to broadly define global standards of excellence for creating and working in the worldwide environment.

Let us propose an analogy. When European settlers first came to North America, they often farmed the soil until it was depleted and then moved west. They based their behavior on the assumption of infinite resources; one simply located oneself and one's family and business in a resource-rich part of the continent. Similarly, many corporations, in moving from domestic to multinational operations, initially acted as if the world offered infinite resources. If the supply of inexpensive labor disappeared from one country, then production could always be moved to another country. If the market stagnated at home, one could always expand abroad. If natural resources became scarce and therefore expensive in one country, one could always purchase them at a good price from suppliers in yet another country. In fact, basic economic competition and the law of supply and demand seemed to dictate that corporations operate that way in order to survive. However, as Harold Williams, chief of the Getty Foundation and former CEO of Norton Simon, has observed (as cited in Magnet, 1986), this classic free-market "concept of 'let the market govern' relieves one of one's sense of responsibility."

Even though the analogy held for the multinational expansion of domestic operations, we question its validity for today's

global corporations. Unlike the firms of the past, global corporations increasingly face a closed system—the international
equivalent of the situation when westward expansion across
North America reached the Pacific Ocean. Simultaneously, corporations face an increasingly reactive environment. For example, corporate employment practices cause worldwide migrations
of expatriate workers (witness, for example, the Filipinos in
Saudi Arabia, the Mexicans in California, and the Turks in
Sweden and Germany). Similarly, product quality standards
cause dramatic shifts in worldwide markets (witness the shift
from American to Japanese cars). Corporate pollution standards
cause government retaliation in the form of new, more restrictive legislation. As corporations recognize the closed-system
nature of global business (captured more accurately in the Disney
song "It's a Small World After All" than in the aforementioned
pioneer spirit) and the extent to which their actions create their
environment, global social responsibility increasingly will come
within their mandate.

Who Is Responsible for the World?

The nature of international business is clearly changing.
With that change comes executives' increasing responsibility for
broader geographical areas and greater cultural diversity. Homogeneous simplicity, a relic of the past, has given way to
heterogeneous complexity.

Domestic business has always challenged executives at the
individual and organizational levels to act with integrity—with
self-integration, principled consistency, and self-candor in relation to a standard of excellence. Today global business challenges
them to do so in relation to a dynamic diversity heretofore unheard of. The difficulty is not in the concept of integrity itself
but, rather, in the added complexity. Within the organization,
integrity now involves the constant open and consistent recognition of diversity. In relation to the external environment,
integrity now demands the rejection of determinism and the
concomitant acceptance of proactive responsibility for a global
reality.

The mandate of acting with integrity at an international level is at once overwhelming and the *sine qua non* of a future, healthy world. This challenge was well captured by Art Wright (1986, pp. 5, 7), director of the Asia Pacific Foundation of Canada and vice-president for Asia of the Canadian International Development Agency:

As we all move toward the twenty-first century, we are indeed on the verge of a major transition in the way global society functions:

- A transition of politics from fostering nationalism as a driving force for unity to appreciation of the common interests of global society.
- A transition in education from reliance on mechanistic and increasingly narrow specialization to holistic learning and recognition of wisdom of diverse cultures.
- A transition, at least in Western societies, from rugged individualism to a sense of global community.
- A transition from exploitative "win/lose" strategies to equity-based "win/win" approaches.
- A transition from isolated, frequently adversarial relations among business, labor, academia, and government to constructive interchange and mutual recognition of diverse but complementary fields of expertise.

11

To Thine Own Self Be True: Coping with the Dilemmas of Integrity

Harry Levinson

Competition brings out the best in products and the worst in people [David Sarnoff, quoted in Jackman, 1985].

Sarnoff's observation might arguably be even more appropriate today. The business world is more complex; corporation leadership has to make larger commitments for research, building plants, product innovation, and adaptation to new techniques that must be amortized over longer periods. The more a corporation promises by its reputation and its advertising, the more important it is that it sustain the public trust. Widespread complaint about American automobiles has led to the successful invasion of Japanese and German automobiles, with their reputations for greater reliability. The failure of the *Challenger* has led to public dismay and disillusionment with NASA. Officials of television broadcasting companies are troubled because children, weaned on advertising from an early age, no longer believe commercials or pay much attention to them (Hornblower, 1986). The rise of the baby boom population to managerial age intensifies the competition among its members for the fewer places in downsized organizations. The shift to leverage as a major means of financing operations, mergers and acquisitions, and the explosion in the use of personal

268

credit maximize the competitive edge of cash flow. Taken together, these and other forces, as Sarnoff said, frequently bring out the worst in people as reflected in newspaper headlines about insider trading, payoffs, hostile takeovers, and arbitrageur manipulations.

In short, we are witnessing an increasing intensity of aggression directed at one another. At the national level there is growing defensiveness, reflected in rising tariffs and the manipulation of the comparative value of the dollar. In everyday business activity, the evidence lies in the expanding number of people who are displaced from their employment, sometimes from organizations in which they have worked for decades.

Meanwhile, the public cries for integrity, meaning that it wishes to be able to depend on businesses for reliability of product and service. Employees yearn for integrity: They want to be able to trust their leadership to give them accurate information quickly, to anticipate crises, to provide retraining where possible, to enable them to share in the decisions that affect their jobs and their lives, and not to repay loyalty with contemptuous abandonment. The government seeks to enforce integrity in businesses, both for reliability and validity of product or service and for environmental impact. All these are expressions of a desire to inhibit, if not contain, what people experience as predatory aggression.

The concept that all creatures are inherently aggressive is not new. As Freud pointed out, sex and aggression are the two fundamental drives. All creatures are significantly motivated by those drives and must evolve modes of tempering and channeling them in the interest of social living. In some cultures, like the Navajo or the Hutterites or certain monastic communities, people have learned to sublimate their aggression and even their sexuality into mutual support and service to others. But sadly, as illustrated by the Holocaust, the Armenian and Kampuchean genocides, the Stalinist mass murders, the slaughters in Africa, and sadistic cruelty everywhere, rampant, uncontrolled aggression is widespread. In societies where it is reasonably controlled, it is here to stay, largely in the form of enlightened self-interest, which, nevertheless, is basically self-aggrandizement.

Seeking advantage is characteristic of all animals. In one of Jacques Cousteau's dramatic films, two male salmon fight for access to a prospective mate. They grasp each other by their respective snouts and wrestle each other around. Finally, one wins and swims off to claim his prize. Suddenly the loser turns on him and bites his tail before darting away. Cousteau captures the ubiquitous phenomenon: males fighting for dominance. (It is equally evident that once one of the combatants communicates the ichthyological equivalent of "Uncle," the victor has no need to destroy him. Man is not so fortunate as to be genetically that inhibited. But not all organisms are so beneficent. Although the competitive males may not destroy each other, there is intraspecies murder. Sociobiologists report that both males and females in some species destroy the young of their species, the males most certainly the offspring of those males they have defeated, and the females those who might compete for food with their own offspring [Anderson, 1986].)

Status competition occurs within all species. Much of the time among humans the pecking order is determined by who has the greatest wealth, whether in gold, in numbers of wives or cattle, or in acres of land. Companies drilling for oil on the North Slope in Alaska used to be chagrined to discover that their male Eskimo employees suddenly disappeared. The reason: The position of a man in an Eskimo village culture is determined by his ability to buy a boat, hire a group of his village friends, and lead them in an expedition to get a whale. Earning money by drilling or pumping oil provided many with the funds to organize a whaling party and thereby to become respected figures in their villages. To attain such status is far more important than simply to make more money to buy material possessions.

Sociobiologists also report that across all cultures, at about the age of six months, infants begin to fear strangers. This rejection of strangers and hostility to the outsider seems to occur among all species, in all groups, and in all cultures. Everywhere there are insiders and outsiders. There is always some form of hostility to the outsider. Even in genteel and gentle New England, people who have lived in a given community for many years often are still defined as outsiders. Hostility to the outsider seems to have a genetic base (Konner, 1986). Among some species, mothers destroy young that smell different than their own.

Everywhere ordinary people make a competition out of anything. In England, for example, there is a competition among sheepherding dogs. Each dog is not only to herd the sheep into a pen but also to guard them until relieved by the shepherd. Even though the competition may be on a hot September day, and the dog has herded his sheep into the pen, he may not leave them even briefly to get a drink from a nearby pond. Duty comes first, even for a thirsty dog.

Polynesians in Tahiti, representing their own tribal units, compete both in boat races and in massed dance groups. In Guatemala, a favorite competition is the amateur rodeo. In county fairs and big state fairs in the United States, there is competition for the fattest pig, the tastiest apple pie, and the most artistic quilt. You name it, someone has made a competition of it. Aggression is turned to constructive ends—pleasure and better products or services.

In industrialized countries, people have become increasingly individually competitive because their aspirations rise from generation to generation. These expectations accelerate partly because children usually try to exceed the achievement of their parents, partly because their parents expect them to be better and do better than they themselves, and significantly because of the distortions of unconscious childhood thinking that lead to unrealistic expectations of self to compensate for feelings of helplessness or inadequacy.

The astronomical increase in technical information and the ability to communicate by satellite instantly all over the world makes more people aware of the vast range of knowledge quickly enough to take advantage of it. The restless young in the Philippines, Pakistan, Korea, and even China and Hungary press for greater freedom to compete and achieve. That pressure is made more intense in the United States by the examples of young, imaginative people, like Steve Jobs and Stephen Wozniak, the founders of Apple Computer, and Noah Bushnell, the founder of Atari. They became wealthy overnight by inventing new devices, aided by the ready availability of venture capital. Many

others fervently wish for the same good fortune. With such stir-
rings and the greater sense of entitlement, individual competitive
urgency soars. When that urgency is suppressed, both people
and organizations suffer. There are already complaints in Japan
about the loss of imaginative initiative because of the overcontrol of young people in Japanese business organizations (Kontkin
and Kishimoto, 1986).

Efforts Toward Mastery

Historically there are two major methods for trying to control aggression.

Self-Control. The first method, self-control, follows the
Old Testament adage "Thou shalt love thy neighbor as thyself"
(Leviticus, 19:18), translated by the first-century philosopher
Hillel into "What is hateful to you, do not do unto your neighbor" (*Encyclopedia Judaica,* 1971, Vol. 8, p. 482) and reformulated
in the New Testament as the Golden Rule. Indeed, all religions
have rules and principles that enable people to live with one
another. All else besides this guideline, said Hillel, is commen-
tary. The "all else" has proliferated into multiple codes of ethics,
exemplified by the Hippocratic oath. Harvard's president, Derek
Bok, notes that "Across the country, thousands of courses now
exist on these subjects. At Harvard alone, there is a requirement in the core curriculum for courses on moral reasoning and
ethical issues; there are required courses on legal ethics in the
Law School, and there are courses on ethical issues in the Business School, the Medical School, and the School of Government.
This year we are also inaugurating a new program to prepare
professors to teach such courses in colleges and professional
schools" (1986, p. 3).

Outside academia, there are centers for the study of ethics
in medicine and business. However, according to the executive
director of the Ethics Resource Center, "In many cases, company representatives arrive with a code of conduct in hand,
noting that even with written standards the company is having
a problem with ethical conduct" (Edwards, 1986, p. 3). In recent years, in many companies, this problem has meant an ex-

amination of corporate values, particularly with a fadlike concern for changing or integrating corporate cultures when companies must change radically or when they reorganize, merge, or acquire others. Yet, there is no accepted body of ethical theory to guide these efforts (Brady, 1986). And clearly criteria external to individuals, like codes of ethics, however useful, do not adequately deal with the ethical problems in any field.

To support individual and organizational self-control, and to retain some semblance of equity in relationships, there are referees of various kinds: government agencies, courts, and self-government by professional and trade associations. There is recourse to suits as exemplified by recent major actions over the Dalkon Shield, asbestos, and the Ford Pinto. Editorialists, columnists, and citizens alike, at this writing, expect to see indictments of E. F. Hutton & Company and General Dynamics Corporation executives.

Before there were official referees, adversarial power spawned countervailing power. There is also a long, sometimes bloody history of balancing managerial power with union power, corporate power with consumer power, and government power with citizen power. Despite consumer organizations and government regulations, people in market-oriented countries are subject to manipulation by advertising, which is a form of attack when it exacerbates feelings of inadequacy, when it stimulates unrealistic beliefs, when it promises near perfection. Individuals, groups, and even whole communities are exploited by economic pirates who destroy organizations for their short-term gain. And, of course, all this undermines identification of people with the organizations that employ them.

Individual and organizational modes of self-control do not work as well as anyone would like.

Being True to Oneself. The second major method for controlling aggression has been summarized by Shakespeare: "To thine own self be true . . . thou canst not then be false to any man" (Hamlet, I, iii, 58). That, it turns out, is not easy to do either, for obvious psychological reasons: Often we do not really know what goes on in our heads, as psychoanalysts and cognitive psychologists have demonstrated.

Anna Freud (1966) has described in some detail a range of mechanisms by which we defend ourselves against information that may threaten us. Melanie Klein (1964) advanced the theory that infants develop paranoid and depressive positions. The paranoid position is the feeling that the world is a hostile and painful place and therefore one must be perennially on guard. The depressive position is the pervasive feeling that one is at fault and therefore deserves self-criticism. It is an old clinical story that most people are always struggling with their critical feelings about themselves. They are only too ready to deflect their irrational anger with themselves into an attack on another person.

Then there is the phenomenon of splitting, the powerful tendency to classify people as wearing white hats or black hats. There is a general propensity for stereotyping people, for painting them in starkly disparate hues to differentiate those who are good from those who might be theatening.

These are among psychological mechanisms which keep people from knowing themselves and which precipitate hostile reactions toward others. There are, of course, many other psychological devices that act in the same ways.

Other forces make it difficult to be true to oneself. In some circumstances gentle people may be stimulated to become more aggressive. Sociological phenomena exacerbate competitive hostility—for example, the various forms of status competition mentioned earlier. Some may be made less aggressive. The aging process in all cultures makes some men the warriors, those who carry on the leadership responsibility for the tribe or group or nation. Others who are older are dependent on the warriors, and those who are really old, in the extreme, go out to sea on an ice floe or travel into the mountains to die so as not to become a burden on the warriors. Cultural values may enhance or diminish the roles and thereby the self-images of their members. Only in some few cultures are the aged still revered because presumably they pass on the wisdom of the tribe, but increasingly the old men don't know what the young men are already skilled in—namely, adapting to the working, trading, bartering money culture of the dominant outside world.

It is difficult for many to behave according to their basic feelings and therefore to be true to themselves. In almost all cultures men are taught to overcontrol their feelings because, as men (warriors), they are not supposed to cry. Furthermore, if they are bonded together as members of an in-group, they share the grandiose feelings (Kohut, 1971) that give them a sense of being "better than" those outside the group. In that case, they may well be truer to the group than to their individual expectations of themselves.

Organizational Stimulants to Aggression

Even if we could live up to the biblical dictum and to Shakespeare's advice, the task of controlling aggression, never easy, is now more difficult. Two of the factors that exacerbate aggression within businesses are invisible to executives and are not seen for what they are. The difficulties they engender are viewed merely as the inevitable, perennial problems of an openly competitive society.

Dilemma of Reward. The first of these is the fact that organizations operate on reward/punishment assumptions. When executives use such assumptions, unconsciously they regard those on whom they exercise that manipulation to be jackasses (Levinson, 1973). In turn, the people on whom the manipulation is used seek to maximize the carrot and to minimize the stick. The resulting mutual manipulation precipitates internal hostility, often reflected in union/management conflict. This conception leads to a heavy emphasis on the bottom line but precious little emphasis on how people get that bottom line. In so many instances only the results count, regardless of the cost to the organization of how they were achieved. When they are obtained fraudulently, as in E. F. Hutton & Company and General Dynamics Corporation, top management denies that it had anything to do with that mode of operating, failing to recognize that its pressure for bottom-line results and individual achievement set in motion the forces for getting those results in any way possible.

Dilemma of Structure. The second executive blind spot is organizational structure. The classical hierarchical model, which dates from imperial Chinese courts and the Old Testament (Exodus 18:13–26), is intended to ensure accountability and adequate control. When corrupted, as it is in most businesses as a system of pay grades (Jaques, 1976), it maximizes dependency and emphasizes power seeking. It also usually exacerbates feelings of threat because members typically get inadequate information about where they stand, what is happening, and what is likely to happen in the organization, since there is nothing in performance appraisal systems that requires, documents, and compensates interactions of managers and their subordinates (Levinson, 1976).

Under these circumstances, the greater the pressure for individual achievement and the pursuit of individual power, the greater the pressure to make it big, no matter what the cost to the organization. Simultaneously there is greater instability in businesses. These two factors, the pay-grade basis for structure and the pressure for individual achievement, maximize self-centeredness at the cost of organizational effectiveness and adaptiveness.

All this is reflected in some of the contemporary metaphors of business. One heard frequently is the phrase *lean and mean.* *Lean* refers to the complaint of many high-level executives that their organizations are (or were) heavily bloated with middle managers. But they, top management, put them there, largely because they gave little or no thought to a psychological logic for organizational structure. And *mean* refers to the fact that increasingly in athletic competition one is not only to play well but also to bruise and injure the opponent to whatever degree possible in any way one can get away with. Competitive athletes easily separate their view of what is acceptable behavior on the basketball court or football field from what is acceptable to them every day as citizens (Bredemeier and Shields, 1985). The athlete who is well-mannered among colleagues and the public at large feels that it is his responsibility to destroy the athletic enemy almost literally if he can get away with it. For those who follow this athletic model, presumably the business task is to compete not just effectively, but viciously as well.

Integrity and the Ego Ideal

But there are also other dilemmas, threats to executive integrity, those of which executives are only too painfully aware. These threats to one's pursuit of one's ego ideal are more germane to students of executive integrity.

The ego ideal is a picture of oneself at one's ideal best toward which one is always striving. The ego ideal is "an ideal conception of selfhood . . . on which the ego seeks to pattern itself. . . . It gives a sense of *promise* and is situated therefore in the future" (Chasseguet-Smirgel, 1985, p. 44). "The imagery of the ego ideal could be said to represent a set of to-be-striven-for but forever not-quite-attainable ideal goals for the self" (Erikson, 1968, p. 210).

The ego ideal is counterposed with the self-image, a picture of oneself as one thinks one may be at any given point in time. People are continuously engaged in advancing their self-images toward their ego ideals. When people feel they are moving in that direction, then their self-esteem rises. This relation may be formulated as:

$$SE = \frac{1}{EI - SI}$$

The wish to like oneself, to narrow the gap between the self-image and the ego ideal, is the most powerful of all motivations. When people feel they are not moving consistently enough or quickly enough toward their ego ideal or are moving away from it, the gap between the self-image and the ego ideal increases, and they become angry with themselves. This is the core of stress. When they become angry with themselves, their feelings of guilt and inadequacy increase. They then become depressed, sometimes momentarily but, if the superego is severe, more often chronically. They may respond by increasing the intensity of their pressure on themselves to do better. Often there is also a spillover effect, projecting the blame on others and rationalizing an attack on those others. People may overcontrol their anger, increasing inner tension and stress. Or they may turn their anger on themselves in the form of accidents, self-defeat, and suicide.

To have a high ego ideal is to have, simultaneously, powerful aspirations. But an inordinately high ego ideal, whether developed primarily out of distortions of childhood thinking or exacerbated by the external environment, increases the intensity of anger with oneself. The same is true when the self-image is lowered. Thus one's greatest asset is simultaneously one's greatest source of vulnerability and stress.

When the self-image and ego ideal are in reasonable juxtaposition, so that the person feels good about himself or herself and is also ready to confront and surmount new challenges, the person experiences a sense of integrity and well being. The person feels whole, in charge of himself or herself, and the master of his or her own fate. When the gap increases beyond the person's comfort to manage the difference, then the person experiences pangs of guilt. When the guilt paralyzes or distorts thinking and action, that usually reflects also underlying unconscious guilt. By definition, this is guilt of which the person is unaware; and by definition, the person is also unaware of the reasons he or she feels that way and cannot act realistically. It is this phenomenon that usually undermines performance appraisal and makes a mockery of most training for appraising performance (Levinson, 1976).

Following are some of the more prominent threats to various executives' ability to approach the ethical aspects of their ego ideals.

1. *Dilemma of loyalty.* It used to be much easier to be true to one's own family, group, or tribe. This overriding consideration, still powerful in many cultures, legitimizes in many other countries what we in the United States would regard as venal nepotism or graft. That is the kind of commitment Jack Nicholson satirically exemplifies in the movie *Prizzi's Honor* when, on his Mafia boss's orders, he kills his own wife. It is also the kind of commitment to one's company that kept some of the long-term employees who were fired by Litton Industries from joining a suit against the company for age discrimination (Faludi, 1986).

Upwards of 90 percent of people at work are employed in organizations. Executives, managers, and even people at the line level are frequently torn between their obligations to their organization and those to other individuals and groups, whether fellow employees, customers, financial institutions, or government. Often executives who have been accused of cheating the government, cheating financial institutions, or turning out inadequate products to increase corporate profits say they did not do it for their own personal gain—they did it for the organization (Stricharchuk, 1986). Indeed, much of the time, that is true. One executive was fired for not giving a government regulatory agency information that it had not asked for when, ethically, he was supposed to do so. There was no personal gain in it for him, he told me; he was just "defending" his company. In his eyes, it shouldn't have fired him.

As a consequence, younger people now tend to identify more with their technical and professional associations than with the organizations that employ them. "Keep your résumé up to date and your network alive" is their byword. According to many surveys, middle management increasingly distrusts top management, and in many organizations managers are waiting for the other shoe to drop, fearing more contraction.

2. *Dilemma of product.* An executive described this problem: His company manufactures decorations. Among other products they make a silver-colored Christmas tree ornament. They learned that the silver paint on the ornament began to tarnish after seven years. Should he continue to allow that ornament to be manufactured? Probably he would not be in his present position for seven years. He might not even be in that company. He and his production superintendent concluded that nevertheless the company standards would not allow them to manufacture that ornament.

Johnson & Johnson and Bristol-Myers pulled capsules from the market, but other companies continue to manufacture products that they know to be dangerous or threatening. Ford was accused of that with its Pinto. What must executives feel who are aware of those dangers?

3. *Dilemma of shutdown.* The retired chairman of a major corporation described his difficulty contracting the size of the organization in the face of an economic downturn because he

knew so many of the people in it, as well as members of their families. He could not bring himself to fire some. Paralyzed by similar feelings of guilt, many executives in the coal, steel, and petroleum businesses could not face the implications of their economic realities until it was too late, and whole communities suffered.

Why must an executive think it is impossible for him or her to contract an organization, or even to do something far less painful, to give somebody else information about his or her performance? To think that one cannot or must not implies that one has deep-seated feelings, akin to terror, about acting. To take either one of those actions seems so terrible that for many people they are intolerable. Those feelings we understand as unconscious guilt (Levinson, 1964).

4. *Dilemma of personal desertion.* This is the usual experience of many entrepreneurs who, having built loyalty to themselves paternalistically, then sell their organizations. When they do, they frequently feel that they have betrayed and abandoned their people and that it is unfair of them to leave their people to strangers when, for reasons of age or estate, they had little choice. In most cases the purchasers are larger and more professionally managed organizations. They streamline the operations, often upgrade them, and are more demanding in their management. That means that many long-term employees who were tolerated by the previous owners can no longer be tolerated. Among such employees one often hears the remark "They don't care. It's just another big company now."

Contemporary entrepreneurs, typified by some in California's legendary Silicon Valley, flush with venture capital and a patented idea, often built loosely managed organizations that seemed more like country clubs than businesses. They attracted around them other young people who shared the enthusiasm for their freedom and their intention to get rich fast. When the advent of sobering reality subsequently required accountability and managerial controls, some acted as if reality should not have intruded. Their subordinates were disillusioned, and their success paled in the face of competition. Some publicly regretted letting their people down.

It is not unusual for managers or executives to have developed highly profitable units, departments, and specialty services for which they and their teams have justifiably attained great respect. They evolved and sustained an *esprit de corps*. Often, with their reputations, they could defend against real and imagined threats from the rest of their organizations. When the company decides to sell that unit or when such a leader retires or goes elsewhere, the rest of the team is likely to feel abandoned. The leader himself will have to live with the feeling that, however justified, his action was not fair to those loyal helpers and followers.

5. *Dilemma of succession.* As the chief executive of a major corporation reviewed the candidates from among whom his successor would be chosen, he said rather sadly that none among them was as good as he. His was not an egocentric remark. His candidates were indeed good. He had chosen them wisely and had nurtured their competence. Yet none would have traversed the same route as he. He had joined the organization when it was comparatively small. His creative leadership built it to major proportions. He knew all of its businesses, having studied some of them carefully before acquiring them and having managed others sometime during his career. However, he could not have rotated his potential successors through the range of businesses that he had been able to experience. The organization had become too big and many components too specialized for that. Indeed, in that sense, none of his possible successors would be as good as he. Although each would bring different perceptions and different skills, and whoever succeeded him would surely grow into that role, he could not leave his organization the competence he felt it deserved. In his view, he could not fully discharge his ethical responsibilities.

Another chief executive was preoccupied with the worry that his successors would not carry on his values. He was a caring, charitable person. His successors were "gung ho" bottom-line-oriented. For economic and other reasons there had not been enough time to develop from within sufficient numbers of potential successors who could carry on his values. He had had to employ several high-level executives from the outside to manage the businesses he had acquired when their entrepreneurs subsequently left. The second-tier executives were good managers, but they had not worked with him long enough to identify with him. They did not yet share his tradition. He felt he was not being fair to his organization. More important to him, he was not being fair to himself, for he had devoted his leadership tenure to advocating and standing for his values. Now the organization would no longer be his monument. Its symbolic banner would be only a tattered rag. He cried his pain.

Every executive who devotes herself to building her organization, whether part of a company or an independent unit, and puts her characterological stamp on it has or will have the same problem as each of these two executives. She will have built or rebuilt. And if she has done it well, rarely will her successor have been as close to the developing organization. Often the successor will have to come from the outside. Inevitably, that person, being different, necessarily will have to do things differently. Each change implies to the predecessor that her successor thinks she didn't do something well enough. Each change is an implied criticism. No matter what anyone says about being unconcerned after he or she has left a role, the fact is that few executives who have been through such an experience are free of such feelings.

6. *Dilemma of personal responsibility.* When the balcony of the Kansas City Hyatt Regency Hotel collapsed, according to press reports, the first impulse of Donald Hall, who was then the chief executive of Hallmark and who had a big stake in that hotel, was to go to the families of those who had been killed and injured. His company and his family were well known in Kansas City for their responsible and compassionate community leadership. However, his lawyers insisted that he not do so because of the corporation's vulnerability to suit. He could not act in keeping with what he felt to be his personal responsibility as traditionally he would have.

In a different context, Warren M. Anderson, then the chief executive of Union Carbide Corporation, wanted to do something immediately for the victims of the Bhopal tragedy in India. In fact, he went almost immediately after the accident to Bhopal. He was quickly forced to withdraw his effort and to allow his attorneys to respond to the many claims against his company.

In both instances the executives could not act to meet what they thought to be their personal and leadership moral obligations. All executives inevitably, at some time in their careers, will be confronted with such incidents. They will have to anticipate being caught up in such a dilemma. For legal reasons and perhaps others, they will have to curb their humanitarian impulses. It will be especially difficult for executives whose values have included a powerful sense of compassion.

7. *Dilemma of fiduciary.* The task of every executive of a publicly held organization is to be accountable to his or her board and, in turn, to the stockholders. The board determines the direction; it can and does fire executives. That poses problems when an executive has to contract or ''downsize'' or close a plant in the interests of the stockholders at the expense of the employees.

An executive, however pained, must act to preserve the organization, even if it means firing loyal, long-term employees and in some instances demoralizing whole communities. One has only to look at the unemployed among the slag heaps of West Virginia, the dying communities of Pennsylvania among the vast, empty, rusting steel mills, and the crumbling oil towns of the Southwest, with their contaminated water tables, to know the social cost. The same problem occurs when the organization must deal with environmental impact and obligations. Midwestern electric power companies are being told that they must purge their sulfur dioxide emissions to prevent acid rain. That means that they must spend billions of dollars for a technology that many think is questionable. In fact, some electric utilities may not survive if they have to spend those billions. Regulatory bodies usually feel that such expenditures must come out of stockholders' pockets, not consumers'.

In both instances, shutdown and pollution, the executive has assumed the responsibility for protecting the financial interests of the owners in the context of a political system that gives priority to property rights. He or she must perforce protect the organization even if it means declaring bankruptcy, as Manville Corporation, Continental Airlines Corporation, and A. H. Robin Company did, to avoid being totally wiped out by damage claims and the costs of prevention and restitution.

Under such circumstances, what is fair? Can an executive afford even to be fair? How will executives feel when they must defend in every possible way, not only to settle present allegations but, more important, to set no precedents and leave no loopholes for future litigants?

8. *Dilemma of sharing power.* Eastern Airlines' attempt at participative management failed. Frank Borman, then Eastern's CEO, was said to be accustomed to an authoritarian style of direction and therefore not to know how to engage in participative effort (Simmons, 1986). A whole era of contemporary executives will be struggling with the same problem while they push the people below them to engage in participative management.

The self-image of the good executive is of one who is in charge, who gives direction, who marshals his or her forces to defeat the competition. The ego ideal of many executives is to do exactly that, for to invite the contributions of subordinates is also to invite debate and dissension, differences and discord, and the possibility that the whole management team will collapse in conflict, the position of the executive as the leader undermined.

If executives are to be involved more actively in participative management, they will have to head teams of specialists having skills which complement and support their own but in which they may not be as well versed as those specialist practitioners. Think, for example, of how few executives know as much about management information systems as management information systems specialists. Yet, if the work of all those people is to be coordinated, the leader will have to encourage discussion and contribution to decision making by all members of the team. As more personnel assert their professional competence, they will tend to regard themselves more as professional colleagues than as subordinates. The leader will have to engage with them while sustaining her leadership role. And in some cases she will have to stand corrected by her team members when she errs.

Executives, increasingly, will have to see themselves as being in leadership, rather than command, roles. Given the contemporary ethos, they will have to delegate responsibility more often than give direction, and to do so responsibly will mean that they will have to engage with those who constitute their teams. In some instances, as in matrix management, those team members will also be given leadership by others. They will be necessarily dependent on all the executives to whom they are responsible. If those executives are not to be in perennial conflict, then they, in their turn, will have to be in close touch with one another. That calls for regular communications meetings and the resolution of differences among executives in those meetings.

9. *Dilemma of obligation.* Traditionally trust officers in banks manage estates for widows and orphans. They are supposed to be conservative and reliable, as their title implies. With the reorganization of banks and their concern for return on investment, return on assets, profitability, and other financial criteria, trust officers were pushed to increase the earnings from their departments. To increase earnings requires them to take bigger risks. To take bigger risks means to them that they can no longer readily assure themselves and their clients of the safety and steady return that they implicitly had offered those who trusted them. Furthermore, when bank functions are divided into commercial banking and consumer banking, neither of those defines a home for the trust officer. How can he or she now meet these multiple obligations?

No doubt there are parallels in other businesses, especially service organizations. How does one balance needs for profitability against quality of service? When financial criteria rather than service criteria become paramount, the client takes the bigger risks. But it is the executive who, like the trust officer, suffers the anguish of being less able to assure himself and his clients of the quality of service that they expected of him.

Coping with the Dilemmas. No doubt managers and executives in all organizations face many similar dilemmas. How can managers and executives cope with such dilemmas? To be more precise, how can they cope with their own feelings of obligation to themselves so that they may continue to like themselves and to remain psychologically whole?

Individuals who are in psychotherapy frequently will spell out such struggles and spill out their feelings. That process helps them clarify their options, weigh them, and choose the most satisfactory. In other contexts support groups, composed of people who struggle with similar problems, often enable participants to choose appropriate options. In organizations, team-building activities allow people to share their problems and to attenuate them, but in many organizations the need to protect the macho image of the executive may militate against such effort, and at times the organizational culture may not allow the flexibility or personal freedom for such expressions. In these cases the individual managers and executives may talk with a consultant to arrive at modes of coping with their feelings. However, often no consultant is available. There is then no alternative to depression and its concomitant, stewing in one's own physiological juices.

The research possibilities are myriad. For example, what is the range of problems of ego-ideal conflict that managers and executives confront? What do they do about them? With what success? What do they wish in retrospect they had done? How do these problems vary by kind of business, size of business, level in the organization, and experience? What inures managers and executives to such strains, and at what cost in loss of sensitivity to their own feelings and to those of others in their organizations? What is the correlation between such strains and the incidence and prevalence of physical symptoms?

How do we understand those conflicts that seem not to be rational or to be less rational than some others? Among these is the unconscious guilt in performance appraisal that results in piling up ratings at the high end of the scale, no matter what is done to attenuate that problem. How, in empirical research, might it be possible to differentiate rational guilt from unconscious guilt? There are many situations, like the one cited earlier, where executives cannot contract their organization even in the face of possible bankruptcy because they are unable to bring themselves to discharge people. Without a theory of personality, there is no room for such phenomena in ordinary, atheoretical, descriptive psychology or what is ordinarily called organizational behavior. Yet the phenomenon is pervasive and probably constitutes the single most destructive influence on executive decision making (Levinson, 1964).

There are no satisfying solutions to ego-ideal conflict, but we can apply an important lesson from our understanding of ambivalence. Ambivalence is the simultaneous presence of two conflicting feelings, positive and negative. One, usually the negative or aggressive feeling, is unconscious. There is necessarily ambivalence in all relationships. Relationships survive when the affectional component outweighs the aggressive. In dealing with ethical conflicts, there is a way of increasing the affectional: by discussion with other interested or concerned persons who thereby provide support. Ethical dilemmas can be tempered when they are shared by those who have a commitment to themselves and their organizations as well as to their customers or clients. Companies can foster commitment in three ways.

1. By having a criterion of an appropriate and effective organization. Jaques (1976) defines a "requisite organization" as one which meets human needs and standards of ethical behavior and which fosters (1) awareness of self and the self of others, (2) the ability to communicate and understand the communication of others, (3) the capacity to cooperate with another in paying attention to the same subject, and (4) the capacity for social and economic exchange relationships. It is the last to which the hidden dilemmas relate most directly, but all require the involvement of all organization participants.

There are many other definitions of effective organizations. Researchers might well test the hypothesis that there are fewer ego-ideal conflict problems in requisite organizations, as Jaques (1976) hypothesizes. Would organizations that meet other criteria of effectiveness have fewer such problems or resolve them more readily?

2. By trying to facilitate commitment. To be an organization, those who are part of it must cohere. Cohesion is a product of the definition of the transcendent purpose of the specific employment organization, exemplified and implemented by the leadership. Purpose is more than a mission statement: It is a statement of values and beliefs which are never achieved and

toward which the organization is always striving. That striving is in pursuit of goals and objectives that are derived from purpose, goals being long-term steps and objectives being short-term steps. Transcendent purpose should differentiate one organization from another, just as an individual's unique ego ideal differentiates that person from others. An idealized statement that is akin to "Motherhood and apple pie" and not supported by specifics of principles, policies, and practices will only make people cynical.

Are there fewer ego ideal conflicts when the transcendent purpose of an organization is clearly defined and the goals and objectives support the movement toward that purpose? Are there fewer dilemmas when performance appraisal systems are developed by employees out of their own experiences? When continuity of organizational values is sustained, or when continuity of ownership and management is consistent over time? Empirical research could help answer such questions.

Can people who teach management also teach not ethics, but an understanding of guilt, particularly unconscious guilt, and will such teaching help graduate students in business or business executives cope better with problems concerning guilt in the future? Those, too, are empirical questions.

3. By recognizing, as some of us have been saying for many years, that all change is loss and all loss must be mourned. Otherwise, chronic low-level depression ensues, which impairs the adaptive capacity of the organization. One can hardly treat organizational depression with drugs. To lift it requires that all the staff recognize the significance of the underlying fear, anxiety, and anger when change occurs, even when that change is highly desirable. This means that people must be able to talk to one another, both within and across departments, about what is happening to them, how they feel about it, how they propose to master the new problems, and how they can have an effect on the decisions to cope with those forces requiring change. They must be able to identify with their leadership in order to be able to identify with one another. Leadership itself must exemplify the purpose of the organization by leading an attack on its problems and creating conditions under which people can identify

with that leadership. In short, purposeful activity must become a cause.

That kind of purposeful leadership that became a cause in their organizations was exemplified by the six major chief executives Levinson and Rosenthal (1984) interviewed. The six were the chief executives of General Electric, IBM, the *New York Times,* Monsanto, Citicorp, and AMAX. In each case, those chief executives saw themselves as stewards. Their task was not only to perpetuate their organizations but also to turn over to their successors organizations that were stronger than when they themselves had taken over. They gave considerable attention to succession and to the development of people who could assume organizational leadership. In at least three cases—General Electric, IBM, and the *New York Times*—there was a very heavy emphasis on corporate values in which purpose was embodied and on the traditions of the organization that reflected those values as the basis for continuity. General Electric executives joked that they had the GE symbol stamped on their behinds. The *New York Times* viewed itself as the daily historian of major world events. It stood for integrity and independence. And IBM's emphasis on quality, service, and consideration for the communities in which it operated, as well as respect for its employees, is widely known.

As documented in that book, each organization faced specific threatening problems, and each leader, in keeping with the values of that organization, sometimes at great risk, led his organization into mastering them. Not without trepidation. Not without anxiety. Not without sometimes horrendous failure. Not without significant disappointment. And above all, not without hope, ideals, and conviction.

Do such executives, organizational stewards, with their heavy emphasis on continuity and regeneration, suffer greater conflict of conscience in their roles because of that orientation, or do the powerful value systems of their organizations buffer them under such circumstances? Neither that study nor others answer that question. It would help to know.

12

Foundations for Executive Integrity: Dialogue, Diversity, Development

Suresh Srivastva
Frank J. Barrett

Even before Socrates beckoned to us to "know thyself" and spoke of the need to examine one's own life, humankind had been struggling with the question of how to live in this world meaningfully, how to live a life that has value.

The individualistic tone of this wisdom is misleading, however, for if we did not have to live *with* one another, the question would never arise. If we could be self-contained and live our lives without needing to relate, or to understand and be understood, the questions of goodness, rightness, and excellence in character would be irrelevant. A life of solipsism and narcissism, in which the self is the center of the universe, oblivious to others' existence, would make the questions of moral choice and value of character irrelevant. Human action would be guided by one consistent principle of self-service without impingement by pangs of awareness of what consequences one's actions have for others. We would not pause to wonder whether the food we had gathered for ourselves meant that a living organism had died or that another would starve. Nor would we hesitate to pass over a deserving employee for promotion or worry about the consequences of ignoring performance appraisal. We would live our lives assuming that the world was consonant with our desires, existing for our pleasure, and our only concern would be our own continued satiation.

This concept of integrity is an effort to acknowledge the crucial role of the other in the shaping of our behavior and our utterances. By placing the word *executive* in front of *integrity*, we mean to say that integrity is not an individual characteristic or state of existence. In our frame it is misleading to speak of a person who "has" integrity, as if it were a possession. *Integrity is an interactive event, an evolving, transformative process that occurs in exceptional moments, moments when individuals step out of the ordinary day-to-day life of self-oriented existence for survival in an effort to attend to the other's development.* We *create* moments of integrity whenever we are able to appreciate what we allow ourselves to see in the other and in such a way that the relationship is furthered and sustained. The "wholeness" that the word *integrity* refers to is the wholeness of the relationship, the wholeness of the interaction.

When we see integrity as a moral quality that certain individuals possess, reflection and discussion usually become frustrating and oppressive because, like all virtues, it becomes a standard never realized. "Integrity" too easily becomes a club to punish oneself and others for shortcomings, and in so doing, it obscures our perceptions. The concept leads to embarrassing admissions that one does not live up to the ideals one hears oneself and others espousing and as a consequence suppresses further inquiry as one attempts to deny the parts of one's experience *not* full of integrity. Almost every discussion of integrity leaves someone feeling inadequate and inferior or angry. When integrity is conceived of in this way, dialogue ends, and with it the very possibility for integrity, because integrity as we conceive it demands sustained interaction, a point we will return to at length.

Such a concept unintentionally promotes a deficiency orientation ranging from self-deprecation to cynicism and diminished expectations for the capacity for moral action among humans. If we succumb to the temptation to see integrity as manifest in a code of ethics, we risk the likelihood of noticing that almost every action we take in the workplace is in violation of some rule. Once such ideas become expressed as platitudes and no longer belong in the arena of imperfect human interaction, they are more likely codes for the gods to live by.

Our concept of integrity as a relational, interactive event is a protest against the view of the person as an isolable, self-contained unit, existing independent of culture and society and occasionally "entering into" relations with other "individuals." Such a view holds the self as authentic when able to separate from the influence of others in order to be "truly oneself." Some have said that a person has integrity to the extent that he or she is fully himself or herself. In fact, the concepts of self and individual are misnomers. We are never "fully ourselves" in our utterances. Nor can we ever remove ourselves from others' influences. *There is no such thing as privacy.* We are a collection of selves, of influential voices that carry on an unceasing dialogue inside our heads, so that it is misleading to say a person has integrity when he or she is truly saying what is on his or her mind. Outer, articulated speech is only an island that emerges from a sea of competing and interweaving voices (Vygotsky, 1986). In this sense *every spoken word is coauthored.* Even the process of thought itself is social. Thinking assumes the form of socially defined conversations with imagined others (Bakhtin, 1981). If all acts and speeches are coauthored, then in order to create conditions in organizations to enhance integrity, organizations must create norms that foster true dialogue, actively promote diversity, and support development.

Fostering Dialogue

I constantly have to remind myself to
stay in the conversation [Neil Simon].

Martin Buber (1947) wrote that the experience of true dialogue is like the "lifting of a spell." The "spell" he spoke of was his perpetual withholding of himself, his impenetrableness and unwillingness "to communicate himself." When he was able to truly enter dialogue, to actively engage another, he felt a sense of freedom, release, and union with another presence. We are engaged in true dialogue whenever we are willing to have our thought interrupted by the other, to be changed by the other. Mutuality and reciprocity occur in a dialogical exchange: Each sees the other as an active center of awareness capable of offering a rich perspective. Dialogue does not translate into surrendering one's point of view in favor of the other's. When a person's position is constantly under revision or when she is always empathic, she cannot engage in true dialogue, because she can contribute nothing to the other.

In our view, dialogue is the operative soul of the integrious human system. In fact, genuine dialogue presupposes the existence of the other conditions for integrity—diversity and development. And yet like oxygen, though vital to the life support of the system, moments of dialogue are invisible and tacit. One can have a dialogical encounter with an influential other even when that other is not present. It is possible to have an ongoing dialogue with an influential other whose voice in our heads persuades us toward some emotion or action. Often we realize another's contribution long after an exchange occurred. Many, for example, continue to struggle with or receive guidance from an influential parent even after the parent is deceased. We will attempt in this chapter to identify some of the characteristics of genuine dialogue, to make the tacit explicit, but since dialogical exchanges cannot be confidently identified or photographed, we can only talk around it and sketch the outline of an elusive, vital process.

To the extent that both parties sustain a presence and remain accessible and open to the emergence of new voices in their exchange, the conditions of integrity are furthered. The more radically different the voice of the other, the more potential for integrity, because there exists more potential to stretch, to surprise, to extend experience. In dialogue, executive integrity is occurring in those moments when we actively respond to the other, who, stimulated by our response, engages further, which, in turn, inspires us to imagine new ideas and invest new energy. If executive integrity were a process that could somehow be color-coded and photographed, it would appear as multiple mini-figures of mutually generating, ascending spirals.

Executive integrity is embodied in dialogical exchanges because it is a recognition of the primacy and richness of the relationship. The evolution of social exchange is not a unilateral

294   Executive Integrity

choice, however. One party's stance influences the other's. That
is, as coauthors, both shape the direction of the exchange and
the range of responses available to each other.

Consider the following exchange, which appeared in the
Cleveland *Plain Dealer* ("Dispatcher Helps Save Choking Child,"
1984, pp. 12A–13A) when Barbara DiDomenico placed an emer-
gency call to the Warminster Township Fire Department to
report that her eighteen-month-old son was choking on an orange
slice. The dispatcher was Robin Thoman:

"Hurry, please, my baby's choking," Barbara DiDomenico told Thoman.
"Please hurry. He's blue. Hurry, please. What can we do?"

After telling Mrs. DiDomenico an ambulance was on the way and
asking what the child was choking on, the dispatcher told the mother to
hold her son close and listen to instructions. Mrs. DiDomenico gave the
phone to her father, Donald Black, sixty-two, at whose Warminster
Township home the family was staying. The conversation, taped as part
of the town's emergency-call procedures, continued:

"Listen to me. I'm going to tell you what to do. Put him over
your hands. Turn him on his stomach over your arms . . . gently press
on his stomach and pat him on the back at the same time and wipe out
his mouth if he starts choking it up so he doesn't swallow it back."

"His jaws are locked," Mrs. DiDomenico sobbed.

"Can you get an ambulance here?" Black asked.

Thoman told him an ambulance was en route, then repeated his
instructions. Finally, he heard a baby's cry.

"Oh, he's starting to cry," Black said.

"OK, all right," Thoman said. "Make sure you wipe it out of
his mouth so he doesn't choke it back down. . . . All right, is he breathing
OK? Is he breathing OK?"

"Oh, he's all right," Mrs. DiDomenico said.

"OK," Thoman said. "The ambulance will be there in a couple
of minutes."

In this dialogue each of the participants tacitly shapes the tone
of the interaction and the direction of the spiral. In a testimony

to the tentative, crystalline nature of interaction, each party contributes something of value to the other. Barbara provides information adequate for the dispatcher that engages his participation. She invites the dispatcher to imagine the victim's condition by presenting a pictorial image ("He's blue") and puts forth an open-ended invitation to enter: "Hurry, please. What can we do?" Robin, the dispatcher, perhaps struggles with his internal dialogue and attempts to "take in" an image of the other. Listen to how he describes what went on in his mind. He tells the news reporter: "The first thing I had to do was get a mental picture of the child. I tried to picture what I would do if my children were choking, and I think it drove me that much faster." He raises the other to a level of significance by struggling, by allowing the language of the other to invoke something in him. There is no closing out of the other, no "slamming of the gate," no reliance on established authority or prescriptive formula to establish a presence before the other. And the caller, on her part, poses no threatening challenge that would stimulate in the dispatcher a hardening urge to establish presence. There are no blinders to impair the immediate, concrete granting of voice of the other and image formation of the victim. The dispatcher slows down the high velocity of the crisis with clear, concrete, physical directions, concurring with Buber's sense that when a person is engaged in dialogue, time seems to slow down: "Listen to me. . . . Put him over your hands. Turn him like on his stomach." He gives deliberate attention to minuscule details as if guiding the other graciously: "Make sure you wipe it out of his mouth so he doesn't choke it back down. . . . Is he breathing okay?" alternating between instruction, deductive logic, taking a barometer of the other's state, he refuses to get lost in the reliance on formulaic prescriptions and checks back with the other, the living, squirming, unpredictable other who at any moment could surprise him with a new, concrete obstacle: "Is he breathing okay?" As if to wonder, "How much of my direction have you been able to absorb?" And, finally, the reassurance: "The ambulance will be there."

Organizations are collections of people with diverse perspectives who are brought together under a shared paradigm

(Pfeffer, 1981). When dialogue is given import, the organization is valuing members' diversity as well as their commonality. One of the characteristics of the "ideal" bureaucracy (Weber, 1946/1961) is that members' forms of responsiveness are limited and limiting. Spans of control, role barriers, hierarchical authority are created and reinforced in service of efficiency so that members perform prescribed tasks by bringing parts of themselves to bear on the job. The "ideal" bureaucracy fosters a monologic mode of interaction to the extent that the organization dictates what behaviors are acceptable and what concerns are legitimately voiced.

Integrity occurs in organizations to the extent that the organization fosters norms which stress that organizing is a verb, that action is in the process of becoming, that members are continuously creating and re-creating the future. Through dialogue and continual interaction free from arbitrary barriers, members exchange ideas and perspectives on reality, inquiring into one another's potential and furthering the emergence of new ideas. Engaging in dialogue is a testimony to members' innate potential to create something new, and when organizations legitimate dialogue, they are furthering the overall sense of the organization as open-ended, evolving, and adaptable.

The spirit of dialogue furthers the executive integrity of the system because membership involves more than just task completion. It involves ongoing learning, a search for and discovery of knowledge and ideas through interaction, a sense of interdependence. Ongoing, restless dialogue furthers the assumption that the unprecedented experiment can be attempted.

> Proposition #1: Dialogue is the consent to grant voice to the other. Dialogue is enhanced to the extent that one addresses the other with the presumption that the other is capable of responding unexpectedly and meaningfully. Executive integrity exists in an organization to the extent that members are willing to be interrupted and make themselves available to engage in dialogue with one another.

Dialogue means the parties invite and join one another

in entertaining the possibility of pursuing ideas and projects; in a sense, they help one another appreciate the potential for the emerging, developing idea. Members can eliminate arbitrary barriers to interaction that create separation in traditionally hierarchical systems such as the traditional division between managers as "thinkers and planners" and workers as "doers." In the integrious system every member is a "thinking doer," and in that sense, every member of the system is an executive.

The integrious system promotes norms which create the sense that the organization is open and becoming, unresolved, unpredetermined, exceeding its own previous boundaries. It is a system of unlikely marriages. Changing relevant issues spur the continual creation and dissolution of temporary ad hoc groups, investigative task forces, and fluid dyadic partnerships. Creating accessibility is the key.

Executives often find subtle ways to maintain inaccessibility. Closed office doors and demands that appointments be made with secretaries during prescribed office hours are certainly necessary to protect one's time and space in a busy world. The CEO of one local hospital, however, has an open policy of "deliberate accessibility"—at any time during the day, any physician can speak with him: "I have a policy that I've made clear. I work for the doctors here. If at any time they need to see me about anything, they can. Whether I'm in a meeting or a planning session, they can come in and interrupt and get me out."

Certainly all members need to limit their range of responsiveness to others to some degree. However, we wish to call attention to the spirit behind this example and the subtle ways in which people withdraw from others. We are not recommending that all executives remove their doors from the hinges and burn their appointment books; we only suggest that fostering dialogue is a deliberate act of accessibility.

> Proposition #2: Executive integrity exists in an organization to the extent that members create new and multiple forms of responsiveness in arenas where members are free to respectfully vocalize perceptions without restraint or fear of reprimand or censure.

Executive integrity is enacted when members know that their perspectives, though not always agreed with, have a legitimate right to be voiced. Organizations need to be aware of the dangers of dogmatism that prevents articulation of the unexpected. When organizations foster norms of dialogue and create arenas of responsiveness, they are valuing the relational, inter-human web of the organization that goes beyond the manifest level, the content of information exchange. Organizations that experiment with multiple forms of responsiveness improve the possibility for multilevel understanding among undiminished voices.

The CEO of one large manufacturing company discovered that executives were hesitant to express some of their ideas and concerns to him, and so he created monthly "executive sessions." The first Saturday of the month, they gather for "casual cocktails" and discuss "whatever comes up." One physician group has semiannual three-day retreats with no agendas. Another senior manager meets bimonthly with a random selection of employees from each department for a two-hour lunch in which members are encouraged to express concerns and ideas. When each member of the organization has had an opportunity, the manager begins the cycle again: "At first I was hesitant to try it because I thought I'd just hear people bitch. And initially that's what happened. But suddenly it turned into lively dialogue sessions. I've gotten some ideas from those lunches. It caught on like wildfire. The funny thing is that they give each other ideas about their departments and I can hardly get a word in edgewise. They do ask tough questions." Another CEO gives every employee in the company his home phone number and invites members to call him.

Organizations need to experiment continually with new ways to facilitate the expression of members' concerns and ideas and create processes that are occasions for discovery. Integrious dialogue involves deliberate invitational efforts, outside a traditional chain of command, where permission is granted to vocalize the unpermissible. In a sense, organizations need to create an "antiorganization," a "time-out" in which anyone is free to say anything, an arena where members are free to parody the formal organization and everyone agrees not to take offense. Organizations need to create a collective carnival, a chance to make the sacred ordinary, to create a parody of the official culture where members can laugh at their own conventions from a safe distance. One academic department in a local university held such an event at a recent holiday celebration where students and faculty members performed a parody of *The Wizard of Oz*. Members were free to laugh at caricatures of themselves and the comic depictions of some of the common departmental dilemmas and coping mechanisms. "Unpermissible" topics usually reserved for private gossip were made public and acknowledged. The anonymous quips, targeted at no one person, provided a collective release of frustration, a temporary group absolution, a catharsis of sorts. Humor is the great equalizer. When we are engaged in laughter together, all status differentials are temporarily erased. We are all characters of comedy. A distinction needs to be made here between humor and sarcasm, and again the critical variable is intent. Sarcasm seeks to subordinate the other indirectly. Humor creates bonds because we laugh at ourselves first and is healing because it is a glance at the comic dimensions of our common survival efforts, our serious attempts to look perfect in an imperfect world. When an organization creates an arena where members engage in play and humor, to momentarily offset the unintended consequences of stratification, executive integrity is furthered because relationships, not distance created by status, are valued as primary.

Norms of ongoing fruitful dialogue that legitimate interruption create a sense that members are coauthors of the organization's future. When organizations create forums where members can imagine and articulate the polar opposite of the declared strategy, genuine dialogue and therefore executive integrity are furthered because dialogue fosters the sanctity of the potential, the yet unrealized but not impossible; dialogue keeps the dialectic creative process alive and fosters a sense that organizational decisions and structures are not inevitable and static but are the result of human choice (Srivastva and Barrett, 1987).

One obstacle to articulating the "underside" of organizational life is the possibility (or likelihood) that someone will take offense. The tendency, especially among middle-level managers, to protect, to feel cautious, to take personal offense is perhaps the largest obstacle to forums for restless, ongoing dialogue. It usually occurs when managers define their jobs as managing and controlling people rather than orchestrating ideas. When managers define their sense of importance in terms of areas of responsibility or the number of people they are responsible for, they are bound to spend a good deal of their life feeling offended or guarding against attack. However, to the degree that they see themselves as midwives helping in the birthing process of new ideas, or as choreographers helping others to dance, they are furthering the possibility for executive integrity because their focus is always on the potential and the tacit. There is less fear of having to share the spotlight, because the spotlight is always on the emerging idea—or, to continue the metaphor, we applaud the dance and not the dancer.

Proposition #3: Executive integrity is furthered when the organization adopts norms that legitimate members' inquiry into all realms of organizational activity.

Executive integrity exists in an organization to the extent that members are free to interrupt monologues, the gradual hardening of positions that, intentionally or not, excludes some important other. When one member engages in monologue, an effort to create a preferred posture without granting voice to another, it is contagious—others become more likely to do the same. Taken to an extreme, monologue is a strategy to eliminate or ignore the other's version of reality. In fact, one could argue that many unethical organizational activities are the result of the gradual exclusion of a point of view, a voice that became so diminished as to be forgotten. Recent disclosure of the decision-making processes that led to the failure of *Challenger* provides a reminder of the seductiveness of urgency as the voices of dissent of engineers at Morton Thiokol were not heard. When members are free to engage in continual questioning, conjecturing, and hypothesizing, wondering about the significance and consequences of their work, the potential for integrity is furthered.

Organizations are prime candidates for such "innocent" ignorance of the other's point of view that spiral later into far-reaching consequences. Organizations are especially prime places to generate justifications for such actions (Weick, 1986). Executive integrity exists to the extent that organizations *deliberately* create processes that allow themselves to be interrupted and create time-outs for reflection and self-awareness. Fostering norms that legitimate members' right to question and provoke at all levels of hierarchy and all stages of activity will further the conditions for executive integrity. In the integrious system *all* questions are fair game, from executive succession to whether the firm should buy nonunion lettuce for the cafeteria, from investments in South Africa to hiring practices.

> Proposition #4: Executive integrity exists to the extent that members promote norms of sustained presence and create a culture marked by a willingness to stay in the process of dialogue with one another.

The typical "dance" of members engaged in monologue is to make assertions and depart. Withdrawal is not always physical, however. Platitudes and clichés, citing reliable authority, citing one's superior position are all strategies to maintain inaccessibility. The rhythm of dialogue is sustained presence and interaction, continuous active debate. If an outsider were to witness an organization having a creative, dialogical exchange, she might mistakenly think she was watching disorganization and conflict. One cannot capture the spirit of the integrious, dialogical organization in a single snapshot, however. Dialogue presumes a history and an imagined future.

For example, an administrator at the Cleveland Clinic described his dismay when, in his first week as a member of the division, he witnessed an intense debate between two prominent surgeons who, in a committee meeting, disagreed sharply on a particular departmental issue. He concluded that they were arguing so intensely that the distance between them was unbridgeable, and he assumed the department would dissolve. He was shocked to find them talking together a few hours later as if nothing had happened. The administrator recounted the experience: "When I first came to this department, I went to a meeting with the chairman and a number of the prominent physicians in the department, and there was some disagreement. It broke into a furious argument. It was a very heated argument with slamming fists and yelling at each other, 'I think you're crazy.' It was very disturbing. And I thought, 'This is it; well, the department will dissolve, everybody's going to leave, these people are going to quit probably this afternoon.' I thought the whole structure had fallen apart and I'd only been here a week. I thought, 'I hope my old job is still available.' Later that afternoon the physicians were sitting around having coffee together talking about some other topic."

Efforts to achieve integrity in relationships are often long and arduous. Integrity is occurring in some nascent form among parties whenever there are attempts at dialogue. Moments are not smooth but jittery: testing and trying, refusing and reconsidering, withdrawing and returning. The ability to debate furiously, to disagree liberally, comes when members have a sustained, dialogical, committed relationship that can withstand moments of divergence. Much organizational literature stresses that in order to resolve conflict among individuals and groups, members must establish a sense of trust, which then allows the accomplishment of interdependent tasks. In our view, the independent and dependent variables are reversed. Cooperative action creates trust, not vice versa. Trust can be defined as repeated success at dialogue.

Promoting Diversity

Executive integrity refers to the *vibrancy* of the collective. Vibrancy connotes a lively, pulsating energy, as in the quivering motion of a tuning fork that vibrates with sound when struck. Executives attend to the integrity of the system and the life of the idea when they are resonators, listening for the resonance and the sympathetic vibrations as ideas and perceptions reverberate among members, when the percussive sound of a proposed idea echoes and prolongs after its original articulation. When executives can attune themselves to the various frequencies, some audible and some inaudible, they are furthering the executive integrity of the system. When we speak of the need to promote diversity, we are referring specifically to the need to deliberately give voice to the inaudible frequencies.

Much recent organizational literature stresses the need for common vision leadership and the powerful potential for organizations that have a common mission, a meaningful culture that drives members' contributions (Srivastva and Associates, 1983; Peters and Waterman, 1982). When members feel that the organization's mission has a sense of destiny, that the organization is doing something significant, it becomes a catalyst for members' commitment and the creation of an egalitarian spirit (Srivastva and Cooperrider, 1986). Diverse individuals and groups depend on a common mission to coordinate activities. Recent leadership literature extols successful leaders who are able to articulate the common mission well (Levinson and Rosenthal, 1984; Bennis and Nanus, 1985).

We would like to speak to the other side of leadership: the need to appreciate diversity within the organization. We recognize that executives are powerful to the extent that they do both simultaneously, helping *diverse* members experience themselves as contributing to a *shared* understanding that drives collective action (Srivastva and Barrett, 1986). To understand the complexity such action entails, it is necessary to appreciate the dynamics of the *group mind*. When we widen the forms of interaction from the dyad to the group or organization, dynamics become more complicated and abstruse and the issue of integrity more elusive. We would like to address some of the dynamics in group life that are usually unseen and unconscious but powerfully affect individual behavior, as a way to call attention to the need for actively appreciating and deliberately promoting diversity in order to further integrity.

When individuals enter a group setting, they begin to behave differently than would be expected. Sigmund Freud noticed that when individuals collect in groups, a collective mind set begins to take over, and individuals regress and relinquish their critical faculties. He looked specifically at highly autocratic, homogeneous groups—the church and the military—but his insights offer explanations for individual tendencies in all groups, from families to mobs. He saw that individuals easily fall under the hypnotic spell of a leader and become like helpless, dependent children following the internalized voices of their parents: "A group is extraordinarily credulous and open to influence, it has no critical faculty, and the improbable does not exist for it . . . agreement with reality is never checked by any reasonable agency. The feelings of a group are always very simple and very exaggerated so that a group knows neither doubt nor uncertainty" (Freud, 1921/1965, p. 16).

Freud theorized that individuals seek homogeneity in groups and relinquish their intellect to an autonomous leader because of the largely unconscious desire to be included and protected by the larger presence of the group. They surrender their "critical faculty" to a highly invested other in order to feel that they belong and that they are protected from a threatening, chaotic world.

What is it within individuals that makes them susceptible to such a costly surrender, that of their autonomous wills? What is it that prepares them to silence parts of themselves and grant automatic voice to an other? It is beneficial to spend a few moments looking at this process and some of its consequences because the very same tendency exists for individuals in organizations. It is necessary to notice the manifestation of this tendency, as executives often do at some tacit level, in order to further the occurrence of executive integrity because if integrity is the granting of voice, and individuals willingly silence their voices in organizations, perhaps "granting" voice is not a strong enough concept to preserve integrity.

The answer to this question lies in our socialization processes and how individual development is curbed by, and in some ways opposed to, the development of civilization. The individual's full expression of his or her natural instincts, especially the erotic and aggressive instincts, would threaten the existence of the human bond (Freud, 1931/1969). The individual needs to develop some sort of automatic mechanism that will curtail impulses. It is the role of the parents in the early development of the child to implant an inner voice that will guide behavior. This "voice" becomes the conscience (or superego), which guides the individual's choices by imposing a sense of right and wrong. According to Freud, the first significant moment when the child "bumps up" against the civilization is when he is toilet-trained. He learns that he creates waste, that parts of himself are bad and unacceptable. His conscience eventually becomes adept, so that parents no longer need to correct his behavior, when the child automatically denies certain impulses and in effect says, "Don't worry, Father, you don't have to punish me anymore. I'll punish myself now" (Becker, 1971). Thus begins an interactive cycle of constriction and self-editing. In the meantime, the child learns to do whatever he can to correct behavior and win parental love and a sense of belonging. The willingness to ignore impulses and silence instincts in order to belong and be accepted is repeated throughout life and helps explain why individuals surrender.

The passion for belonging is strong and has guaranteed the survival of the family and of civilization, but when it takes advantage of the individual's readiness to deny too much of his autonomy, it can become dysfunctional. *When individuals become members of an organization, deliberate efforts must be made to support their autonomy while not sacrificing their membership, their bonds with one another.*

In group life, dialogic exchanges must be *very* deliberate and conscious events, because there are many forces in group life outside conscious awareness that drive members not to take full responsibility for their actions. In fact, the truth is that members often *want* monologue, they want pronouncements and rules. So when we call for the creation of opportunities for dialogue, that often means creating something people say they do no want. The job of the executive in the integrious system appears more complicated on closer inspection.

When we say that organizations need to "promote" diversity, we want to capture the sense that "to promote" is to move to the forefront, to elevate to a higher position, to actively stir up interest in, as in when legislators "promote" legislation through backstage lobbying. Executives promote diversity by actively stirring up dissension and disagreement by legitimizing the articulation of differences. The active seeking of dissent means crossing the borders of members' silence and acquiescent smiles of approval.

> Proposition #5: Integrious moments in group life occur when, among the cacophony of voices, a voice emerges that ministers to the group in such a way that members can see the evolving development of the group as a unit and the significance of their contribution toward the whole. The more the group or organization can accept an uncommon voice and promote the voicing of dissent, the greater the executive integrity of the system.

There is no one successful method to promote or stir up members' voices to be sure people do not become entrapped in the net of conformity. One of the most striking themes that emerged in our study of CEOs was their puzzlement over this very issue—why people hesitate to surface dissent. We present three examples of CEOs' efforts to get their directors and vice-presidents to express disagreement. The CEO of a large insurance company yearns for people who express divergent views:

Well, it's a cliché to say it's lonely at the top. . . . We've had a spectacular record for a long time, so no one here is going to argue with me much. So people respond to my ideas—"Whatever you decide." That's the answer. I say, "I've got a problem, what do you think?" I get, "Whatever you want to do is okay with me." I get that answer way too much. I have to work to draw people out all the time.

The leader of a major trucking and transportation firm cannot understand why people are afraid to express disagreement and why, although he explicitly rewards those who openly dissent, people hesitate to speak up:

Management is an art. My VPs will have different perceptions of what to do. I will accept that. Walk through my door, I tell them. Don't think that because you can't reach an agreement is a negative. Come in and let's get it resolved. It's a tremendous battle to get that understood. . . .

I try to make it comfortable for them. If I were to say, "I would consider it a weakness if you guys can't reach consensus," then I could understand why they wouldn't. . . . I don't know why they do it. It absolutely destroys me that mature people can't view the management of events and transactions without getting all cluttered up with some imagined threat if [they disagree] with the chairman or one of the VPs. . . . I tell them, "I will give you a gold star if you come to me with those kinds of problems."

The chairman of a manufacturing and tool company admits that the ease with which he reached conclusions in forming a strategic plan has made him suspicious and he needs to actively seek out alternative views that no one has been willing to express thus far:

I worry about becoming a little bit arrogant and saying these conclusions [about strategic planning] are right. I've been very forceful in forming them, and I haven't found anybody to really fight with me on it, which makes me nervous. But on the other hand, I really believe the conclusions are so obvious and so supportable, at least by the data, that they're difficult to argue with. . . . I'm going to the guys who run the divisions to talk about these conclusions, and I'm going to say, "*If you see it differently*, let me know."

We were left with the impression that the attentive CEOs were continually making efforts to "draw people out," trying whatever personal approach, whatever stimuli it took to make people feel safe and comfortable enough to speak their minds. Keep in mind that these are not middle-level managers and their subordinates. These are CEOs talking about their *top lieutenants* (an ambitious group of males who did not achieve their status by being reticent). These CEOs were genuinely confused and perhaps unaware of the effect their status and authority have on people around them. And perhaps there are other ways that they subtly reward people for agreeing with them. What is clear is that this hesitancy to speak out, this reluctance to pursue alternative perceptions and tendency to leave it to highly invested others, occurs at every level of the organization.

The effort to surface diverse views therefore needs to occur at all levels of the organization, in whatever areas create a successful context for members' abilities to get in touch with their own perceptions and ideas, autonomy and responsibility. And it needs to be occurring continually, using whatever methods support individual members' articulation. It is the *constant search* for a supportive context, not the outcome, that marks the integrious human system.

Organizational norms promote diversity when every voice is valued, when precautions are taken not to form premature judgments that might eliminate possibilities and variety. The value of a shared mission is not the outcome of the shared agreement itself but the opportunity it creates for the tolerance of discord, for creative individual expression. A shared mission creates more certainty about the direction in which the organization is heading and allows for more individual deviation in what actions need to be taken. Agreement, in fact, is never identity, and so even the appearance of unanimous agreement is only a comforting fiction.

When members actively promote diverse expressions, the group becomes more resilient. Members are more likely to see their part within the whole; their satisfaction becomes less contingent on whether they agree with the outcome. It is not the content of the exchange that is central but *the experience of being taken in and heard,* which not only affirms the legitimacy of one's way of looking at the world but then allows one to begin letting go of some defensiveness because the experience of affirmation increases one's capacity to affirm others. We recall the words of Milan Kundera, who captured this sense that what looks like human aggression is in fact a search for reception: "All men's life among men is nothing more than a battle for the ears of others" (1980, p. 80). "Love," he concludes, "is a constant interrogation" (p. 163), a continuing curiosity about the other. Once we feel heard, we become empowered to hear others. When members can appreciate one another's diversity, they further the integrity of the system.

So the test of integrity in an organization is not whether monologic exchanges, the unintentional closing out of others, occur but whether the organization provides opportunities to catch itself, to break through the mounting temptation to exclude dissent. One recent example of an integrious moment occurred when one of the divisions of a client organization gathered *en masse* to discuss the future strategic plan. After a few of the leaders described their plans, one woman spoke up: "I'm excited about the future of the department and I like everything I've heard so far, but I'd just like to say that I notice that it's been five white males who've spoken up so far. I hope that in the future we begin to hear female leaders emerging around here." Her interruption disturbed some people and momentarily stopped the smooth flow and coziness of the meeting. At first the results were silence, some offended executives, and a few defensive explanations. Her comment must have reverberated within people, because eventually individuals who were usually silent noncontributors, many of whom were minorities, began to speak up passionately. The one-hour meeting continued for three hours. And by the end, the department agreed to take steps to include "outsiders" in future planning. Some called it the most productive meeting in recent memory.

> Proposition #6: The greater the organization's efforts to include radically different others, the greater the executive integrity of the system.

Groups commonly experience xenophobia, the fear of outsiders. We need to recognize that in collectives our initial instinct is to exclude others whom we perceive as different. Self-perpetuation, however, is impoverishing. As the Russian linguist Mikhal Bakhtin (1981) observed, we transform others so that we learn nothing by making them a version of ourselves. Executive integrity is a call for global awareness, for awareness in executives that expands in widening concentric circles to imagine including spheres of previously unimagined others.

For example, Best Western International, Inc., instituted one of the more creative employment programs we are aware of. In its effort to promote diversity, it hired women prison inmates as reservation clerks. We quote from the report by the Council on Economic Priorities (Lydenberg and others, 1986, p. 291).

In 1981 Best Western's headquarters in Phoenix, Arizona, initiated a program to employ inmates at the Arizona Center for Women, a minimum-security prison seven miles from its offices. Best Western installed a complete reservations center at the prison at a cost of $10,000, trained prisoners in computerized phone reservation work at a cost of $1,900 each, then hired them at salaries equivalent to those of reservation agents at its headquarters. One third is set aside in a trust fund for inmates when they are released; and one third is paid out as disposable income, which can be sent outside for family support. Through mid-1985 the program has employed 134 inmates at the prison. Of those subsequently released, Best Western has hired approximately 30 as regular staff. The headquarters offices in Phoenix and in Winston-Salem, North Carolina, have received local Employer of the Year awards for hiring the handicapped on company time.

We can barely imagine under what conditions this creative idea was first proposed and the initial resistance some must have voiced to such a crazy proposal as giving opportunity to women prisoners, social deviants who have demonstrated irresponsibility. Most members would probably think of dozens of reasons that such an idea would be impossible and unreasonable. When we speak of executive integrity as *vibrancy,* we refer to the efforts to keep the reverberations of such creative ideas alive, the willingness of members to entertain the possibility, to suspend disbelief long enough to incubate the early life of a delicate, quivering idea. To the extent that organizations are incubators, life-support systems for seemingly crazy proposals to include radically different others and thus to promote diversity, the greater the executive integrity of the system. Integrious systems keep crazy ideas alive at least for a few more hours.

Encouraging Development

The one quality of the human animal that is unique among living organisms is the capacity to initiate action, to conceive of and enact something new, not predicated on any previous event. The capacity to interrupt and begin the new in the human sphere is celebrated when we encourage development, because we are recognizing the human capacity for growth, the innate potential of every human to do the startlingly unexpected. The beginning of every new action is in a sense a miracle because it introduces the unexpected into a world that values certainty and predictability. *When we encourage development, we acknowledge the boundless potential of human action.*

One of the characteristics of human action is its unpredictability and irreversibility once initiated. One can never know the consequences of a deed once done—how others will react to and be affected by one's deeds. We know that each action begins a chain reaction. Every process begins new processes. If humans have capacity for initiating new actions, and we can never know the reactions and reverberations that will follow a deed, what does this mean for organizations? Certainly some boundaries must be created to curtail the unpredictability of consequences of action. Bureaucratic, hierarchical systems, however, are often guilty of overbounding human action. When organizations foster norms that constrict individuals in roles, they are in danger of overbounding and stagnating members' potential. Efforts to bound human action are efforts to create artificial closure. Imposing closure on action is often redundant anyway. Left to our own devices, we are often too suspicious to follow our own inclinations and we rarely act with unsuppressed spontaneity. To the extent that organizations allow spontaneous action and foster learning by experimentation and serendipity, they further the occurrence of executive integrity in the system because they are acknowledging the richness of individuals' inner promptings.

By granting members public presence, a space for initiating action, an organization offsets the human tendency toward *role constriction*. We need to be aware of our complicity in limiting others' development. It is impossible to see everything in everyone. Constricting what we see in others is necessary so that we can reduce complexity, perceive simply, and act decisively. It is a convenient fiction, a closure that creates a sensible space. We can ignore the innumerable details and capacities of the other and speak to the other as *the* waitress, *the* police officer, or *the* accountant.

Attending to the role rather than penetrating to the person

is usually an unconscious choice that we make (Goleman, 1985), especially in bureaucratic organizations. Consider this example of a nurse/manager in a hospital: "I talked to the family of one of our child patients. They were so concerned about what was happening with their baby, and Dr. Jones told me I was wrong. I shouldn't be doing that. 'That's not your job,' she said. 'Just do the blood tests.' *I was shocked.* What could possibly be more important than providing information to the family, to help them feel comfortable? That's the most important thing I could possibly do.''

   This sense of being redirected to "role only" comes from a feeling that one cannot bring one's entire self to bear on the situation. Role constriction is a testimony to the power of others as coauthors to constrict development. If we take in the image of the other as "holding us back," we feel limited in the range of responses available. To constrict the other's voice and rely on prior descriptions is to hinder the development of integrity for both parties; one actively denies the other's potential while posturing oneself on a perch of privilege. Moments of integrity become possible when we make ourselves aware of our complicity in shaping others' experience of themselves in the world. Because so much of this complicity is tacit and unconscious, it takes a deliberate effort to bring it to awareness. We are reminded of Mother Teresa's statement: "I began my ministry when I realized there was a bit of Hitler in me." The reason integrity becomes possible in these moments of self-reflection is that we are then free to focus on potential.

> Proposition #7: Organizations encourage development and further executive integrity when they support experimentation and serendipity as a legitimate mode of learning because they are supporting members' potential for discovery of the new and creation of the unprecedented act.

Executive integrity occurs in those exceptional moments when the unexpected happens, when members are able to perform in a way that was previously unimaginable, when they are inspired to surpass their previously perceived limitations. Consider the following experience of an employee who works at a local prestigious hotel. We asked him why he plans to stay: "I haven't always done well here. About two years ago, Dick (my boss) asked me to research a new compensation system for the salaried employees. I had never been given an opportunity like that before. I was practically an office clerk. I really didn't know anything about it, but he gave me the chance to develop something. I researched it for months and proposed three options, one of which was eventually adopted. This place has been so good to me. I love this organization."

Serendipity is the creation of public space: calling on the other to do the unexpected, providing a space that the other has not "proved" his or her capacity to fill. Executive integrity occurs in such relationships to the extent that individuals validate each other by bringing out each other's potential. Like a lightning bolt, the organization sends a charge out to one party, who, enlivened in some way, sends a charge back to the originator.

In order to focus on another's potential, we need to live with unreduced complexity. We need to give up the comfort of creating fictions of closure on human action, the urge to oversimplify as a way to create boundaries, the tendency to see individuals in terms of their history, their demonstrated capacities rather than their potential to do the unexpected. When we meet complexity and unpredictability, the natural human reaction is fear and hesitancy. Organizations need to acknowledge the presence of fear in their members, fear of the unknown consequences of all complexity. As March and Simon (1958) pointed out, members are likely to introduce procedures that reduce choice making and complexity: They construct bounded worlds of rationality. We would rephrase that to say they create fictions of closure.

If members are expected to forgo the innate instinct to put closure on complexity and are to live with seeing the other's potential rather than seeing the other's history, something deliberate must be done to allay members' fears.

Proposition #8: When the organization rewards cooperative action, it encourages reciprocity and mutual support of development and thus furthers executive integrity.

We can all think of examples of strong, intelligent individuals who were unable to create coalitions of support for joint action, whose initial actions created chain reactions of resistance rather than resonance. Such individuals, to the extent that they cannot generate coactivity, are impotent.

Since every action initiates reactions and consequences that can never be predicted, we can never know the life of an idea or action in advance. Only in retrospect can the effects of action be estimated. Even then the meaning of particular actions cannot be known. Only historians can reconstruct a semblance of the story of action (Srivastva and Barrett, 1987). Heroes can be acknowledged only from a distance, by someone who can see the complex web of relationships. In this sense the concept of achievement is misleading. At no point can we actually isolate and identify the achievement of an idea or action. Irretrievability of deeds and unpredictability of reactions make the effort to identify achievements a flimsy effort at creating meaning. When organizations acknowledge individual achievement, they are creating comforting fictions, attempting to put false closure around an expansive phenomenon. When members seek to be acknowledged as sole authors, they begin to make themselves impotent.

When an organization creates awareness of the dynamics of coaction by rewarding coauthorship, when it rewards catalytic receptivity, it will encourage development, because members become aware of the fragile fabric of relationships that is necessary for the development of any potential. An organization encourages development and furthers integrity when it creates conditions such that the advancement of one member or group is not contingent on the recession of another. The physicians at the Cleveland Clinic, deciding that collaboration was one of the key requirements for successful task performance, created a peer review process in which each manager is rated by his or her colleagues (Srivastva and Cooperrider, 1986). A collective reward system was initiated so that one member's advance was not contingent on another's failure, furthering a high level of cooperation between individuals and departments.

Proposition #9: To the extent that members are able to forgive each other for unforeseen consequences of initiated action and the inevitable trespassing on each other's territory, they encourage development of potential and they further the executive integrity of the system.

That boundaries will be violated and turf trespassed on is inevitable in organizations. The issue is what members do once the infringement happens. Since initiation of action sets off unpredictable consequences, no wonder organizations are overbounded. Because the doer himself can never know the consequences of an action he begins and can never be completely aware of what he is disclosing about himself, we choose to collude in role constriction. In some ways we do not appreciate the courage and boldness required to initiate actions, because by definition one can never know how one is revealing oneself, how one is affecting others, or who will be crossed. Maybe ignorance is a blessing. If we were aware of too much, we would be paralyzed, endlessly attempting to imagine and sketch out unintended consequences. We would resolve the dilemma by choosing not to act.

Of all the dynamics within organizations that weaken the power of the system and hinder the development of integrity, turfism is the most destructive. Protecting one's turf and fearing that someone else's star will shine more brightly curtails the possibility that members can facilitate and support the activation of one another's potential. When members perch themselves as border guards, they hinder the development of action and discourage the realization of potential. It is inevitable that consequences of actions and sets of reactive processes will "bump up" against another's border. As long as action is occurring, trespassing is inevitable. As Hannah Arendt (1958) noticed, the one antidote to the predicament of unpredictability of action is forgiveness. Forgiveness is the release of the other for the consequences of actions that could not be foreseen, the one intervention in the chain of reactions that is unexpected and can break a cycle of vengeance. If we advocate spontaneous action and serendipity in organizations, members must be willing to forgive each other for consequences of ideas and actions that they could not predict. Without forgiveness, we need tightly bound bureaucracies to ward off trespassers.

Moments in human history when enemies and competitors stop the monologic spiral of conflict and vengeance and offer peace and forgiveness are the most miraculous, most graceful actions humans are capable of, because there is no rational reason whatsoever for such actions within the current frame.

If we have had difficulty suggesting what organizational conditions foster dialogue and promote diversity, we are truly at a loss for suggesting how organizations further forgiveness. Forgiveness goes beyond any rational intervention, for it never follows as a deductive conclusion from the facts. The facts of the history of a relationship call for reaction or vengeance and a furthering of the chain reaction. Facts support turfism. Events call for the continuation of rivalry because every member is "guilty" of some infringement on someone's turf almost every time an action is initiated.

Perhaps one suggestion is finding ways to further members' sense of their own competence. One study (Krebs, 1970) showed that participants were able to engage in altruistic acts and initiate care for each other only after they were convinced of their own competence after experiencing success at a task. Sibling rivalry in families and turfism within organizations are very serious interpersonal "games" with very high stakes. What is at stake is esteem. And although esteem is ultimately something one only grants oneself, organizations can further the likelihood of individuals' coming to conclusions about their own competence and esteem by supplying evidence of members' capacity, by reminding members of what they have a difficult time remembering themselves. Even this, of course, is no guarantee: Some individuals cannot generate self-esteem in spite of volumes of evidence of their own worth. But it is clear that we cannot, on our own, convince ourselves of our competence and worth. We continually need evidence and experience of success. The greater the extent to which members supply evidence of one another's competence, the greater the probability that members will come to feel esteem, and consequently the greater the likelihood of altruistic efforts, cooperative actions, and forgiveness of others for the inevitable violations of boundaries. Without forgiveness, organizations should make themselves very bureaucratic and create an excess of borders to curtail chain reactions and unpredictable consequences. Excessive organizational segmentation and interpersonal distance are a surrendering to the law of vengeance.

Conclusion

In the behavioral sciences we rarely speak of integrity, referring as it does to some ephemeral, spiritual quality that has no home in a discipline modeled on the empirical sciences. Among executives we rarely speak of integrity proudly, although we occasionally apply its name to deplore its absence. Seldom does the word appear except in contexts of censure. Ironically, we seldom notice executive integrity when it is present, perhaps because we need a framework to celebrate its occurrence. One barely notices the climate of a room unless something happens to disturb comfort, and it is then, half annoyed, that one begins to inquire whether the furnace or air conditioner is broken. We have attempted here to build a framework in which to notice executive integrity, to identify what is happening among groups of people when integrity is occurring so that we can see this process before the room temperature draws attention, before the fragile fabric of human relationships is strained.

Executive integrity is embodied in the organization's spirit of interaction. Most conflicts in organizations stem from different perceptions of reality—from members' telling different stories, selecting different relevant details, using different methods of expert analysis—in an effort to further positional preferences and convincing conclusions. Integrity comes to focus when we ask questions that probe beyond the manifest level of information exchange. Executive integrity exists to the extent that members pay attention to the delicate web of the relationship, attend to its ongoing development. Executive integrity occurs when members see through the illusion of solo performance as the mode of development and recognize the inherent coauthorship of every utterance, every idea, and every action. Aggressiveness and achievement are qualities usually rewarded in organizations; and yet executive integrity is promoted when members feel acknowledged for their responsiveness to one another, their receptivity and creative efforts to understand others' perspectives as well as articulating their own.

The great danger, as well as the great excitement, of the celebrated capitalist notion of self-determination and self-expression is that it permits an exaggeration of individual pursuit and an expansion of certain interests to the exclusion of others. We humans are a strange sort of magical thinkers, easily addicted to self-indulgent dreams of endless consumption. Even once satisfied, our hunger knows no bounds. We create invulnerable, convoluted rationalizations that justify behavior aimed at seeking preferred spots at the podium. With an eye still on Piaget's notion that children are jolted out of egocentric thought once they realize that everyone does not automatically understand them and the world is not a playground for their unfettered satiation, we contend in this chapter that integrity becomes possible when we are *willing to have our fantasies so interrupted by the awareness of the other.*

In organizational life much of the time we seek to deliver monologues, to establish a favored identity, making assertions and withdrawing into some invulnerable space. In the integrious system efforts are made to foster dialogue, to create arenas of accessibility wherein members can affirm and amend, can actively respond to one another. Given the nature of group dynamics, the net of conformity lures us to surrender our autonomous wills, to divest full or partial responsibility for actions and place it in the hands of highly invested, perhaps even charismatic, others. To bring the members back to life—the ongoing task of the integrious system—to surface members' perception, to draw out the unspoken wisdom, deliberate efforts must be made to appreciate and promote diversity and the legitimate voicing of dissent. Lastly, out of the need to reduce complexity, members collude to constrict themselves and one another into manageable roles; and out of the need to strive for mastery of turf, members guard against intrusions to border off claimed areas. In the integrious system, efforts are made to appreciate potential and to support and encourage members' development and capacity to initiate actions heretofore unimagined.

The propositions we put forth here are an attempt to create bifocals, a set of glasses that allow for dual focus, so that we can *see* processes that heighten executive integrity and actively promote it. Executive integrity exists insofar as organizations foster dialogue, promote diversity, and encourage development. It is occurring when the organization is in "full voice."

References

----◆----

Adams, G., and Rosenthal, S. Z. *The Invisible Hand: Questionable Corporate Payments Overseas.* New York: Council on Economic Priorities, 1976.

Alabanese, J. S. "What Lockheed and La Cosa Nostra Have in Common." *Crime and Delinquency,* Apr. 1982, *28,* 211–232.

Albrecht, K., and Zemke, R. *Service America!* Homewood, Ill.: Dow Jones–Irwin, 1985.

Alverno College Faculty. *Liberal Learning at Alverno College.* Milwaukee, Wis.: Alverno Productions, 1985a.

Alverno College Faculty. *Assessment at Alverno College.* Milwaukee, Wis.: Alverno Productions, 1985b.

Alverno College Valuing Department. *Valuing Education Materials.* Milwaukee, Wis.: Alverno Productions, 1984.

Anderson, D. M. "The Delicate Sex." *Science 86,* Apr. 1986, pp. 42–48.

Andrews, K. R. *The Concept of Corporate Strategy.* Homewood, Ill.: Irwin, 1971.

Arendt, H. *The Human Condition.* Chicago: University of Chicago Press, 1958.

Argyris, C. *Reasoning, Learning, and Action: Individual and Organizational.* San Francisco: Jossey-Bass, 1982.

Argyris, C. *Strategy, Change, and Defensive Routines.* Boston: Ballinger, 1985.

321

Argyris, C. "Reasoning, Action Strategies, and Defensive Routines: The Case of the OD Practitioner." In W. Pasmore and R. Woodman (eds.), *Research in Organizational Change*. Vol. 1. Greenwich, Conn.: JAI Press, forthcoming.

Argyris, C., and Schön, D. A. *Theory in Practice: Increasing Professional Effectiveness*. San Francisco: Jossey-Bass, 1974.

Argyris, C., and Schön, D. A. *Organizational Learning: A Theory of Action Perspective*. Reading, Mass.: Addison-Wesley, 1978.

Astin, A. W. *Four Critical Years: Effects of College on Beliefs, Attitudes, and Knowledge*. San Francisco: Jossey-Bass, 1977.

Bailyn, L. "Autonomy in the Industrial R&D Lab." *Human Resource Management*, 1985, *25*, 129–146.

Bakhtin, M. *The Dialogic Imagination*. Austin: University of Texas Press, 1981.

Barnard, C. *The Functions of the Executive*. Cambridge, Mass.: Harvard University Press, 1938.

Bateson, G. *Steps to an Ecology of Mind*. New York: Ballantine Books, 1972.

Baumhart, R. S. J. *An Honest Profit*. New York: Holt, Rinehart and Winston, 1968.

Bebeau, M. "Teaching Professional Ethics." *Encounters: A Publication of the Science Museum of Minnesota*, 1983, *6* (5), 19–20, 36–37.

Becker, E. *The Birth and Death of Meaning*. New York: Free Press, 1971.

Becker, E. *The Denial of Death*. New York: Free Press, 1973.

Beeman, D. R., and Timmins, S. A. "Who Are the Villains in International Business?" *Business Horizons*, Sept.–Oct. 1982, pp. 7–10.

Bell, D. *The Cultural Contradictions of Capitalism*. New York: Basic Books, 1976.

Benjamin, J., Dascher, P., and Morgan, R. "How Corporate Controllers View the Foreign Corrupt Practices Act." *Managerial Accounting*, Nov. 1979, pp. 43–48.

Bennis, W. "A Goal for the 80's: Organizational Integrity." Unpublished working paper, Graduate School of Business, University of Southern California, 1984.

Bennis, W., and Nanus, B. *Leaders: Five Strategies for Taking Charge*. New York: Harper & Row, 1985.

Bernard, G. *Why You Are Who You Are: A Psychic Conversation.*
New York: Destiny Books, 1985.

Bird, F., and Waters, J. A. "The Nature of Managerial Moral
Standards." *Journal of Business Ethics,* 1987, *6* (1), 1-13.

Bok, D. *Harvard University Gazette,* Oct. 10, 1986, p. 3.

Bok, S. *Lying: Moral Choice in Public and Private Life.* New York:
Pantheon Books, 1978.

Bok, S. *Secrets.* New York: Pantheon Books, 1982.

Boorstin, D. J. *The Discoverers.* New York: Random House, 1985.

Botkin, J., Elmandjra, M., and Malitza, M. *No Limits to Learning.* Elmsford, N.Y.: Pergamon Press, 1979.

Boyatzis, R. *The Competent Manager.* New York: Wiley, 1982.

Brady, F. N. "Aesthetic Components of Management Ethics."
Academy of Management Review, 1986, *11* (2), 337-344.

Bredemeier, B. J., and Shields, D. L. "Values and Violence
in Sports Today." *Psychology Today,* Oct. 1985, pp. 23-32.

Brennan, B. A. "Amending the Foreign Corrupt Practices Act
of 1977." *Journal of Legislation,* Winter 1984, *11,* 56-89.

Buber, M. *Between Man and Man.* New York: Scribner's, 1947.

Burns, J. M. *Leadership.* New York: Harper & Row, 1978.

Burrell, G., and Morgan, G. *Sociological Paradigms and Organizational Analysis.* London: Heinemann, 1979.

Burrough, B. "Oil Field Investigators Say Fraud Flourishes from
Wells of Offices." *Wall Street Journal,* Jan. 15, 1985, p. 1ff.

Cavanagh, G. F., Moberg, D. J., and Velasquez, M. "The
Ethics of Organizational Politics." *Academy of Management Review,* 1981, *6* (3), 363-374.

Chasseguet-Smirgel, J. *The Ego Ideal.* New York: Norton, 1985.

Chewning, R. C. "Can Free Enterprise Survive Ethical Schizophrenia?" *Business Horizons,* Mar.-Apr. 1984, pp. 5-11.

Churchill, W. H. *Thoughts and Adventures.* London: Thornton
Butterworth, 1932.

Clinard, M., and Yeager, P. *Corporate Crimes.* New York: Macmillan, 1980.

Clinard, M., and others. *Illegal Corporate Behavior.* Washington,
D.C.: National Institute of Law Enforcement and Criminal
Justice, 1979.

Cohen, R. "How the Mob Is Using Financial Institutions to
Disguise Its Gains." *Wall Street Journal,* Mar. 12, 1985, p. 1ff.

References

Cooperrider, D. L. "Appreciative Inquiry: A Methodology for Knowing and Contributing to Social-Organizational Innovation." Unpublished doctoral dissertation, Department of Organizational Behavior, Case Western Reserve University, 1985.

Culbert, S. A. *The Organization Trap.* New York: Basic Books, 1974.

Culbert, S. A., and McDonough, J. J. *The Invisible War: Pursuing Self-Interests at Work.* New York: Wiley, 1980.

Culbert, S. A., and McDonough, J. J. *Radical Management: Power, Politics, and the Pursuit of Trust.* New York: Free Press, 1985a.

Culbert, S. A., and McDonough, J. J. "Empowerment and the Politics That Precede Trust." Paper presented at the meetings of the Academy of Management, San Diego, Calif., Aug. 1985b.

Culbert, S. A., and McDonough, J. J. "How Reality Gets Constructed in an Organization." In R. Tannenbaum, N. Margulies, F. Massarik, and Associates, *Human Systems Development: New Perspectives on People and Organizations.* San Francisco: Jossey-Bass, 1985c.

Dalton, G., and Thompson, P. *Novations: Strategies for Career Management.* Glenview, Ill.: Scott, Foresman, 1986.

DeBack, V., and Mentkowski, M. "Does the Baccalaureate Make a Difference? Differentiating Nurse Performance by Education and Experience." *Journal of Nursing Education,* 1986, *25* (7), 275–285.

Dentzer, S., and Malone, M. "M.B.A.'s Learn a Human Touch." *Newsweek,* June 16, 1986, pp. 48–50.

"Dispatcher Helps Save Choking Child." *Plain Dealer,* Apr. 6, 1984, pp. 12A–13A.

Doherty, A., Mentkowski, M., and Conrad, K. "Toward a Theory of Undergraduate Experiential Learning." In M. T. Keeton and P. J. Tate (eds.), *Learning by Experience—What, Why, How.* New Directions for Experiential Learning, no. 1. San Francisco: Jossey-Bass, 1978.

Durkheim, E. *The Division of Labour in Society.* (G. Simpson, trans.) New York: Free Press, 1933. (Originally published 1893.)

Earley, M., Mentkowski, M., and Schafer, J. *Valuing at Alverno: The Valuing Process in Liberal Education.* Milwaukee, Wis.: Alverno Productions, 1980.

Edwards, G. "Making Corporate Ethics a Reality." *The President,* Mar. 1986, pp. 3–4.

Emery, F. E., and Trist, E. L. "The Causal Texture of Organizational Environments." *Human Relations,* 1965, *18,* 21–32.

Encyclopedia Judaica. Jerusalem: Keter, 1971.

Erikson, E. H. *Identity, Youth and Crisis.* New York: Norton, 1968.

Erikson, E. H. *The Life Cycle Completed.* New York: Norton, 1982.

Evarts, H. *The Competency Program of the American Management Associations.* New York: Institute for Management Competency, American Management Association, 1982.

Faludi, S. "Put out to Pasture." *Houston Chronicle,* June 1, 1986, p. 14.

Feinschreiber, R. "Liberalizing the Anti-Bribe Rules." *International Tax Journal,* 1982, *8,* 429–433.

Feldman, K. A., and Newcomb, T. M. *The Impact of College on Students.* San Francisco: Jossey-Bass, 1969.

Fingarette, H. *Self-Deception.* London: Routledge & Kegan Paul, 1965.

Freire, P. *Pedagogy of the Oppressed.* New York: Seabury Press, 1974.

Freud, A. *The Ego and the Mechanisms of Defense.* New York: International Universities Press, 1966.

Freud, S. *Group Psychology and the Analysis of the Ego.* New York: Bantam Books, 1965. (Originally published 1921.)

Freud, S. *Civilization and Its Discontents.* London: Hogarth Press, 1969. (Originally published 1931.)

Friedman, M. "A Friedman Doctrine—The Social Responsibility of Business Is to Increase Its Profits." *New York Times Magazine,* Sept. 30, 1970, p. 32ff.

Friedman, M., and others. *Validating Assessment Techniques in an Outcome-Centered Liberal Arts Curriculum: Valuing and Communications Generic Instrument.* Milwaukee, Wis.: Alverno Productions, 1980.

Fritzche, D. J., and Becker, H. "Linking Management Behavior to Ethical Philosophy: An Empirical Investigation.'' *Academy of Management Journal,* 1984, *27* (1), 166–175.

Gallup, G., and Gallup, A. M. *The Great American Success Story.* Homewood, Ill.: Dow Jones–Irwin, 1986.

Giencke-Holl, L., and others. *Evaluating College Outcomes Through Alumnae Studies: Measuring Post-College Learning and Abilities.* Milwaukee, Wis.: Alverno Productions, 1985.

Gladwin, T., and Walter, I. *Multinationals Under Fire.* New York: Wiley, 1980.

Goffman, E. *Asylums: Essays on the Social Situation of Mental Patients and Other Inmates.* New York: Doubleday, 1968.

Goleman, D. *Vital Lies, Simple Truths.* New York: Touchstone, 1985.

Graham, J. L. "Foreign Corrupt Practices." *Columbia Journal of World Business,* 1983, *18* (3), 89–94.

Gypen, J. "Learning Style Adaptation in Professional Careers: The Case of Engineers and Social Workers." Unpublished doctoral dissertation, Department of Organizational Behavior, Case Western Reserve University, 1981.

Hall, N. *The Making of Higher Executives: The Modern Challenges.* New York: New York University Press, 1958.

Handy, C. *Gods of Management.* London: Souvenir Press, 1978.

Harrison, R. "Understanding Your Organization's Character." *Harvard Business Review,* 1972a, *50* (3), 119–128.

Harrison, R. "When Power Conflicts Trigger Team Spirit." *European Business,* Spring 1972b, pp. 57–65.

Harrison, R. "A Practical Model of Motivation and Character Development." In *The 1975 Annual Handbook for Group Facilitators.* La Jolla, Calif.: University Associates, 1975a.

Harrison, R. "Diagnosing Organization Ideology." In *The 1975 Annual Handbook for Group Facilitators.* La Jolla, Calif.: University Associates, 1975b.

Harrison, R. "A Practical Model of Motivation and Character Development." In J. E. Jones and J. W. Pfeiffer (eds.), *The 1979 Annual Handbook for Group Facilitators.* La Jolla, Calif.: University Associates, 1979.

Harrison, R. "Strategies for a New Age." *Human Resource Management,* 1983, *22* (3), 209–235.

Harrison, R. "Leadership and Strategy for a New Age: Lessons from Conscious Evolution." In J. D. Adams (ed.), *Transforming Work.* Alexandria, Va.: Miles River Press, 1984.

Heath, D. *Maturity and Competence.* New York: Gardner Press, 1977.

Hirschman, A. *Exit, Voice and Loyalty.* Cambridge, Mass.: Harvard University Press, 1970.

Hornblower, M. "The U.S. Video Generation: Images and Impressions Are What Count; Not Words." *International Herald Tribune,* June 5, 1986, p. 3.

"How Business Schools Deal with Moral Issues." *Chronicle of Higher Education,* January 15, 1986, p. 42.

Hughes, E. "The Study of Occupations." In R. K. Merton, L. Broo, and L. S. Cottrell (eds.), *Sociology Today.* New York: Basic Books, 1959.

Ittig, J. "Conducting Business Under the Foreign Corrupt Practices Act." *World Oil,* July 1982, *195,* 207-221.

Jackman, M. *The Macmillan Book of Business and Economic Quotations.* New York: Macmillan, 1985.

Jacob, P. *Changing Values in College.* New York: Harper & Row, 1957.

Jacoby, N., Nehemkis, P., and Eells, R. *Bribery and Extortion in World Business.* New York: Macmillan, 1977.

Jacques, E. "Taking Time Seriously in Evaluating Jobs." *Harvard Business Review,* Sept.-Oct. 1979, pp. 124-132.

Janis, I. *Victims of Groupthink.* Boston: Houghton Mifflin, 1972.

Jansen, E., and Von Glinow, M. A. "Ethical Ambivalence and Organizational Reward Systems." *Academy of Management Review,* 1985, *10* (4), 814-822.

Jaques, E. *A General Theory of Bureaucracy.* New York: Halsted, 1976.

Jensen, T. A. "Leadership and the Physician Executive." *Medical Group Management,* forthcoming.

Johnson, H. L. "Bribery in International Business." *Journal of Business Ethics,* 1985, *4,* 447-455.

Jung, C. G. *The Integration of Personality.* London: Routledge & Kegan Paul, 1950.

Jung, C. G. "Two Essays on Analytical Psychology." In C. G.

Jung, *Collected Works.* Vol. 7. Princeton, N.J.: Princeton University Press, 1966. (Originally published 1923.)

Jung, C. G. *The Portable Jung.* (J. Campbell, ed.) New York: Viking Press, 1971.

Kerr, S. "Some Characteristics and Consequences of Organizational Reward Systems." In B. Schneider (ed.), *Facilitating Work Effectiveness.* Lexington, Mass.: Lexington Books, 1987.

Kidder, T. *The Soul of a New Machine.* Boston: Little, Brown, 1981.

Kim, S. H. "On Repealing the Foreign Corrupt Practices Act." *Columbia Journal of World Business,* Fall 1981, pp. 16–21.

Kirk, D. "Japanese Money Politics." *New Leader,* Dec. 1981, pp. 3–5.

Klein, M. *Mourning and Its Relation to Manic-Depressive States: Contributions to Psychoanalysis, 1921–1945.* New York: McGraw-Hill, 1964.

Klemp, G., Jr. *Job Competence Assessment.* Boston: McBer, 1978.

Knefelkamp, L. "Developmental Instruction: Fostering Intellectual and Personal Growth in College Students." Unpublished doctoral dissertation, University of Minnesota, 1974.

Kohlberg, L. *The Philosophy of Moral Development: Essays in Moral Development.* Vol. 1. San Francisco: Harper & Row, 1981a.

Kohlberg, L. *The Meaning and Measurement of Moral Development.* Worcester, Mass.: Clark University Press, 1981b.

Kohut, H. *The Analysis of Self.* New York: International Universities Press, 1971.

Kolb, D. A. *The Learning Style Inventory.* Boston: McBer, 1976.

Kolb, D. A. *Experiential Learning: Experience as the Source of Learning and Development.* Englewood Cliffs, N.J.: Prentice-Hall, 1984.

Kolb, D. A., Rubin, I., and McIntyre, J. *Organizational Psychology: An Experiential Approach to Organizational Behavior.* (4th ed.) Englewood Cliffs, N.J.: Prentice-Hall, 1984.

Kolb, D. A., and Wolfe, D. M. (eds.). "Professional Education and Career Development: A Cross-Sectional Study of Adaptive Competencies in Experiential Learning." Final Report, NIE Grant No. NIE-G-77-0053, 1981. (ED 209 493 CE 030519)

Konner, M. "The Stranger." *The Sciences,* Mar.–Apr. 1986, pp. 6–7.

Kontkin, J., and Kishimoto, Y. "Theory F." *Inc.*, Apr. 1986, pp. 53–60.

Krebs, D. L. "Altruism: An Examination of the Concept and a Review of the Literature." *Psychological Bulletin,* 1970, *73* (4), 258–302.

Kuhmerker, L., Mentkowski, M., and Erickson, V. L. (eds.). *Evaluating Moral Development and Evaluating Educational Programs That Have a Value Dimension.* Schenectady, N.Y.: Character Research Press, 1980.

Kundera, M. *The Book of Laughter and Forgetting.* New York: Penguin Books, 1980.

Lane, H. W., and Simpson, D. G. "Bribery in International Business: Whose Problem Is It?" *Journal of Business Ethics,* 1984, *3* (1), 33–42.

Lawler, E. E., III. *High-Involvement Management: Participative Strategies for Improving Organizational Performance.* San Francisco: Jossey-Bass, 1986.

LeBoeuf, M. *Imagineering.* New York: McGraw-Hill, 1980.

Leitko, T. A., and Kowalewski, D. "Industry Structure and Organizational Deviance." *Contemporary Crisis,* May 1985, pp. 127–147.

Levinson, D. J. *The Seasons of a Man's Life.* New York: Knopf, 1978.

Levinson, H. *Emotional Health: In the World of Work.* Cambridge, Mass.: Levinson Institute, 1964.

Levinson, H. *The Great Jackass Fallacy.* Cambridge, Mass.: Harvard University Press, 1973.

Levinson, H. "Appraisal of What Performance?" *Harvard Business Review,* July–Aug. 1976, p. 30.

Levinson, H., and Rosenthal, S. *CEO: Corporate Leadership in Action.* New York: Basic Books, 1984.

Loacker, G., Cromwell, L., and O'Brien, K. "Assessment in Higher Education: To Serve the Learner." In C. Adelman (ed.), *Assessment in Higher Education: Issues and Contexts* (Report No. OR 86-301). Washington, D.C.: U.S. Department of Education, 1986.

Loevinger, J. *Ego Development: Conceptions and Theories.* San Francisco: Jossey-Bass, 1976.

Loevinger, J., Wessler, R., and Redmore, C. *Measuring Ego*

Development. Vol. 1: *Construction and Use of a Sentence Completion Test.* San Francisco: Jossey-Bass, 1970.

Loevinger, J., and others. "Ego Development in College." *Journal of Personality and Social Psychology,* 1985, *48* (4), 947–962.

Loxley, J., and Whiteley, J. *Character Development in College Students.* Vol. 2: *The Curriculum and Longitudinal Results.* Schenectady, N.Y.: Character Research Press, 1986.

Lublin, J. "U.S. Charges Connor with Defrauding VA by Padding Mobile-Home Invoices." *Wall Street Journal,* Mar. 25, 1985, p. 1ff.

Lublin, S. "Measuring Job Complexity." Unpublished doctoral dissertation, Department of Organizational Behavior, Case Western Reserve University, 1986.

Lydenberg, S., and others. *Rating America's Corporate Conscience.* Reading, Mass.: Addison-Wesley, 1986.

McClelland, D. C. *Power: The Inner Experience.* New York: Irvington, 1975.

McClelland, D. C. *A Guide to Job Competency Assessment.* Boston: McBer, 1976.

McLaughlin, J. B., and Riesman, D. "The Shady Side of Sunshine." Unpublished paper, Cambridge, Mass., 1985.

McQueary, G., and Risden, M. "How We Comply with the Foreign Corrupt Practices Act." *Managerial Accounting,* June 1979, pp. 43–45.

Magnet, M. "The Decline and Fall of Business Ethics." *Fortune,* Dec. 8, 1986, pp. 65–72.

Maier, N. R. F. *Problem Solving and Creativity in Individuals and Groups.* Monterey, Calif.: Brooks/Cole, 1970.

Maisonrouge, J. "How a Multinational Corporation Appears to Its Managers." In G. W. Ball (ed.), *Global Companies.* Englewood Cliffs, N.J.: Prentice-Hall, 1975.

March, J. G., and Simon, H. A. *Organizations.* New York: Wiley, 1958.

Marcuse, H. *Eros and Civilization.* New York: Vintage Books, 1962.

Maruyama, M. "Mindscapes and Science Theories." *Current Anthropology,* 1980, *21* (5), 589–600.

Maslow, A. H. *Motivation and Personality.* (2nd ed.) New York: Harper & Row, 1970.

Maslow, A. H. *The Farther Reaches of Human Nature.* New York: Viking Press, 1971.

Massarik, F. "Human Experience, Phenomenology, and the Process of Deep Sharing." In R. Tannenbaum, N. Margulies, F. Massarik, and Associates, *Human Systems Development: New Perspectives on People and Organizations.* San Francisco: Jossey-Bass, 1985.

Meier, B. "Against Heavy Odds, EPA Tries to Convict Polluters and Dumpers." *Wall Street Journal,* Jan. 7, 1985, p.1ff.

Mentkowski, M. "Creating a 'Mindset' for Evaluating a Liberal Arts Curriculum Where 'Valuing' Is a Major Outcome." In L. Kuhmerker, M. Mentkowski, and V. L. Erickson (eds.), *Evaluating Moral Development and Evaluating Educational Programs That Have a Value Dimension.* Schenectady, N.Y.: Character Research Press, 1980.

Mentkowski, M. *College as an Enabling Institution.* Milwaukee, Wis.: Alverno Productions, 1984.

Mentkowski, M., and Doherty, A. *Careering After College: Establishing the Validity of Abilities Learned in College for Later Careering and Professional Performance* (Final Report to the National Institute of Education). Milwaukee, Wis.: Alverno Productions, 1983. (ED 239 556–239 566)

Mentkowski, M., and Doherty, A. "Abilities That Last a Lifetime: Outcomes of the Alverno Experience." *American Association for Higher Education Bulletin,* 1984a, *36* (6), 3–6, 11–14.

Mentkowski, M., and Doherty, A. *Careering After College: Establishing the Validity of Abilities Learned in College for Later Careering and Professional Performance* (Final Report to the National Institute of Education: Overview and Summary). Milwaukee, Wis.: Alverno Productions, 1984b. (ED 239 556)

Mentkowski, M., and Loacker, G. "Assessing and Validating the Outcomes of College." In P. T. Ewell (ed.), *Assessing Educational Outcomes.* New Directions for Institutional Research, no. 47. San Francisco: Jossey-Bass, 1985.

Mentkowski, M., Moeser, M., and Strait, M. *Using the Perry Scheme of Intellectual and Ethical Development as a College Outcomes Measure: A Process and Criteria for Judging Student Performance.* Vols. 1 and 2. Milwaukee, Wis.: Alverno Productions, 1983.

Mentkowski, M., Much, N., and Giencke-Holl, L. *Careering After College: Perspectives on Lifelong Learning and Career Development* (Final Report to the National Institute of Education, Research Report Number Eight). Milwaukee, Wis.: Alverno Productions, 1983. (ED 239 564)

Mentkowski, M., O'Brien, K., Cleve, L., and Wutzdorff, A. *Assessing Experiential Learning: The Learning Incident as an Assessment Technique.* Milwaukee, Wis.: Alverno Productions, 1983.

Mentkowski, M., O'Brien, K., McEachern, W., and Fowler, D. *Developing a Professional Competence Model for Management Education.* Milwaukee, Wis.: Alverno Productions, 1982. (ED 239 566)

Mentkowski, M., and Rogers, G. *A Longitudinal Assessment of Critical Thinking in College: What Measures Assess Curricular Impact?* Milwaukee, Wis.: Alverno Productions, 1985.

Mentkowski, M., and Strait, M. *A Longitudinal Study of Student Change in Cognitive Development, Learning Styles, and Generic Abilities in an Outcome-Centered Liberal Arts Curriculum* (Final Report to the National Institute of Education, Research Report Number Six). Milwaukee, Wis.: Alverno Productions, 1983. (ED 239 562)

Mines, R. "Student Development Assessment Techniques." In G. R. Hanson (ed.), *Measuring Student Development.* New Directions for Student Services, no. 20. San Francisco: Jossey-Bass, 1982.

Morgan, G. "Paradigms, Metaphors, and Puzzle Solving." *Administrative Science Quarterly,* 1980, *20,* 605–622.

Much, N., and Mentkowski, M. *Student Perspectives on Liberal Learning at Alverno College: Justifying Learning as Relevant to Performance in Personal and Professional Roles.* Milwaukee, Wis.: Alverno Productions, 1982. (ED 239 563)

Much, N., and Mentkowski, M. *Student Perspectives on Learning and Development in College.* Milwaukee, Wis.: Alverno Productions, 1984.

Noonan, J. *Bribes.* New York: Macmillan, 1984.

Nord, W. A. "The Failure of Current Applied Behavioral Science—A Marxian Perspective." *Journal of Applied Behavioral Science,* 1974, *10* (4), 557–578.

Opinion Research Corporation. "Codes of Ethics in Corporations and Trade Associations and the Teaching of Ethics in Graduate Business Schools." A survey conducted for Ethics Resource Center, ORC Study No. 65302, June 1979.

O'Toole, J. *Vanguard Management.* New York: Doubleday, 1985.

Ouchi, W. G. *Theory Z.* Reading, Mass.: Addison-Wesley, 1981.

Pace, C. R. *Measuring Outcomes of College: Fifty Years of Findings and Recommendations for the Future.* San Francisco: Jossey-Bass, 1979.

Parcel, T. L., and Mueller, C. W. "Occupational Differentiation, Prestige and Socio-Economic Status." *Work and Occupations,* 1983, *10* (1), 49–80.

Perrow, C. *Normal Accidents: Living with High Risk Technologies.* New York: Basic Books, 1984.

Perry, B. *Enfield: A High-Performance System.* Bedford, Mass.: Educational Services Development and Publishing, Digital Equipment Corp., 1984.

Perry, W., Jr. *Forms of Intellectual and Ethical Development in the College Years: A Scheme.* New York: Holt, Rinehart and Winston, 1970.

Perry, W., Jr. "Cognitive and Ethical Growth: The Making of Meaning." In A. Chickering and Associates, *The Modern American College: Responding to the New Realities of Diverse Students and a Changing Society.* San Francisco: Jossey-Bass, 1981.

Peters, T. J., and Waterman, R. H. *In Search of Excellence.* New York: Harper & Row, 1982.

Pfeffer, J. "Management as Symbolic Action." In L. L. Cummins and B. M. Staw (eds.), *Research in Organizational Behavior.* Vol. 3. Greenwich, Conn.: JAI Press, 1981.

Piaget, J. *The Language and Thought of the Child.* New York: Meridian Books, New American Library, 1955.

Piaget, J. "Intellectual Development from Adolescence to Adulthood." *Human Development,* 1972, *15,* 1–12.

Presidential Commission on the Space Shuttle Challenger *Accident.* Washington, D.C.: U.S. Government Printing Office, June 6, 1986.

Rauch, J. "The Foreign Corrupt Practices Act." *National Journal,* 1981, *13,* 1422–1425.

Read, J. "Alverno's Collegewide Approach to the Development of Valuing." In M. L. McBee (ed.), *Rethinking College Responsibilities for Values.* New Directions for Higher Education, no. 31. San Francisco: Jossey-Bass, 1980.

Reisman, M. W. *Folded Lies.* New York: Free Press, 1979.

Renner, J., and others. *Test of Cognitive Development.* Normal: University of Oklahoma Press, 1976.

Rest, J. *Development in Judging Moral Issues.* Minneapolis: University of Minnesota Press, 1979.

Rest, J. *Moral Development: Advances in Research and Theory.* New York: Praeger, 1986.

Revans, R. W. "Action Learning and Development of Self." In T. Boydahl and M. Pedlar (eds.), *Management Self-Development.* London: Gower Press, 1981.

Richman, B. "Can We Prevent Questionable Foreign Payments?" *Business Horizons,* June 1979, pp. 14–19.

Romaneski, M. "The Foreign Corrupt Practices Act of 1977." *Boston College International and Comparative Law,* Summer 1982, *5,* 405–430.

Sanford, N. "Notes Toward a Theory of Personality Development at 80." In J. R. Starde (ed.), *In Wisdom and Old Age.* Berkeley, Calif.: Ross Books, 1981.

Schön, D. A. *The Reflective Practitioner: How Professionals Think in Action.* New York: Basic Books, 1983.

Schott, B. "Self and Organization in Mid-Life: A Study of Inner/Outer Developmental Stages." Unpublished doctoral dissertation, Department of Organizational Behavior, Case Western Reserve University, 1981.

Scott, W., and Mitchell, T. "The Moral Failure of Management Education." *Chronicle of Higher Education,* December 11, 1985, p. 35.

Selznick, P. *Leadership in Administration: Sociological Interpretation.* New York: Harper & Row, 1957.

Sheehan, J. "Moral Reasoning and Clinical Performance." Paper presented at the annual meeting of the American Educational Research Association, Montreal, Apr. 1983.

Sheehan, J., and others. "Structural Equation Models of Moral Reasoning and Physician's Performance." *Evaluation in the Health Professions,* 19, *8* (4), 379–400.

Sheehy, G. *Passages: Predictable Crises of Adult Life.* New York: Dutton, 1974.

Shepard, H. A. "Changing Interpersonal and Intergroup Relationships in Organizations." In J.G. March (ed.), *Handbook of Organizations.* Skokie, Ill.: Rand McNally, 1965.

Siedel, G. J. "Corporate Governance Under the Foreign Corrupt Practices Act." *Quarterly Review of Economics and Business,* Aug. 1981, *21,* 43–48.

Simmons, J. "Frank Borman's Eastern Experiment." *Boston Globe Magazine,* Mar. 30, 1986, pp. 14ff.

Sims, R. "Kolb's Experiential Learning Theory: A Framework for Assessing Person-Job Interaction." *Academy of Management Review,* 1983, *8* (3), 501–508.

Solomon, R., and Hanson, K. *Above the Bottom Line: An Introduction to Business Ethics.* San Diego, Calif.: Harcourt Brace Jovanovich, 1983.

Srivastva, S., and Associates. *The Executive Mind: New Insights on Managerial Thought and Action.* San Francisco: Jossey-Bass, 1983.

Srivastva, S., and Barrett, F. J. "Functions of Executive Power: Exploring New Approaches." In S. Srivastva and Associates, *Executive Power.* San Francisco: Jossey-Bass, 1986.

Srivastva, S., and Barrett, F. J. "A Role for Human Cosmogeny in Organizations." Unpublished working paper, Department of Organizational Behavior, Case Western Reserve University, 1987.

Srivastva, S., and Cooperrider, D. L. "The Emergence of the Egalitarian Organization." *Human Relations,* 1986, *39* (8), 683–724.

Stewart, A. J., and Winter, D. G. "Self-Definition and Social Definition in Women." *Journal of Personality,* 1974, *42* (2), 238–259.

Stricharchuk, G. "Businesses Crack Down on Workers Who Cheat to Help the Company." *Wall Street Journal,* June 13, 1986, p. 25.

Suzuki, D. "Declaration on Science and Social Responsibility." *Bulletin, Canadian Commission for UNESCO,* June 1986, p. 3.

Vaillant, G. *Adaptation to Life.* Boston: Little, Brown, 1977.

Vogel, D. "The Study of Social Issues in Management: A

Critical Appraisal." *California Management Review,* 1986, *27* (2), 142-151.

Vroom, V., and Yetton, P. *Leadership and Decision Making.* Pittsburgh: University of Pittsburgh Press, 1973.

Vygotsky, L. *Thought and Language.* Cambridge, Mass.: MIT Press, 1986.

Walton, R. E., and Lawrence, P. R. *Human Resource Management: Trends and Challenges.* Boston: Harvard Business School Press, 1985.

Waters, J. A. "Corporate Morality as an Organizational Phenomenon." *Organizational Dynamics,* Spring 1978, pp. 3-19.

Waters, J. A. "Of Saints, Sinners and Socially Responsible Executives." *Business and Society,* Winter 1980, pp. 67-73.

Waters, J.A. "The Moral Dimension of Organizational Culture." *Journal of Business Ethics,* Fall 1986.

Waters, J. A., and Bird, F. "Attending to Ethics in Management." Working paper, York University, 1986.

Waters, J. A., and Bird, F. "The Moral Dimension of Organizational Culture." *Journal of Business Ethics,* 1987, *6,* 15-22.

Waters, J. A., Bird, F., and Chant, P. D. "Everyday Moral Issues Experienced by Managers." *Journal of Business Ethics,* Fall 1986, pp. 373-384.

Waters, J. A., and Chant, P. D. "Internal Control of Management Integrity: Beyond Accounting Systems." *California Management Review,* Spring 1982, pp. 60-66.

Watson, G., and Glaser, E. *Critical Thinking Appraisal.* San Diego, Calif.: Harcourt Brace Jovanovich, 1964.

Weber, M. "The Three Types of Legitimate Rule." In A. Etzioni (ed.), *Essays on Complex Organizations.* New York: Holt, Rinehart and Winston, 1961. (Originally published 1946.)

Weick, K. "The Demystification of Organizing: Discovered Threads." Paper presented at Academy of Management, Chicago, Aug. 16, 1986.

Weinraub, B. "How Donald Regan Runs the White House." *New York Times Magazine,* Jan. 5, 1986, pp. 12-15ff.

"What Ever Happened to Ethics?" *Time,* May 25, 1987, pp. 14-29.

Wiener, N. *The Human Use of Human Beings.* New York: Doubleday, 1954.

Winter, D. G., McClelland, D. C., and Stewart, A. J. *A New Case for the Liberal Arts: Assessing Institutional Goals and Student Development.* San Francisco: Jossey-Bass, 1981.

Wolfe, D. M., and Kolb, D. A. "Beyond Specialization: The Quest for Integration in Mid-Career." In C. B. Derr (ed.), *Work, Family and the Career.* New York: Praeger, 1980.

Wright, A. "Toward the Year 2000." *Issues,* 1986, *1* (3), 1–8.

Index

―――◆―――

A

Abstractions: and bottom-line mentality, 148–149; and exploitative mentality, 150–152

Accentuation, in advanced professional development, 73

Active engagement, and leadership, 163

Adams, G., 254n

Adaptation: primary and secondary, 155–158; primary, reinforced, 162–163

Adler, N. J., 19, 23–24, 243, 246n

Adults, development and maturation of, 161–169

Advocacy: inquiry coupled with, 207–208, 212–213; results of, 204–207; self-serving, 236

Afghanistan, and violence, 243

Age of Endarkenment, 45

Age of Terror, 1

Aggression: control methods for, 272–275; organizational stimulants to, 275–276; and personal

integrity, 269, 271, 273–275; and self-control, 272

AIDS epidemic, 243

Alabanese, J. S., 254n

Albrecht, K., 62

Alignment: attributes of, 225–228; attunement balanced with, 46, 58–67; categories of, 226–227; concept of, 225–226; and development of integrity, 11; and executive integrity, 228–230; and high-integrity management, 239; resistance to, 227–228; and schisms, 231–235; and search for integrity, 22; and truth, 238–239, 240

Alumnae: integrated performance by, 107–108; self-sustained learning in, 117

Alverno College: Alverno Institute at, 95n; curricular impact at, 96–103; cyclical development at, 103–105; education for integrity at, 13–14; education for personal growth at, 89n, 92–119; inte-